FIGHTING
BACK

D1452643

FIGHTING BACK

LITHUANIAN JEWRY'S ARMED RESISTANCE TO THE NAZIS, 1941–1945

DOV LEVIN

TRANSLATED FROM THE HEBREW BY
MOSHE KOHN AND DINA COHEN

FOREWORD BY
YEHUDA BAUER

HM

HOLMES & MEIER

NEW YORK   LONDON

First published in the United States of America 1985 by
Holmes & Meier Publishers, Inc.
160 Broadway   New York, NY 10038
Reprinted in paperback with a new preface 1997

Book design by Stephanie Barton

Library of Congress Cataloging in Publication Data
Levin, Dov, 1925 Jan. 27–
    Lithuanian Jewry's armed resistance to the Nazis,
1941–1945.
    Bibliography: p.
    Includes index.
    1. Jews—History—Lithuania—20th century.   2. Jewish
soldiers—Lithuania.   3. World War, 1939–1945—Underground
movements, Jewish—Lithuania.   4. Holocaust, Jewish
(1939–1945)—Lithuania.   5. Lithuania—Ethnic relations.
I. Title.
DS135.R93L5554   1985   947'.5004924   83-12605
ISBN 0-8419-1389-7

Manufactured in the United States of America

CONTENTS

PART III
IN THE GHETTOS AND LABOR CAMPS

PART IV
IN THE FORESTS—PARTISAN WARFARE

FOREWORD

Dr. Dov Levin has become known in Israel as one of the foremost researchers in the area of Holocaust history. The book he now presents is the result of many years of research into one of the most important aspects of this history, namely, the story of the resistance of Lithuanian Jews to the Nazis both inside Lithuania and in the ranks of the so-called Lithuanian Division in the Soviet Army.

After the first six months of the frightful murder of most of the Lithuanian Jews in 1941, four ghettos remained in Lithuania, and only 40,000 Jews lived in them out of the quarter of a million who had lived in the country prior to the war. Resistance groups slowly organized in all four ghettos. Their story and the fate that befell them is told by Dov Levin against the background of the relations between the Jews and their Gentile neighbors.

Those few thousands who had managed to flee before the advancing German armies became a source of manpower for the Lithuanian Division in the Soviet Army. Dov Levin shows how the Lithuanian Division, in fact a Jewish division with Lithuanian officers and a Lithuanian minority among its soldiers, fared during the severe fighting that ended in the liberation of Lithuania by the Soviets.

It is a story which not only contradicts the accepted image of Jewish passivity during the war, but also presents the dilemmas of collective responsibility and family relations under severe stress of traumatization. Levin's book is therefore a major contribution to our knowledge of the period.

Yehuda Bauer

PREFACE
TO THE NEW EDITION

THIS NEW EDITION SUPPLEMENTS WHAT THOUSANDS OF visitors learn from the Kovno Ghetto exhibition at the United States Holocaust Memorial Museum (USHMM) in Washington, DC after its opening late in 1997. The importance of the Kovno community lies not only in the central place it held for Lithuanian Jewry between the two world wars, but also in the significant role played by members of this community as part of the anti-Nazi fighting forces of Lithuanian Jewry. Moreover, in the complex reality of Lithuania during the Second World War in general, and under Nazi occupation in particular, those who came from the Kovno community found themselves fighting together with members of other communities in Lithuania within the framework of a joint fighting force, whether in the conventional army or in partisan units.

When this book first appeared, in 1985, forty years had passed since the main events of World War II and, more specifically, the active involvement of the Jews of Lithuania. At that time there still existed an "Iron Curtain" between the superpowers. In the Soviet Union, including Soviet Lithuania, significant portions of archival material relevant to the armed struggle of Lithuania's Jews against the Nazis were made unavailable. Nonetheless, at that time we made a supreme effort to utilize, in the most intensive manner, the available information from Jews who had survived the underground organizations in the ghettos of Lithuania, the partisan units that operated in the forests of that land, and from the soldiers of the Lithuanian Division of the Soviet Army who fought against the German invaders beginning with the "Center" front in Russia and ending at the ports of the Baltic Sea in the last days of the war.

By comparing the factual material cited in the original edition with the material found after the collapse of the Soviet Union in the archives of the newly independent Lithuania (after 1991), we can conclude that, in general, the original account was valid. We had succeeded in presenting a faithful reconstruction of the reality that formed the background from which the Jewish struggle took shape, as well as in describing its various aspects. With the help of confirmed statistical data, we have succeeded more recently in assessing the degree of military activity of the fighters (mainly in the underground and partisan frameworks) and the cost in bloodshed (in dead and wounded) claimed by this action.

With the political changes in the former Soviet Union, and the immigration of almost all the Jewish fighters from Lithuania to Israel, we have been able for the first time to arrive with optimal accuracy at the number of losses inflicted on the Jewish soldiers who fought in the framework of the 16th Lithuanian Division of the Soviet Army. Thus it is possible to note with certainty that out of about 5,000 officers and soldiers who fought as part of this division, about 40%—that is, about 2,000—died. For 1,724 of them, many personal details—such as first and last names, names of father or mother, year of birth, military rank, date and place of death— have been uncovered thus far. Even greater is the number of soldiers wounded (one or more times), though their total number has not been verified to this day and may never be determined. No information has been uncovered up to now regarding the fate of the Jewish soldiers and partisans who were captured by the Nazi Army or its allies.

Below are the data on the combat dead among the Jewish soldiers who fought in the 16th Lithuanian Division in the Soviet Army, according to the sources of information on their deaths and according to the sub-divisions in which they served.

Based on Semitic names from official sources
in the military archives in Podolsk, Russia

	Number of Men and Women
The 156th Rifle Regiment	306
The 167th Rifle Regiment	325
The 249th Rifle Regiment	408
The 224th Artillery Regiment	48
Other Units	129

According to personal lists
from sources of public organizations

In Rifle, Artillery and other Regiments	510
Total	1,724

The Hebrew University, Jerusalem
Passover Eve, 5757 / 1997

PREFACE
TO THE FIRST EDITION

IN THE LAST THREE DECADES, BOTH JEWISH AND NON-Jewish historiographers have published a great deal of information about Lithuanian Jewry during the Holocaust. Most of this information, however, has been incomplete, unclear, or tendentious. Unrelated compilations of facts have not adequately filled in the background nor explained the causes of events, partly because the Lithuania known to history has been destroyed and because the country's present is so very different from its past.

The purpose of this book is to help rectify this, by summarizing the role played by the Lithuanian Jews in every form of active combat against the Nazis in World War II. It attempts to describe the different forms of their resistance and defense and explain and analyze the nature, scope, and effectiveness of each, on the basis of evidence drawn from all available sources.

For the purposes of this study, the expression "Lithuanian Jewry" refers not to the Jews living in the truncated state of Lithuania as it was between the wars, but to the Jews living in the Socialist Republic of Lithuania, whose temporary capital was Kovno (Kaunas) and whose borders were established in 1940 and still remain intact today. These borders comprise Vilna (Vilnius), Svencian (Švenčionys), Troki (Trakai), and Eishishok (Eišiškės), and a number of other places. Though these areas were annexed to Lithuania at the beginning of World War II only eighteen months before the German conquest, the whole of Lithuania within these frontiers remained under one civil administration for most of the war, although by turn Lithuanian, Russian and German. Because the Jews there shared a common fate during the Holocaust, the story of Lithuanian Jewry's war against the Nazis can be treated, for practical purposes, within the framework of these frontiers.

The Nazi occupation of Lithuania began on June 22, 1941—the day the Germans invaded the Soviet Union. It ended on January 27, 1945, the day the Red Army, with the Lithuanian Division in its ranks, drove the Germans out of the port of Klaipėda (Memel), the German's last stronghold in Lithuanian territory. But even before the invasion of June 1941, the Jews of Vilna had already taken an active part in fighting against the German troops in the brief campaign of September 1939, in the ranks of the Polish Army. And Jewish soldiers and partisans from Lithuania continued to fight the Germans and their allies until the German surrender on May 8, 1945, almost four months after the liberation of Lithuania from Nazi rule.

This book also treats the activities of Lithuanian Jews who reached Soviet Russia in one fashion or another after the outbreak of war and before Russia was partially occupied by the Germans, for Lithuanian Jewry's resistance was not confined to their homeland. In fact, the Jews of Lithuania concentrated their forces and did a great deal of their fighting in a large, triangular patch of land in the central and western European region of the Soviet Union. With its base along the Baltic and its two sides stretching eastward and its apex at the city of Gorki on the Volga, this triangle fanned out from the central region of the Soviet Union and encompassed parts of Byelorussia, Latvia, and eastern Prussia, as well as the territory of Lithuania itself.

This volume is divided into an introduction and four parts. The introduction describes the social, economic, and cultural background of Lithuanian Jewry as a whole, stressing the period from the 1930s until the eve of the collapse. Special attention is accorded to the factors causally connected with Lithuanian Jewry's active fight during the Holocaust period, such as the visible deterioration of the relationship between the Jews and the non-Jewish population, which led to the non-Jewish population's active participation in the mass murder of Lithuanian Jewry. In this section, emphasis is also placed on the special quality of Lithuanian Jewry—primarily its cultural and national unity—that later shaped both the form and content of their campaign against the Nazis.

Part I describes the problems that beset Lithuanian Jews and their reactions to the Soviet takeover in 1940 and 1941. In the struggle, both open and hidden, waged at that time by the Jewish minority in Lithuania (including the Jews of Vilna), the new, young cadres sprang up that later would constitute the main reserve forces of the underground movement, as well as of the regular army. Part I also describes the Nazi invasion of Lithuania and the division of Lithuanian Jewry into those who remained in Lithuania and those who reached the

Soviet Union. It also describes the mass immigration of Lithuanian Jews to Central Asia. The central themes here are the Jews' attempts to reach Eretz Yisrael (Palestine) and their desire to participate actively in the struggle against Nazism.

Part II is concerned with the Lithuanian Jews who reached the Soviet Union and actively participated in the war in the ranks of the Red Army. The stress here is on the Lithuanian Division, where, at least at a certain stage, Jews were a plurality if not a majority. The special character of the Lithuanian Division, as well as of Lithuanian partisan warfare, will become clear from an explanation of how the division was established, an analysis of its political, historical, and military background, and a description of its functions and its command. This should also help explain how the status of the Jewish soldiers in its ranks made this division unique in the whole of the Red Army. Furthermore, the statistical analyses that appear in the different chapters, and which have been constructed from different starting points, illustrate the "inner strength of the biological-sociological cells of Jewish society" to which Prof. Benzion Dinur rightly attributes a great role in the Jews' power of resistance in the light of the extreme conditions during the Holocaust.

In contrast with the very full treatment of the Lithuanian Division, other military formations are more summarily reviewed; they are dealt with mainly by way of comparison, in order to illuminate still more sharply the special character of the Lithuanian Division, as well as for the sake of comprehensive treatment of the subject. A detailed account is also given of the events in this region, which centered with increasing intensity on the Soviets' unrelenting attempts to regain their foothold on the eastern shore of the Baltic.

Part III concerns those Jews who remained in Lithuania under the murderous German occupation, and mostly those who survived the riots, deportations, and systematic exterminations. While the history, motives, and methods of the resistance movement in the four major ghettos that survived—Vilna, Kovno (Kaunas), Shavli (Šiauliai), and Svencian—are treated in depth, only marginal attention is paid to manifestations of passive resistance, though these were of tremendous intrinsic importance. The central theme is the spontaneous display of active resistance to the murderers.

The clandestine organizations in these four ghettos are analysed and compared with the following in view: (1) to select facts and data connected with the theme of resistance in every organization throughout Lithuania, making quantitative summation possible for the first time; (2) to study the various characteristics of the different organizations; and (3) to determine the common characteristics of the resistance movements and their organizers in all the ghettos of Lithuania.

Part IV provides a similar overall survey of the various forms of partisan warfare in which Lithuania Jews participated and describes the national content of each and the conditions under which they fought. In the margin, as it were, we shall also present a detailed portrait of one of these combat units, primarily relying on one document *sui generis*. Our critical analysis of this unit shows it to be representative, to a certain degree, of all the Jewish and mixed partisan units active on the eastern marches of the territory with which we are concerned.

THE SOURCE MATERIALS

The treatment of the subject as outlined above is of added significance in view of the attempt by Soviet historiography to ignore, or at least minimize, the role of the Jews in general, and of Lithuanian Jewry in particular, in World War II. For from the Soviet viewpoint, every additional fact brought to light concerning the contribution of Jews to the war effort against the Germans must diminish the part played by the Lithuanian people, which in any case was small enough. (See my "Facts and Problems in the Study of the Fighting of the Jews of the Soviet Union in World War Two," in *Jewish Resistance During the Holocaust*, [Jerusalem: Yad Vashem, 1971], pp. 392–403.)

New facts, relevant to the present study, were found in documentary material published in spite of the above-mentioned Soviet tendency to distort the picture. This material includes transcripts of trials of Lithuanian collaborators and photograph albums and memoirs published by the man who was the Lithuanian Division's Political Commissar. Another source includes articles published by Jews in newspapers and journals in the Soviet Union, Eretz Yisrael, and elsewhere, while the events were taking place. I have also drawn from documents written during the Holocaust, mostly by Jewish individuals and groups, including posters, leaflets, internal circulars, logs reporting the manpower and weapons situations, letters written by the Jewish underground organization in the Vilna Ghetto, fifty-two issues of the Vilna Ghetto's weekly news bulletin in Yiddish, *Geto Yedies*, diaries kept by the inmates of the Vilna and Shavli ghettos, the almanac and issues of the *Nitzotz* newspaper of the Kovno Ghetto's *Irgun Brit Ziyon* (I.B.Z.), and memoirs later written by survivors. Considerable use has been made of such unique documents as the diary written in Yiddish by a Jewish soldier of the Lithuanian Division, a battle log kept by a partisan detachment (battalion) of Jewish partisans in the Vilna region, and an annotated list of Jews and some Russians from another partisan detachment in the same region, with personal data on each fighter.

At a certain stage in our research, we realized that even if we had had all the existing documentary material at our disposal, it would still not cover many of the unique facts about the Jewish participation in the war effort that we had set out to study. To fill this gap, we used existing testimonies of survivors and recorded further interviews. In Israel, we made real use of forty-five testimonies from the Yad Vashem Archives and twenty from the Moreshet Archives. However, the bulk of the interviews used were those we planned and conducted ourselves, designed to provide information on specific episodes about which few facts were known, and to answer questions and deal with assumptions that we had posited at the outset of our study, or that arose in the course of it.

We conducted 200 interviews with 165 persons, holding as many as six sessions with some survivors. Thirty-five of the interviews were in Yiddish; the rest were in Hebrew. The interviewees may be classified as follows:

- Twelve Lithuanian Jews who served in the Lithuanian army or were active in self-defense
- Sixteen Lithuanian Jewish refugees or expelees in the Soviet Union, some of whom were active in the smuggling of Polish refugees to safety
- Sixty Jewish members of the Red Army's Lithuanian Division, including twenty-five from the rank of corporal up
- Fourteen Lithuanian Jews who served in other Red Army units or in various Polish forces
- Sixty-three underground members and partisans from the Vilna, Shavli, and other ghettos

These interviews, all of them taped, were conducted at the Oral History Division of the Institute of Contemporary Jewry at the Hebrew University of Jerusalem. The tapes were transcribed and then catalogued according to the names or sobriquets of the interviewees and according to serial numbers based on the chronological order in which they were made. All this material, whose general designation is (12), can be found in the Oral History Division's archives.

The technique of these interviews was based on the experience of interviewing ninety persons for our previous study, on the underground organization in the Kovno Ghetto (Z. A. Brown and D. Levin, *Toldoteha shel Mahteret, Ha'irgun Halohem shel Yehudei Kovno Bemilhemet-Ha'olam Kovna Hasheniah*, (The Story of an Underground: The Resistance of the Jews of Kovno (Lithuania) in the Second World War) (Jerusalem, 1962). However, adjustments were always made to deal with the dynamics peculiar to each of the fighting organizations covered in the present study. (Thus, for example, group interviews were conducted and closed questionnaires distributed at two mass meetings held in Tel Aviv, one in December 1968, of former partisans in the eastern-border forests of Lithuania, and the other in February 1969, of veterans of the Lithuanian Division.) Z. A. Brown and - D. Levin explain the interview methods in a joint article, "Problems Relating to a Questionnaire on the Holocaust," in *Yad Vashem Studies III*, (Jerusalem, 1959) pp. 91–118.*

*This volume is based on a doctoral dissertation, *The Participation of the Jews of Lithuania in the War against the Germans in World War II*, submitted to the Senate of the Hebrew University of Jerusalem in 1970. The interested reader can find exact copies of the full dissertation, with its unabridged text, full complement of footnotes and references, and the bibliography of books, journals and documents on which the present work is based, in the following libraries: Jewish National Library (Jerusalem), Yad Vashem (Jerusalem), and the YIVO Institute (New York).

ACKNOWLEDGMENTS

$\mathbf{A}$S ONE OF THE FEW LITHUANIAN JEWS WHO HAD THE privilege of actively participating in the war against the Germans and their allies, reaching Eretz Yisrael (as an "illegal") at the end of World War II, and fighting in Israel's four wars, I regarded this research project, which occupied me for many years, as a mission if not as my life's work. I was motivated principally by the desire to uncover as many facts as possible about Lithuanian Jewry's participation in the struggle against the Germans; to analyze the substantive and functional relations between the different data; and to record the events and the names of the participants for posterity as accurately and faithfully as possible.

It is doubtful whether I would have succeeded in my undertaking to the extent I did without the help of various individuals and institutions. First and foremost, I wish to express my gratitude to the late Shaul Esh, of blessed memory, who was killed tragically. He was not only my teacher but my comrade, and directed me in the early stages of this project. I am profoundly grateful to Professor Yehuda Bauer, who continued to direct me and, together with Professor Jonathan Frankel, gave me much advice and encouragement. Professor Bauer also rushed publication of this book in Hebrew and in English.

I wish also to thank the following: Rabbi Joel S. Geffen for his kind help and encouragement; my friend, the poet Abraham Sutzkever, who supplied me with the document to which the analysis of Chapter 23 is devoted; my comrade in arms and pen, Professor Zvi A. Brown (Bar-On), who gave me inspiration and the benefit of his experience and knowledge when we worked together on "*Toldoteha shel Mahteret*" and continued to do so whenever I consulted him in connection with the present study; my dear friend David Gavish, who made valuable comments on the statistical aspects of this study; the translators of the present work, Moshe Kohn and Dina Cohen; Dr. David Geffen and Dr. Cynthia Haft Levin, who reviewed the manuscript with me to help make the text clearer; and Mrs. Melna Charin and Ms. Linda Alcalay for typing all my correspondence with the publisher. Thanks also to Mrs. T. Soffor for drawing the maps.

In particular, I want to single out two persons to whom I am especially indebted: my dear aunt, Mrs. Rivka Gutman, of Blessed Memory, who warmly hosted me at her home in Tel Aviv during my frequent trips there to conduct interviews and search for documentary material; and, last but not least, my wife Bilha, who not only inspired and encouraged me, but also typed the original Hebrew manuscript and, while doing so, made valuable stylistic suggestions.

My deep gratitude extends also to the hundreds of people mentioned in the appendixes, who readily agreed to interviews and cooperated with me all along the way, and to others, still living in the Soviet Union, who in various ways sent me valuable documents and information.

Finally, I wish to pay tribute to the memory of all those who fell in the struggle against the Nazis.

T HE TRANSLATION OF THIS BOOK INTO ENGLISH WAS made possible by Mr. Bert Lewyn in memory of his parents, Yohanna and Leopold Lewyn.

FIGHTING BACK

THE PUBLICATION OF THIS BOOK WAS MADE POSSIBLE BY the Alexander Silberman International Scholarship Foundation; the author is an Alexander Silberman International Fellow at the Institute of Contemporary Jewry, Hebrew University.

INTRODUCTION
LITHUANIAN JEWRY BEFORE WORLD WAR II

EVER SINCE 1251, WHEN LITHUANIA BECAME A CHRISTIAN monarchy under its first king, Mindaugas, it has been contested territory, struggled over primarily by Prussia and Russia. Then, in 1795, the date of the third partition of Poland, to which Lithuania was politically linked, most of the country was annexed to Russia, and the remainder to Prussia. For the next 120 years of Russian occupation, when Lithuania was known as Russia's "Northwestern Region," Lithuanians resisted Russian national and cultural oppression in various ways, including fighting in the great Polish uprisings of 1831 and 1863 and, at the Lithuanian conference held in Vilna near the end of the 1905 Russo-Japanese War, going so far as to demand immediate national autonomy.

By the time the Germans conquered Lithuania in 1915, there were some 200,000 Lithuanians in the Russian interior, most of whom were either soldiers in the Russian army or people who had been banished to the interior on the eve of the Russian retreat. But it was not until February 16, 1918, after a delegation of 336 Lithuanians met at the close of the February 1917 Russian Revolution to demand an independent state in ethnic Lithuania, and after the German-sponsored Lithuanian National Council, the *Taryba*, was elected in Vilna, that the Taryba proclaimed the independent state of Lithuania.

The struggle, however, was not over. In 1920, the legions of the Polish General L. Zeligowski captured Vilna, Lithuania's capital, along with the surrounding towns and annexed them to Poland. As a result, Lithuania lost its common border with Poland as well as with the Soviet Union (see Map 1), and was plunged into a dispute with

3

Poland that lasted until 1938. Lithuania's second largest city, Kovno with a population in 1939 of 140,000, became the country's temporary capital. The League of Nations, of which Lithuania became a member in 1922, took up the Lithuanian question many times.

On the other hand, Lithuania also gained some territory during this time. In 1923, it annexed the harbor of Klaipeda (Memel) and its environs, which the Versailles Treaty had cut off from Germany, and granted its 140,000 German inhabitants a certain measure of auton-

MAP 1   Location map of Lithuania between the two World Wars

T. Soffer , Geography Dept. H. U.

omy. Therefore, independent Lithuania comprised 21,489 square miles and a population of 2,421,570 of whom 84 percent were Lithuanians (mostly farmers and Catholics); 7.6 percent Jews; 2.7 percent Poles, Russians, and Byelorussians; 1.4 percent Germans; 0.7 percent Latvians; and 0.5 percent others. Outside the country, the greatest concentration of Lithuanians was and still is, in the United States.

Between the two World Wars, Lithuanians supported themselves mainly by farming and the manufacture of agricultural by-products, which were also the country's main export item. The economy was also bolstered by 600,000 Americans of Lithuanian origin who, by investing in enterprises there, contributed to the nation's funds, or assisted their relatives. On the other hand, ties between the motherland and the 45,000 Lithuanians in the Soviet Union were very loose.

Lithuania could maintain neither social nor economic stability, however, and as a result, the democratic system instituted at independence did not last very long. In the six years following the Constituent *Seimas* (Diet) in 1920, there were three parliamentary elections and seven governments. In 1926, a military coup brought the fascist movement to power, abolished the 1922 democratic constitution, and dissolved the Third Diet, in which seven national minorities were represented. Three years later the fascists were overthrown by the nationalists, who ruled until Lithuania lost her independence in 1940.

Ever since its War of Independence (1918–1920), Lithuania maintained an armed establishment of 50,000 men. This included three infantry divisions, four artillery regiments, three cavalry regiments, one air force regiment, and several special units. Most of the officers were ardent nationalists and supporters of the regime, especially those who had trained in Germany or Czechoslovakia, as well as some who had served in the Czarist armies.

There have been Jewish communities in Lithuania since the fourteenth century, and when the Duke Vytautas granted them religious liberty and the freedom to engage in commerce and handicrafts, in 1388, their numbers increased. Although these privileges were later withdrawn, mainly because of pressure from burghers, they were eventually restored by the kings and nobles of united Poland and Lithuania. In the 16th century, the growing Jewish communities consolidated themselves and established the "Council of Lithuanian Lands," an organization comprising representatives from five of the major Jewish communities—Grodno, Pinsk, Brest-Litovsk (Brisk), and later Vilna and Slutzk. The Chmielnicki insurrection of 1648–1649 and the Russian and Swedish invasions hit some of these communities quite hard, however, and in 1764, the "Lands Council" was abolished.

Between the Russian annexation of Lithuania in 1795, and World War I, Lithuanian Jewry was steadily subjected to discrimination, pressure, and pogroms by the Czars. This, of course, persuaded tens of thousands of Lithuanian Jews to migrate to North America, South Africa, and other countries. Yet, even so, Lithuania, and especially Vilna, became a major center of Jewish religious, cultural, and intellectual life and of Zionist and Jewish social-revolutionary movements. Then, on the eve of World War I, the Russian military, uneasy and angry about their own forthcoming retreat, ordered pogroms and the mass expulsion of 120,000 Jews to the Russian interior. The rest remained under the harsh German occupation until 1918. These were the Jews who, with the small number who returned from the interior at the end of the war, ultimately constituted independent Lithuania's Jewish community, which in 1923 numbered 153,743.

The Jews and Lithuanians in Czarist Russia had worked together in the elections of three *Dumas* (National Assemblies) since 1906. Furthermore, Jewish leaders had had extensive contact with Lithuanian statesmen during the last months of World War I. As a result, Jews played a prominent part, in Lithuania and in the international arena, in the country's successful struggle for independence and then in the struggle to consolidate that independence. In the first Lithuanian government formed in Vilna in December 1918, Dr. Jacob Wygodzki was named Minister for Jewish Affairs, and two Jews were named Deputy Ministers: Dr. S. Rosenbaum (Foreign Affairs) and Dr. N. Rachmilevitz (Commerce and Industry). Furthermore, the Jews were promised national autonomy in a "Declaration of Principles" handed down by the Lithuanian delegation at the Versailles Peace Conference on August 5, 1919. This declaration had the approval of the Lithuanian government and of the three main parties represented in the Constituent Diet. It was given legal sanction by Section 73 of the Lithuanian Constitution of August 1, 1922: "Citizens belonging to national minorities and constituting a segment of the population are entitled by law to conduct their own cultural, public education, social welfare, and mutual aid affairs in an autonomous manner, and, towards this end, to elect representative institutions in a manner to be laid down by law." Section 74 goes on to state: "The minority groups are entitled, within a suitable legal framework, to levy taxes on their members for cultural purposes, and to receive from the national and local governments an equitable share of the monies earmarked for popular education."[1]

Jewish rights, along with those of other minorities in Lithuania, were clarified in the Lithuanian delegate's declaration on the eve of the country's admission to the League of Nations, as follows: "All citizens, without distinction of religion or language, are equal before the law, and religious differences need not be an obstacle to their obtaining posts in governmental service. Neither shall there be any restrictions on their use of their own languages in commercial life and the like." These rights were largely implemented during the term of the Constituent Diet (May 15, 1920–November 13, 1922), which included six Jewish members.

A conference of the Jewish communities, which were entitled to levy taxes on their members, elected a "Jewish National Council in Lithuania" consisting of thirty-four members to serve as the supreme body of the autonomous communities. The Council, headed by an executive and a praesidium, also nominated the person who was to be the Minister for Jewish Affairs in the national government, and maintained close touch with the Jewish faction in the Diet. The Council appointed economic, cultural, health, social welfare, and other civic committees and hired a staff to handle these matters. The Council also helped establish a network of popular banks, headed by the Central Jewish Bank.

The Council functioned primarily in the socioeconomic sphere. The Ministry for Jewish Affairs, on the other hand, concentrated on the legal consolidation of the autonomous body, on the supervision of activities in Lithuania's more than 120 reorganized Jewish communities, and on the establishment, maintenance, and development of Jewish education. Since these institutions had official status, the government gave them franking privileges and subsidized the salaries of their workers. Their official language was Yiddish, but their emblems, seals, and stationery were in Hebrew and Lithuanian.

During this period, known as the golden age of Lithuanian Jewry, Jews served in senior governmental and municipal posts, with some also attaining officer's rank in the armed forces and the police. However, as Lithuania consolidated itself politically and the problem of Vilna remained unresolved, its dependence on Jewish moral and diplomatic support decreased. This, combined with the heightening competition between Jews and Lithuanians for economic positions and endemic anti-Semitism among a portion of the Lithuanian populace, brought about a steady deterioration of the general attitude toward Jews and an erosion of their rights.

Two early signs of this process were the abolition of the official status granted to minority languages (in the wake of which Dr. M.

Soloveichik [Solieli] resigned as Minister for Jewish Affairs) and the abolition of the budget of the Ministry for Jewish Affairs. In September 1924, the Ministry and the Jewish National Council ceased to function. In March 1926, the Jewish communities were stripped of their right to levy taxes, register births, and so forth. With the demise of the Council and the delegitimation of the communities, the major representative body of Lithuanian Jews became the Jewish faction in the Diet. Then, when the Third Diet was dissolved by the fascist junta in December 1926, Lithuanian Jewry was left with neither a central organization nor representation. The local Jewish communities no longer had the power or means to do more than fulfil religious needs. Furthermore, new restrictions in municipal elections drastically reduced Jewish representation in the city councils.

Despite the patriotism and loyalty displayed by most Lithuanian Jews, Lithuanians frequently cast slurs on them precisely because of their loyalty. At the very time when thousands of Lithuanian Jews, many of them volunteers, were actively participating in the Lithuanian War of Independence and dozens of them were being killed in the fighting, Lithuanian troops were staging pogroms in Ponevezh (Panevėžys) and other places. In spite of such occurrences, which were relatively rare in Lithuania, and in spite of their disappointment over certain restrictive policies, the Jews of Lithiuania were fully aware that they were better off than the Jews of neighboring countries. It is, therefore, easy to understand their general inclination to serve in the armed forces and such patriotic associations as the Vilna Liberation Committee and why the pupils of the Hebrew high school in Kovno, for example, volunteered to serve in the Lithuanian "Sharpshooters Units" against the Polish legions that had attacked Vilna. The Association of Jewish Veterans of the Lithuanian War of Independence, established in 1933 and comprising more than 3,000 members in thirty-three branches, repeatedly stressed in its Lithuanian-language newsletter, *Apžvalga*, and elsewhere, the Jewish contribution to Lithuanian independence and development. At the same time, it tried to "serve as a central address for Lithuanian Jewry," in the absence of a recognized general Jewish representative body.[2]

The Hebrew educational system, however, did survive from the period of autonomy, and it distinguished Lithuanian Jewry between the two World Wars from all other Jewish communities, except that in Eretz Yisrael.

In 1937, the Jewish public school network in Lithuania embraced 13,856 pupils in 107 of its own schools, in addition to the 2,106 students attending forty-five "Jewish classes" in the public schools. Since

9,699 of these students attended Zionist-sponsored *Tarbut* schools, where the language of instruction was Hebrew (as compared with 6,217 in the 1926–1927 school year), and others attended religious, Zionist-sponsored *Yavneh* schools, the Hebrew school network constituted 85 percent of the Jewish schools, Yiddish the other 15 percent. In addition, there were more than 3,000 pupils attending fourteen privately run Jewish high schools, of which eleven also used Hebrew as the language of instruction.

Hebrew was spoken not only in the schools, but also in the Zionist youth movements, some Zionist institutions, and Zionist *hachsharah* agricultural training camps, as well as in intellectual circles and a small but substantial number of homes. This—in spite of the fact that Yiddish was the vernacular of the overwhelming majority of Lithuanian Jewry and the language of the six daily newspapers and a number of weeklies and other periodicals that Lithuanian Jewry produced.

Lithuanian Jewry was also distinguished by its Yeshivot (Orthodox rabbinical schools), some of the more famous of which were the Slobodka (Vilijampolė) Knesset Yisrael Yeshiva in Kovno and those in Telsh (Telšiai), Ponevezh, and Kelme.

The Jewish national and religious character of Lithuanian Jewry was reflected not only in its school system but also, very strongly, in its political and ideological life. Except for the country's tiny Communist Party, in which the Jewish membership sometimes reached 50 percent, with some Jews occupying key party positions,[3] there were practically no Jews in the general Lithuanian political parties and organizations. There were 5,010 members in the Zionist youth movements in 1929 and 8,625 two years later. In 1938, there were 215 registered Jewish institutions and associations (28 percent of the country's total), including seventy-eight for mutual aid, forty-five for culture, forty-three for social welfare, and sixteen for the economy.[4]

According to the first and only census taken in independent Lithuania, the 153,743 Jews in the country in 1923 represented 7.6 percent of the total population, the country's largest national minority. Two-thirds of them lived in the cities. Between 1923 and 1938, 20,000 Jews left the country, half to go to Eretz Yisrael.[5] Because of this and a decline in the birth rate, the Jewish population decreased in both absolute and relative terms.

In 1923, the Jews constituted an overwhelming majority of the mercantile class. But in the wake of the government's policy of encouraging cooperatives and of concentrating import-export activities in government companies, their role in both wholesale and retail business gradually declined until the 1930s, when constant official harassment, reaching a peak during World War II, made Jewish participation in industry, the handicrafts, commerce, and the free professions even more difficult. Because prospects for securing positions even after completing school were slim, enrollment in institutions of higher learning also decreased. Hence, anti-Jewish restrictions and the difficult economic situation turned Lithuania "into a cage without hope for the Jewish youth." Forced to study abroad, many did not return.

Especially serious was the plight of the 60,000 Jews of Vilna and the 30,000 of the surrounding towns, including Troki, and Eishishok. After the conquest of this area by Zeligowski's Polish legions in 1920, these Jews were almost completely cut off from the rest of Lithuanian Jewry, including their families. According to a socio-economic study conducted in each of the Jewish communities of this region in the late 1920s, "the Jewish *shtetl* is hovering between life and death."[6] And yet, despite the impact of the Polish educational system, Yiddish remained the vernacular of the Jews of Vilna, as it was of the rest of Lithuanian Jewry.

FAR-REACHING CHANGES ON THE EVE OF WORLD WAR II

The situation of Lithuanian Jewry deteriorated even more rapidly after 1938, as a number of political developments affected the country's integrity and sovereignty. In the new constitution of 1922, the last vestiges of the autonomous period were omitted. Furthermore, a "Lithuania for Lithuanians" campaign was launched, principally by farmers and urban economic organizations. They demanded that Jews who had entered the country after 1918 be expelled and that the remainder of the Jews be prohibited from selling beer, flour, grains, flax, and seeds and from operating restaurants, cafes, and hotels. They also demanded that Saturday, the traditional Jewish day of rest, be declared the official market day, that all trade be prohibited on Sunday, and that the Jews' ritual slaughter of animals for food be banned. In spite of reassuring pronouncements to the Jews by a number of key Lithuanian statesmen, the government in fact adopted a number of these demands, mainly those of an economic nature.

This anti-Jewish agitation was accompanied by physical assaults on Jews, to an extent hitherto unknown in independent Lithuania. Incidents like the smashing of Jews' windows simultaneously in a number of towns suggest that this was a centrally organized operation. The same applies to the wave of fires that hit dozens of Jewish communities during that period.

In response to these developments, the Jewish extreme Left expanded and took control of the daily *Folksblat* (People's Paper). On the other hand, the Zionist movement, including its youth affiliate, began to wane. There was also a sharp decrease in the number of youths in the *hachsharah* training camps of the *Hehalutz* movement, where the waiting period for a British certificate to enter Mandatory Palestine was now three to five years. In the wake of the growing restrictions imposed on Jews seeking admission to medical, agricultural, and engineering programs, and especially in view of the virtual impossibility of finding jobs in these fields, the enrollment of Jews at Kovno University continued to decline. Furthermore, there were now fewer possibilities of emigrating to South Africa or to the Americas, the traditional destinations of Lithuanian Jewish emigrants. Only the boom caused by the country's preparations for war alleviated the economic lot of Lithuanian Jewry. Otherwise, the Lithuanian Jews were confronted with needs and circumstances radically different from those they had experienced in the relative calm and stability of the previous decades.

THE REUNION WITH VILNA JEWRY

With the return of the Vilna region to Lithuania, the country's Jewish population increased by 100,000 to a total of 250,000, or 10 percent of the whole population.[7] (These numbers were altered, however, when, during their six-week control of Vilna [from September 18 to October 28, 1939], the Soviets arrested and banished a number of prominent Jews, and then, they withdrew, carrying off a number of industrial plants. For a variety of economic and political reasons, approximately 360 Jewish workers of the Elektrit factory and their families accompanied their employer to Russia. In addition, several thousand young Jews, primarily Leftists who had served in the militia or in the Workers' Guard, also went along.[8])

Despite public and political experiences they shared during the struggles for Lithuanian independence and Jewish autonomy and despite the family connections between them, nineteen years of separation created some differences between the Jews of Vilna and the Jews of Kovno, especially in terms of their political and cultural approach. For, while Lithuanian Jewry and its leaders admired the Jews of Vilna for their public-mindedness and for the sophistication of their political institutions and organizations, they often considered Vilna Jewry as "a starving pauper but still a respected relative." During the short period before the war, they could develop only a brief relationship based on mutual aid, the exchange of information, and courtesy visits. It took their common fate—the coming Holocaust—to bind them solidly together.

The Jews of Vilna, however, were not the only ones to return to Lithuania at this time. In addition to the 1,500 Jews of the Suwalki region who had been banished to the no-man's land between Lithuania and Poland by the Germans and who were later absorbed into the towns of southern Lithuania, hundreds of Jewish soldiers of the Polish army were ransomed by the Jews of that region from prisoner-of-war camps. Furthermore, some 15,000 Jewish refugees from the Soviet and German occupation areas streamed into Lithuania via Vilna. These included hundreds of political and communal leaders, writers, and intellectuals, about 2,500 young Zionist *halutzim* in their *hachsharah* training-camp formations, and about the same number of *yeshivah* students and teachers.

Members of these various groups were later to play a prominent role in the underground organizations of the ghettos and labor camps of Lithuania during the Holocaust. On the whole, the refugees, were flexible and particularly adept organizers, and many persisted in their efforts to flee Lithuania and Europe as quickly as possible, for Eretz Yisrael or elsewhere.[9]

Contact with such diverse groups of such high caliber was a rich and surprising experience for Lithuanian Jewry, which shook many out of their relative complacency. As one of them put it to a refugee from Poland: "We're lost. With the Russians on one side of us, and the Germans on the other, we're going to be ground to dust." Now Lithuanian Jews, too, began leaving the country in great numbers. Shortly after the Red Army left Vilna at the end of October 1939 and the Lithuanians took over the city, the situation for the Jews hardly improved. With the encouragement of the Lithuanian police, a pogrom was staged, killing one Jew and wounding nearly 200. Eyewitnesses reported that the pogrom was in part "a reaction to the activity of the Jews during the short period of Soviet rule." As a result of vigorous protests by leading Jews who threatened to request outside intervention, however, the pogrom was stopped after one day.

During the pogrom in Vilna, there had not been sufficient time to organize a defense.[10] But in view of the danger of future pogroms, a number of Jewish organizations met in Kovno to discuss setting up a program for Jewish self-defense. A detailed plan was drawn up, which included fixed tours of guard duty, a communication network, and an arsenal of pistols, and some discussed radical political changes that might free them from the potential danger of the unstable situation. In the midst of this tension, tainted by the dread possibility of a Nazi takeover of Lithuania, Red Army infantry and armored units invaded Lithuania, on June 15, 1940, and within seven weeks turned the country into a Soviet republic. These events in fact also came to mark the end of five hundred years of strong, traditional, and organized Jewish life in Lithuania.

PART I
IN THE SOVIET SPHERE OF INFLUENCE

CHAPTER 1
THE SOVIET TAKE-OVER

IN THE PEACE TALKS BETWEEN GERMANY AND RUSSIA
held at Brest-Litovsk at the close of World War I, Leon Trotsky rejected
the German demand that Lithuania, Latvia, and Estonia be permitted
to secede from Russia. He argued that this would happen only by free
elections, after all foreign military presence had been gone.[1]

As a result, a Subcommissariat for Lithuanian Affairs was set up
by the Soviet People's Commissariat for National Affairs. Its principal
task was to oversee the 200,000 Lithuanians then residing in the
Soviet Union as war refugees or as soldiers demobilized from the
Czarist army. But, among other things, it was also responsible for
"cultural activity"—that is, for spreading Bolshevik propaganda
among the Lithuanians and for "training cadres for life in independent Lithuania."[2] Therefore, after the Lithuanian *Taryba* (Council) proclaimed the independent state of Lithuania, Bolshevik activists and
members of the Lithuanian Council began infiltrating the country and
hiding themselves among the thousands of Lithuanian refugees returning from Russia. Once in Lithuania, they laid the groundwork for
the Lithuanian Communist Party and, acting in vigorous opposition
to the National Government, proclaimed in December 1918 the establishment of the "Revolutionary Government of Workers and Peasants
in Lithuania," which the Soviet Union officially recognized on December 22.

This regime was most powerful in northeastern Lithuania, where
it succeeded in passing a few laws concerning economic and social
issues. It was, however, very quickly threatened by the armed forces
of A. Voldemaras's National Government, which was in control in the
southwest near the German border, and which was supported with
political, technical, and military assistance by the United States, Great
Britain, France, and Germany.

The Lithuanian and Byelorussian Defense Council waged a rear-guard action against the growing attacks of the Lithuanian National Army, supported by regular German units, armed bands, and Pilsudski's Polish legions.[3] The Council, on the other hand, was supported by the Red Army and by a number of units that had been created in Lithuania proper.[4] In the course of seven months of bitter fighting, the Red Army was gradually forced to retreat from Lithuanian soil. Lithuania was now in the German, Western European, and American sphere of influence, and remained independent until 1940.

Relations with the Soviet Union were regularized by the Moscow Pact of July 12, 1920. Russia recognized the sovereignty of independent Lithuania over the Vilna-Grodno region, agreed to expedite the return of Lithuanian refugees still in the Soviet Union, and consented to the exchange of political prisoners between the two countries. But after the German invasion of Poland on September 1, 1939, and the division of Poland between Germany and the Soviet Union, the Soviet Union again tried to gain sway over Lithuania. Taking steps to insure that Lithuania did not become a German satellite, Soviet diplomats managed with intense effort to amend the first section of a secret appendix to the Ribbentrop-Molotov Pact of August 23, 1939, which, with little warning, had been designed to help Russia include the Baltic countries in her sphere of influence. Signed on September 28, the revised section now read: "The territory of the Lithuanian State fell to the sphere of influence of the U.S.S.R." As a result, Lithuania regained her capital, Vilna. But the Soviet Union was now "permitted to maintain at her expense, at certain vantage points in the Republic of Lithuania, land and air units of the Soviet armed forces of certain limited strength."[5]

On June 15, 1940, the day Paris fell, Soviet troops entered Lithuania—one day after the Soviets issued an ultimatum to the Lithuanian government. Two days later a "People's Government," headed by Paleckis, was formed. It immediately granted amnesty to all political prisoners and declared the Communist party legal. Inspired by the Communist party, elections were held for a "People's Diet," which at its first session on July 21, 1940, proclaimed the Lithuanian Soviet Socialist Republic and decided to apply to the Russian Supreme Soviet for admission into the Union of Soviet Socialist Republics.[6] The Supreme Soviet approved their application on August 3. The next step was a special order proclaiming the Lithuanian army a "People's Army," and appointing General F. Baltušis-Žemaitis commander-in-chief. Later, the Lithuanian People's Army was fully integrated into the Red Army as the 29th Territorial Corps. In the same manner, Latvia and Estonia became Soviet Socialist Republics.

Germany granted political asylum to the president of Lithuania, as well as to many cabinet ministers and to members of the army and police who successfully escaped. Officially, however, Germany rejected Lithuanian, Latvian, and Estonian protests against their annexation to the Soviet Union, although the United States continues to recognize the accredited representatives of Lithuania, Latvia, and Estonia to this day.

CHAPTER 2
THE LITHUANIAN JEWS AND THE SOVIET REGIME, JUNE 15, 1940 TO JUNE 26, 1941

SOVIET RULE IN LITHUANIA DID DEFER THE HOLOCAUST there for twelve months and seven days, but ultimately it heightened the tragedy. For, because the Jews played a significant role in the country's sovietization, both willingly and unwillingly, they later bore the brunt of the patriotic Lithuanians' anger. In addition, Lithuanian Jewry suffered because most of the businesses and buildings that had been nationalized by the Soviets belonged to Jews. Of the 986 plants that the People's Diet had nationalized on July 19, 1940, 560, or 57 percent, were owned by Jews. They also owned 1,320, or 83 percent, of the 1,595 businesses that were nationalized at the end of September. This included every enterprise with an annual turnover of at least 150,000 *litas* (then the equivalent of $15,000), along with the assets and bank accounts of their owners. Moreover, the thrust of the agrarian reforms hit Jewish landowners more than others, because the authorities contended that the Jews did not work their lands and thus were not entitled to retain them. Furthermore, many small shopkeepers, upon whom heavy taxes were imposed and who were subjected to severe restrictions in obtaining fresh supplies, had to close their shops, and some of them were banished from the big cities to the small towns. Thus, sovietization of business and industry had a profound effect on the Jews.

At the same time, most of the Jewish craftsmen were integrated into the economy through the craft cooperatives, while others were permitted to continue working independently. Members of the liberal professions were also freely accepted into government and municipal jobs. Those who fared best, however, were the salaried workers and the manual laborers, who received considerable emoluments and promotions.

Just a few weeks after the Red Army entered, the editors of the Jewish newspapers were replaced, and most of the papers were closed down, leaving only the *Vilner Emes* in Vilna and the *Der Emes* in Kovno. The Hebrew libraries were liquidated and the Yiddish libraries absorbed by the municipal libraries.

All the Jewish schools were placed under the aegis of the Commissariat of Education, and, before the 1940–1941 school year, all teachers were obliged to undergo a special course in Soviet educational methods, with the exception, of course, of those who were no longer permitted to teach. Yiddish became the language of instruction in the schools, and all courses in Hebrew were eliminated. Semitic Studies in the University were replaced by a Yiddish Language department.

Since all education was now free, and the *numerus clausus* was abolished, Jewish youth streamed *en masse* to the universities and the technical schools. Vilna and Kovno now had state Yiddish theaters. But such "advantages" were mitigated by the fact that Sunday was made the one official day of rest and Saturday a mandatory day of work. This hit both Orthodox Jews and Traditionalists hard, and Jews felt discriminated against in this respect, vis-à-vis Christians.

The Soviet regime, of course, also had an immediate political impact on Jews. There were two Jewish ministers—of Health and of Industry—in the People's Government, and two Jewish deputy commissars—of Industry and of Commerce—in the Communist government, which ratified the annexation to the Soviet Union. And at the beginning of 1941, 355 members of the Lithuanian Communist Party, out of a total of 1,968, were Jewish. The new regime also employed a relatively large number of Jewish administrators and other specialists, especially in the implementation of its economic policy. Furthermore, we know the names of twenty-four Jewish officers of company commander's rank who were political commissars in the People's Army and in the 29th Territorial Corps, and of ten Jewish officers who worked on the editorial and administrative staffs of the army journal, *Karių Tiesa* [The Truth of the Soldier].

On the other hand, the authorities did not hesitate to deal harshly with Jewish individuals or groups whom they considered unreliable, hostile, or dangerous. This was undertaken in coordination with the Communist party's minorities bureau, headed by Genrikas Ziman (Zimanas), who eventually played a crucial role in the armed resistance of Lithuanian Jewry during World War II.[1] On June 28, 1940, an order was issued liquidating all national, cultural, and economic organizations in Lithuania, including, of course, the Jewish ones. At the same time, pressures were applied and incentives offered to induce the members of these organizations to join the Communist party, or at least to enter its sphere of influence. A number of their leaders were arrested, some to be freed only after the German invasion a year later.

Furthermore, in many areas Jewish shopkeepers whose businesses had been nationalized had to perform forced labor on public works projects, while factory owners and some businessmen were banished from the large cities. Among the Jews classed as "ideologically dangerous," "anti-Soviet," and "counter-revolutionary" were leaders and members of Zionist and Bundist organizations, and of such military groups as the Jewish war veterans association, "Betar," and the Revisionists. Then, on June 14, 1941, just a week before the German invasion, 35,000 people from all over Lithuania, including 7,000 Jews, were arrested or banished.[2] The expellees—including party and organizational activists, factory owners, and even small shopkeepers—were taken on freight trains to various labor camps in Siberia and far north of the Russian Soviet Federated Republics. Put to work under extremely harsh conditions cutting trees, laying rail lines, and working in mines and fisheries, many of them died of frost, hunger, and illness.

TENSION BETWEEN LITHUANIANS AND JEWS

In spite of the fact that the majority of Lithuanian Jews were no less affected than the general population by sovietization, many Lithuanians identified Jews as a whole with the long-hated Soviet regime. Whereas in independent Lithuania there had been no mass anti-Semitism, other than a certain degree of hostility stemming from economic and professional rivalry, under Soviet rule, raw anti-Semitism came to the fore and tainted the relations between the Lithuanians and the Jews.

If, for instance, a young Jew became an officer in the Soviet militia, Lithuanians accused him of ingratitude and treachery, especially if, in the line of duty, he was involved in the arrest and expulsion of any Lithuanian the public deemed patriotic. Many Lithuanians also took the rise of several hundred Jews to managerial positions in businesses that previously had not hired Jews, personally and were offended by the enthusiasm for the Soviet regime displayed by many young Jews, who as one writer suggests, "did not always behave with the necessary tact."[3]

Since the Soviet regime prohibited the Lithuanians from staging pogroms, they had to content themselves with grumbling and verbal threats of revenge, most forcefully led by the nationalist underground movement, the Lithuanian Activist Front (*Lietuviŋ Aktyvistŋ Frontas*— LAF). Organizing itself systematically, on German soil under the aegis of the German counterintelligence agency, the *Abwehr*, and throughout Lithuania with the support of the local populace, the LAF threatened to exterminate the country's Jewish population "when the time comes."[4]

JEWISH REACTIONS TO THE SOVIET REGIME

During the first few months of the Soviet takeover, the Jews' reactions could be categorized as follows: relief that Lithuanian Jewry had been saved from a Nazi take-over and that the Soviet regime became the lesser of two evils; enthusiasm, motivated by ideology, social sensibility, or emotion, at the prospect of living under a Soviet regime; hope for a liberal, democratic regime under Soviet auspices, or of a flexible Soviet regime; opposition to a Soviet regime, stemming primarily from the fear of persecution.

As the Soviet regime settled in and began to clash frequently with traditional values and frameworks, the enthusiasm and hope waned. At the same time, the German threat and the Jews' awareness that the Lithuanians would seize the first opportunity for revenge intensified the realization that, when all was said and done, the Soviet regime was the lesser evil. Thus we can readily understand why most Lithuanian Jews were inclined to accept and even adapt to the situation, or, at least, to avoid open clashes with the regime and with public opinion.

This feeling was expressed in the priority that was given to clandestine activities throughout Lithuania. In addition to trying to cross the Baltic Sea and escape to Eretz Yisrael, some secreted Hebrew books before the Soviet authorities could seize them, while others risked publishing Hebrew bulletins. They also carried Jewish education underground, teaching the forbidden Hebrew language and literature, Jewish history, and Eretz Yisrael studies, observed Jewish holidays, and disseminated Jewish symbols. Furthermore, both the Leftist Zionist *Hashomer Hatza'ir*,[4] and the rightist Zionist *Betar*,[5] stayed intact, sharing the policy of refraining from anti-Soviet activity, even though the Betar at first continued its routine weapons training.

It was at this time, also, that such underground youth organizations as *Herut*, consisting of *Hehalutz Hatza'ir, Deror* and *No'ar Ziyoni Halutzi*, (NZH or Nezah), and the *Irgun Brit Ziyon* (IBZ) were created "to unite Jewish youth in the preservation of Jewish national and cultural values."[6] These groups were spurred on by the national consciousness of the youth; the affinity to Jewish tradition as envisioned by each of the groups; and, finally, the romantic aura of underground activity. More importantly, perhaps, they reacted against the impotence of Zionist leadership, against the Zionist movement's factionalism, and "against the mechanization of Zionism in the Diaspora and the conversion of the movement into a technical tool of an immigration bureau."[7] For unlike other groups, the established leadership of the Zionist organizations not only made virtually no attempt to deal with the ferment and to retain its authority, but, for personal and security reasons, they completely ceased to function and engaged in no clandestine political activity. Gradually, then, the youth began to take over the leadership, and later, occupied the central role in the Jewish armed resistance.

CHAPTER 3
LITHUANIAN JEWS IN RUSSIA

THE GERMAN INVASION

Early on Sunday Morning, June 22, 1941, after heavy shelling, German forces from East Prussia and Memel charged across the borders of Soviet Lithuania and, before the day was out, conquered considerable areas in the west and the south.[1] Taken by surprise, the Red Army forces retreated rapidly, battling not only the Germans but also the Lithuanian Armed Forces and other Lithuanians, who harassed them from the rear and seized strategic and public installations.

Frantic evacuation of the governmental and Communist party staffs followed, but because of the Germans' rapid advance, only 2,553 government and party members (55.2 percent of the party) and 2,200 Komsomol (Communist Youth Organization) members (15.7 percent) got away.[2] Among the successful evacuees were most of the cabinet ministers, the Party Central Committee, the heads of the security agencies and the militia, Leftist intellectuals and writers, and a number of lower officials and militia men. At the same time, many of the Lithuanians who had worked for the Soviets or had lately joined the Communist party went into action against the collapsing Soviet regime. This was especially true of the 12,000 officers and soldiers of the Twenty-ninth Territorial Rifle Corps, most of whom deserted either immediately or during the retreat. Only 3,000 men, including 355 of the 1,000 cadets from the Infantry Officers School in Vilna, reached the Soviet Union.[3] A considerable number of these evacuees, especially among government and party members, were Jews.

The Jews who stayed behind, however, in the middle of this chaos, and in the middle of the open preparations nationalist gangs were making for massacres, left to their own resources. They had

27

some idea as to what to expect from the Nazis, and in family circles, at gatherings among friends and neighbors, and in the Zionist underground circles, everyone discussed what to do. This was, indeed, a difficult question, because the alternatives were few and uncertain: they might go eastward in the wake of the retreating Red Army, to areas still under Soviet control; they might seek temporary shelter in Lithuania's forests and villages, evading the German army and the Lithuanian gangs; or they might remain and see what would happen.

It became clear almost immediately, however, that the second possibility was impractical, because the roads were controlled by nationalist gangs who missed no opportunity to harm Jews who happened their way and because the Jews were totally unprepared to wage guerrilla warfare. The best alternative, then, was to flee eastward by any possible means, even if this meant—as it did in most cases—the breakup of families and exposure to aerial bombardments and attacks by nationalist gangs. The *Hashomer Hatza'ir* decided to enlist in the Red Army, while keeping Abba Kovner, Chaika Grosman, and Moshe Balush in Vilna.[4] In spite of the danger and the uncertainty about how Soviets on the Russian-Lithuanian and Latvian-Lithuanian borders would receive them, masses of other Jews streamed eastward and northeastward, hoping to reach the border.

The eastward trek embraced tens of thousands of Jews, representing every social class and political persuasion. Most of them were of army age; a small portion were women, children, and elderly. There were also many groups from the youth movements and the former Zionist *hachsharah* training camps, who stood out because they began the march in an organized fashion and tried to stay together all the way. Most of them went on foot in the blazing summer sun, carrying valises and knapsacks.

And yet, since the Soviet border sentries did not always have clear instructions, many of the refugees were forced to turn back.[5] As a result, thousands were murdered by Lithuanian nationalists waiting in ambush, or killed in the heavy bombardments. Many thousands more never set out at all, for family, medical, and other reasons.

LITHUANIAN JEWISH REFUGEES IN THE SOVIET UNION

In the end, only some 15,000 Jews succeeded in crossing the Soviet border or the front line, reaching the interior of the Soviet Union in the summer of 1941 and settling in *kolkhozes* or finding work in factories or in urban centers.[6] Then in the fall, the "evacuees" (as they were now officially called) spontaneously began to migrate individually and in groups from hundreds of localities toward Central Asia. As their testimonies show, the evacuees had a number of reasons for this migration, which later played such a crucial role in the creation of the Lithuanian Division and in the effectiveness of the Division's recruitment.

For numerous Lithuanian Jews who moved to Soviet Central Asia and eventually enlisted in the Lithuanian Division, there were three very tangible reasons for migrating: Central Asia was "warmer, cheaper (plenty of fruit), and far from the front." Others left in hope of finding relatives or friends from whom they had become separated during the flight from Lithuania. Since "everybody meets in Tashkent," the chances of locating relatives or friends were good there. Another, though rarer, reason was: "It's not far to the border, and there may be a chance of getting out, namely to Eretz Yisrael." Finally, there was the desire to be "where there are a lot of Jews."

Apparently not interested in, or capable of, controlling the situation, the authorities contented themselves with directing this traffic to the areas the government was most interested in, including Central Asia. But the capacity of the Central Asian towns to which the Jews flocked (among them, Tashkent, Samarkand, Kokand, Ashkabad, Stalinabad, and Alma-Ata) to absorb the migrants was not unlimited. And after typhus epidemics broke out in these centers, the authorities began redirecting newcomers to villages or kolkhozes in the region, both by "advising" them and by threatening arrest if they did not leave within twenty-four hours.[7] The refugees obeyed, and almost no one harassed them or interfered in their internal affairs. In these circumstances, a group at the Kaganovich Kolkhoz near Samarkand was able to form a Zionist halutz, consisting of fifteen members of the "Zayd" and "Gesher" hachsharah training groups from Kovno.[8] This Kolkholz then became both a meeting place and a haven for members of the Polish Hechalutz, as well as the mailing address for aid packages sent from Eretz Yisrael via Teheran. Furthermore, the refugees got some help from the Soviet Lithuanian government at this time. It provided economic assistance, although irregularly, maintained six children's homes in the Gorki, Tashkent, and other regions, and encouraged writers to pursue their work.

Meanwhile, the refugees who had gone to the Iranian and Afghanistani borders of Central Asia because they hoped to reach Eretz Yisrael looked for ways to realize their dream. Some, such as the members of the youth movements and the Zionist organizations con-

tinued the quasi-legal activities they had undertaken with some success in Soviet Lithuania before the German invasion. Those not
affiliated with any organization, mainly unmarried young men and
women of Zionist background, also saw the possibility of getting to
Eretz Yisrael. But since this meant illegally crossing the Soviet border,
a grave offense especially in wartime, many did not try.[9]

WHY JEWS ENLISTED IN THE RED ARMY

At the very height of the mass escapes from Lithuania, many young
Jews tried to join the Soviet armed forces, either out of a sense of
patriotism and duty, or for personal reasons. Because of the chaos
reigning in the local government offices and in the army itself, however, these volunteers were sent away. The authorities were not even
able to implement the call-up order they had issued for men born
between 1905 and 1918.

Nevertheless, in a few instances the local authorities did issue
arms to young Jewish members of Komsomol (Communist Youth
Organization), so that they could guard installations and institutions.
These young people also provided cover for convoys of Jewish refugees, and some were cited for bravery in action against Lithuanian
nationalist gangs.[10] These, however, were isolated episodes. When
these armed formations reached Russia in the general retreat from the
German invaders, they were immediately disarmed, because of the
general atmosphere of distrust and because of the suspicion that they
might be German saboteurs disguised as Jews.

Organized attempts made by young Jews fleeing from Lithuania
to Latvia to enlist in the Red Army were also rebuffed, primarily
because Jewish and non-Jewish Lithuanian citizens who reached the
Russian Soviet Federated Socialist Republic were classified as
"evacuees from the western areas." Their status determined their fate
in many respects, including their right to enlist in the army.

Jews who had been expelled from Lithuania on June 14, 1941, a
week before the war broke out, and had been incarcerated in labor
camps, also sought to enlist. When the news of the German invasion
reached the camps, many Jewish refugees appealed to the camp authorities to be mobilized into the Red Army so that they "might fight
against the common enemy of the Jewish and the Soviet peoples."
The response of the authorities was categorically negative. In one
camp, the inmates were read an official government announcement,
the gist of which was: "We'll manage without you." Jewish refugees

who appeared at local recruitment offices were given similar answers: for example, "When we need you, we'll call you." This, despite the fact that the Soviet war effort could well have used the additional manpower.

At the end of 1941, however, the authorities decided to create a Lithuanian Division under Red Army command. And whereas relatively few people had been involved in the efforts to volunteer described above, Jews now streamed *en masse* to enlist in the Lithuanian Division. Not only those of draft age went to the recruitment offices, but also youngsters of sixteen and seventeen, men over forty-one, people whose jobs in the war economy exempted them from army service, and people with physical disabilities, which they tried to hide from the recruitment boards, tried to enlist.

Several factors motivated the mass volunteering: first, the desire to escape a badly deteriorating situation, as well as the loneliness of the remote *kolkhozes* and villages. In the Lithuanian Division, they hoped that they would "find plenty of Jews, including friends." Many also felt they "simply didn't want to remain in areas where people pointed fingers at us as shirkers who 'want to fight in Tashkent.' "[11] Furthermore, many believed they would return home to Lithuania "more quickly with the Division than with any Russian unit." But reports that people were finding their brothers and fathers in the Lithuanian Division raised the greatest hopes.

There is no doubt, however, that for all of them, whatever else motivated them, the desire to fight against the Nazis and to take revenge "for all those who were killed in Vilna, Kovno, and other towns and villages in Lithuania" was the most significant factor. This theme recurs again and again in the testimonies of veterans of the Lithuanian Division. Of course, the importance of this motive varied from person to person, depending on his life history and political attitude. It should also be noted that in some instances, enlisting in the army meant renouncing a relatively solid economic position, which adds credibility to the claim of those who say they enlisted on ideological grounds.

Not everyone enlisted, however. Some did not waive their war industry exemptions; and if there were many who tried to hide physical disabilities which might have disqualified them from military service, in rare instances, some exaggerated real disabilities or feigned illness when appearing before the conscription boards.

The Soviet Lithuanian military authorities, the Communist party, and government institutions conducted a continuous recruitment campaign among the Jewish refugees not yet enlisted in the Lithua-

nian Division. They used written manifestos as well as both Jewish
and non-Jewish speakers, including Justas Paleckis himself, the President of the Lithuanian Supreme Soviet. Since not all these Jews
understood Lithuanian, they were also addressed in Yiddish and
Russian.

The basic appeal was a general one, aimed at the patriotic in-
stincts of all Lithuanians of all religious and political creeds, though
several points were designed to appeal especially to the Jews, and
included the following main points:

1. It was important to have a representative Lithuanian unit that
   would participate actively in the liberation of the homeland
2. The members of the Lithuanian Division would form the nucleus of the reconstruction of the homeland after its liberation
   from the Nazis
3. The Soviet government and the Red Army command, having
   created the Division, would supply it with all that was necessary to carry out its assigned task
4. It would be possible to learn new skills and advance voca-
   tionally during service in the Division
5. There was hope of finding relatives and friends in the Division
6. Service in the Division would give the Jews an opportunity to
   participate in the general war against Nazism

PART II
IN THE RED ARMY

CHAPTER 4
THE LITHUANIAN DIVISION

**THE POLITICAL SIGNIFICANCE OF ESTABLISHING THE
LITHUANIAN DIVISION**

ALONG WITH HER LIFE-AND-DEATH STRUGGLE AGAINST
the Germans, the Soviet Union also had to engage in a fierce battle
against them for the hearts of the Lithuanian people to retain its
influence in the Baltic countries.

Since the Germans now had the entire country under their control, the Russians could rely on only a relatively small number of
Lithuanian citizens, including Jewish refugees in the Soviet Union,
far from their homeland. The members of the Soviet Lithuanian government, of the Central Committee of the Lithuanian Communist
party, and of the Komsomol (Communist Youth Organization), constituted a potential state apparatus from the moment they reached the
Soviet Union. The first few weeks, however, were rather wretched
ones for them, and because of the chaos prevailing on the roads and
possibly also because of the negative attitude of the military towards
the Lithuanians, army patrols did not hesitate to disarm and
confiscate the vehicles of these high-ranking officials. Some of them
were even arrested, and their lives placed in jeopardy. Several members of the Lithuanian government accepted administrative jobs in
local factories. Only key figures were granted official status and better
conditions in order to maintain the nucleus of the Lithuanian republic's three central institutions: the Supreme Soviet, the government,
and the Communist party. In addition, the permanent Lithuanian
representation (which later would be joined by the headquarters staff
of the Lithuanian partisan movement) continued to function by turns
in Moscow and in Kuibishev.

These institutions gained importance and were granted considerable scope, especially after December 1941, when the Soviet campaign to assure its future hold on the Baltic countries was intensified. On one hand, they played a representational role, symbolizing the continuity of the autonomous Lithuanian Soviet Republic. On the other, they were quite active, instigating the Lithuanians' social, political, and military struggle for the liberation of their homeland, then temporarily occupied by the Germans. In addition, the Russian authorities took a number of steps designed to preserve the framework of Lithuanian security on a governmental level. These steps concerned the remnants of the 29th Territorial Rifle Corps, the Infantry Officers School in Vilna, and the several hundred militiamen in Soviet-controlled areas.

On December 18, 1941, the State Defense Committee decided to establish a Lithuanian infantry riflemen's division within the framework of the Red Army. According to official Soviet Lithuanian history, the unit was composed of Lithuanian citizens who had fled to the Soviet interior. Its nucleus consisted of "Party and Soviet activists, cadets from the Infantry School in Vilna, and soldiers of the 29th Lithuanian Territorial Rifle Corps." It also included "a sizeable group of Lithuanian veterans of the Red Army, who had fought in Red Army ranks for many years, and now brought its glorious tradition to the Lithuanian Division."[1]

The Lithuanian Infantry Division was only one of hundreds of new units being created within the Red Army at the time. There is no doubt, however, that the motive for its creation was political: to assure the resumption of Soviet hegemony in Lithuania. It was thought that the Lithuanian Division could serve this purpose by (1) showing world governments and public opinion that the Soviet Union intended to return to Lithuania by any means; (2) showing "the whole world that the Lithuanian people, like all the other Soviet peoples, had not laid down their arms, and that they approved of the Soviet Government and the Communist Party"[2]; and (3) making the restoration of Soviet hegemony in Lithuania seem more probable, since it enjoyed the support not merely of a handful of Lithuanian communists, but of an entire division comprising Lithuanian citizens with various political leanings.

At the same time, the division was to serve a number of military and administrative purposes, even though in the long run, these too would prove to be primarily of political importance. It was to be a reservoir of manpower to be trained for special tasks in the military, administrative, and political spheres, and after education and indoctrination, would play an important role in the restoration of Soviet hegemony, when the time came. Unlike the abortive attempt to establish a regime in Lithuania in 1918, this time the Soviet partly succeeded. They largely determined the structure of the division, "which was more than a mere military unit." Moreover, they played a significant role in determining the fate of the division's Jewish soldiers.

The decision to create the division was not made in a vacuum. Most of the Lithuanian refugees had shown their readiness to enlist in the Red Army. And although the Soviet authorities certainly still retained some doubts about their loyalty and, consequently, their reliability on the battlefield, political considerations and the realization that they would be able to keep the thousands of Lithuanian citizens now concentrated in Central Asia under tight security and political surveillance, helped them overcome their reservations. Another factor in the decision to create the Lithuanian Division was the success of the Latvian Division, which had been created a short time before. The establishment of Polish and Czech armies on Soviet soil, to a certain extent also influenced their decision. Moreover, the existence of national units in the Red Army did not run counter to any dogma and was already widespread long before the outbreak of World War II. The creation of the Lithuanian Division in World War II, in fact, was a repetition of what had been done in 1918–1919.

THE CONDUCT OF RECRUITMENT

Immediately after the order was issued creating the Lithuanian Division, work also began to set up the machinery to implement it. The new unit was designated the 16th Infantry Rifle Division, and in its early stage was under the aegis of the "Moscow Military District." The first senior officers were veterans of the effort to establish a Soviet regime in Lithuania during the 1918–1919 civil war and officers of the 29th Territorial Rifle Corps who, in the wake of the German invasion, had been interned temporarily in special Soviet camps, together with some of their troops. These included Major-General V. Karvelis. The organizational base of the Lithuanian Division was the barracks in the vicinity of Balakhna, on the Volga River in the Gorki district. Once the Lithuanian Division's general staff and reception centers were set up there at the end of December 1941, the first recruits began to arrive.

Since the major source of potential manpower for the division, the Asian Soviet republics, were far from Balakhna, a special commission, headed by Eliah Bilevitz, was established by the Central Asian Regional Military Command (CARMC) to deal with recruitment in that region. Its task was to plan recruitment, oversee the absorption of the recruits into the Lithuanian Division, and then supervise their activities. In coordination with the CARMC, local induction boards processed those reporting to recruitment boards near their places of residence, as well as those who had previously been signed up by representatives of the Lithuanian government and new volunteers.

After undergoing general physical examinations, prospective recruits were asked routine personal questions and interviewed about their activities during and before the war. Special attention was paid to the candidates' political past and to any possible contradictions between their past activity and professional desire "to enlist in the fight against the Nazis."[3] As a result of these interviews, a number of candidates were rejected because of their social backgrounds and political views. Those who were accepted were assembled and given administrative and technical instructions about the trip to the divisional base at Balakhna. Pending the train's arrival, they were released to do as they pleased and to make their own sleeping arrangements. "Since there were no barracks and no reception center, it was necessary to take their word for it" that they would be back at train time. For the journey, which sometimes took three to four weeks, they were issued dry rations and occasionally petty cash and new clothes. Each group was placed in the charge of some "reliable" person, usually someone who previously had held military rank, who was entrusted with the tickets and travel orders for the entire group, and who made sure that the train changes were duly made (sometimes five or six per trip) and that all the men in his charge were accounted for. At times, these groups waited several days between trains at some intermediate station, and when the group was a large one, the waiting period was used for preliminary training and drill. En route, these groups often were joined by other recruits, a large majority of them Jews.

This is how the Lithuanian Division's recruits, 4,000 from Central Asia alone, reached Balakhna in the first four months.

STRUCTURE

When the Lithuanian Division was created, divisions were the principal tactical units in the Red Army infantry.[4] Because of the difficult military situation at that time, dozens of divisions were formed hastily throughout the Soviet Union, and after a brief training period, nearly all of them, even before reaching full strength, were sent to the front to fill a dangerous breach, or to be available as replacements or reinforcements.[5] And yet, as noted above, military necessity was not the only consideration in the creation of the Lithuanian Division. This fact affected the pace of its organization, the duration of its training, and, to a certain extent, its internal structure and size. At its peak, it comprised more than 12,000 men, as the following table shows.[6]

TABLE 1[6]

Manpower of the Lithuanian Division (January 20, 1942–January 1, 1943)

Ranks and Jobs	Date						
	1/20/42	*2/11/42*	*2/16/42*	*3/9/42*	*3/28/42*	*5/22/42*	*1/1/43*
Privates	1,174	2,299	3,435	4,707	5,572	9,794	6,771
Political cadres	38	78	104	134	134	—	153
Sergeants	293	389	698	741	855	1,685	2,455
Officers	205	246	348	439	495	919	872
Total	1,710	3,012	4,585	6,021	7,056	12,398*	10,251

*Not including the political cadre.

As customary in the Red Army infantry, the basic composition of the Lithuanian Division included three rifle brigades and one artillery regiment. Major-General F. Baltušis-Žemaitis was appointed commander of the division, and J. Macijauskas was made political commissar. Both had served with the Red Army in Lithuania in 1918–19. The commander of the 167th Rifle Regiment, the first in the division, was Captain L. Buber, a Jew and a Soviet war hero from the Russo-Finnish War.

The division's 167th, 156th, and 249th Rifle Regiments were composed of between 2,000 and 2,500 men each, and were usually divided into three rifle battalions, comprising between 600 and 800 men each and commanded by a major and a commissar. A rifle battalion consisted of three rifle companies, a machinegun company, and a mortar company, each comprising 180 to 200 men and headed by a captain and a company commissar. Each rifle company consisted of three rifle platoons, a mortar platoon, and a six-man antitank detail. A rifle platoon comprised up to sixty men, commanded by a lieutenant or master-sergeant, and was organized into three to five rifle squads, each usually consisting of nine riflemen and a machinegunner, commanded by a sergeant or corporal.[7] Most of the Lithuanian

Division's commissars, *Partorgs* (Party Organizers), *Komsorgs*, (Komsomal Organizers), propagandists, and other political workers, were veteran Communist party members who had been imprisoned during the independent Lithuanian period.[8] The 224th Artillery Regiment comprised some 900 men, divided into three battalions, each equipped with two cannon batteries and one Howitzer battery.

On February 1, 1943, just before setting out for the front, the Lithuanian Division possessed 7,072 rifles, 150 automatic rifles, 911 submachineguns, 220 light machineguns, 108 heavy machineguns, 9 antiaircraft machineguns, 228 antitank guns, 74 cannons, and 188 mortars.[9]

All Red Army infantry divisions had a political section, but the one in the Lithuanian Division played a relatively more important role than the others. Like those in other divisions, the Lithuanian political section recruited through its representatives in the various units new members for the Communist party and the Komsomol. In this task it had notable success, especially during the fighting. It also conducted an ongoing and systematic program of indoctrination and information, concerning the situation on the battlefronts and within the division, and participated in all festive and solemn occasions. In addition, the political section of the Lithuanian Division played a decisive role in the selection of candidates for the division's "Special Company" and for the courses that trained what was to be an administrative cadre for liberated Lithuania. This company was, of course, unique to the Lithuanian Division. The majority of its officers and men were drawn from the ranks and were trained to operate as partisans, propagandists, and intelligence agents behind the enemy lines, primarily in German-occupied Lithuania.

The division also had agents from the Soviet counterintelligence unit in each of its units. The intensity of their activity was largely a function of the fact that the Lithuanian Division had accepted a large number of men from what was actually a foreign country, many of whose citizens, during the Soviet hegemony and the early days of the war, were considered sworn enemies of the Soviet Union.

The 2nd Lithuanian Special Reserve Battalion served as a permanent reception center for the thousands of soldiers who passed through the Lithuanian Division, especially during the fighting, which seriously depleted its ranks. The battalion, based at Balakhna most of the time, also absorbed some of the wounded and crippled men after they had recovered. With this constant stream of men passing through the battalion, it sometimes had more than 1,000 members, well over the standard battalion strength. When the division entered Lithuania in 1944 and began to mobilize local people *en masse*, the Second Battalion was disbanded and replaced by the Fiftieth Reserve Division.

The Lithuanian Division also fostered a good deal of cultural activity, particularly drama and music—both instrumental and choral. Plays were presented in various Lithuanian dialects and frequently developed a controlled patriotic theme: the desire to liberate the homeland from the brutal German oppressor. The division's choral productions were also well known and on the recommendation of the government and the Communist party, the army released 200 men to form the Soviet Lithuanian State Choir. Lithuanian writers and artists were equally active and frequently came to the division to present their works on patriotic themes. Wall newspapers were encouraged, and the division published a newspaper, *Tevyne Šaukia* (The Homeland Calls).

HISTORY OF THE LITHUANIAN DIVISION FROM ITS ESTABLISHMENT UNTIL THE END OF THE WAR

The history of the Lithuanian Division, in the forty-four months from its establishment until the triumphal parade into Vilna at the end of the war, may be divided into three major military and chronological periods, which in turn may be divided into several subperiods, corresponding to geographic landmarks (see map 2).

The first period, devoted to organization and preparation, extends from December 18, 1941, to February 20, 1943—an extraordinarily long time compared to the time Red Army units usually had to prepare themselves for battle during World War II. The duration of this initial stage fortified the assumptions that the main purpose of the division was to liberate Lithuania and that they had been sent previously to other fronts only because of unexpected circumstances. This long period of relative stability for the Lithuanians also made the organizational and social consolidation of the division possible and gave them time to balance their different ethnic elements. The end of the official training period, the relative comfort of the living quarters, and the fine pastoral atmosphere encouraged a good deal of social activity among the troops.

Five months after the division had planted its flag in the Balakhna region, its fighting units had their full complements, staffs,

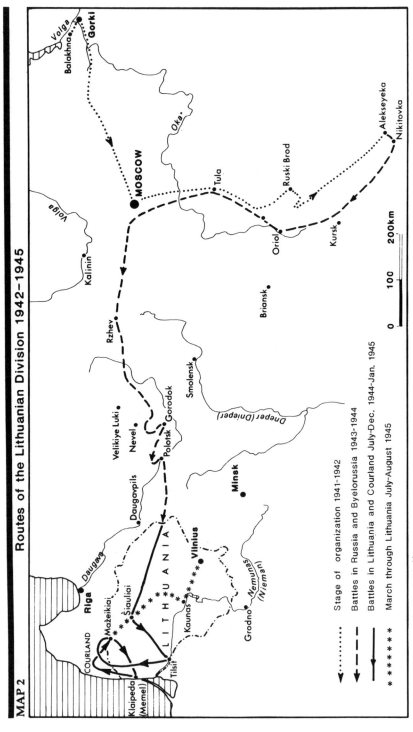

Routes of the Lithuanian Division 1942–1945

MAP 2

Legend:
.... Stage of organization 1941–1942
— — — Battles in Russia and Byelorussia 1943–1944
→ Battles in Lithuania and Courland July–Dec. 1944–Jan. 1945
* * * * * March through Lithuania July–August 1945

0   100   200km

T. Soffer, Geography Dept. H. U.

42

and political units. After the ceremonial distribution of arms to the soldiers in mid-April 1942, and their swearing in on May 1, the division began intensive training. At this time, the division was augmented by ninety-eight cadets from the Vilna Infantry Officers School, who had completed their studies at Stalinsk (Novokuznetsk) and were immediately given middle-command posts in the fighting units. On August 15, the entire division was sent by rail from Balakhna, via Gorki, Moscow, and Serpukhov, to the forest region east of Tula.

At the end of December 1942, with bitter fighting continuing in the Stalingrad region, the Lithuanian Division was attached to the Third Army at the Briansk front. After exhausting night marches through violent snowstorms, the division reached the Glebovo region not far from Orel (Oriol), which was then under assault by the Red Army. There was fear that the fierce German counterattacks would succeed in breaching the front in this area. The Lithuanian Division was ordered to rush to the relief of the 6th Guard Infantry Division, which was suffering heavy losses. On February 14, 1943, the Lithuanian Division began to move towards its destination, southwest in a long column extending many miles.

During this five-day march through deep snow, the troops did not receive any warm food; the quartermaster unit, with all its vehicles and wagons, got stuck in the snow. The artillery units and their arsenals dragged far behind. The exhausted, footworn troops, carrying not only their personal equipment, but also auxiliary weapons parts, suffered from hunger and thirst, and many licked at the snow and nibbled their dry iron ration. Others fell asleep in the deep snow, through which not even the vehicles and horses could pass.[10] Utterly exhausted, depressed, desperate for sleep—to sleep even in the blinding, freezing snow—the division's infantry columns arrived at their destination—the village of Alekseyevka in the Pokrovski region of the Orel (Oriol) district—on February 19, their field kitchens and artillery a two- or three-days' march behind them.

Two days after arriving at Alekseyevka, without a real chance to rest and refresh themselves, and without artillery support, the Lithuanian Division was thrown into the first line on the Central Front. The objective was to break through the enemy's defense line towards Zmeyovka, and from there to join the Red Army assault on Orel at the Central Front. The fighting lasted from February 21, 1943, to May 8, 1945.

Exploiting their topographical advantage and superiority, the Germans, entrenched west of Alekseyevka, inflicted heavy losses on the division's infantry units, which were easy targets for the German machineguns and mortars as they came charging, wave after wave, across the snow-white plain. Because of organizational shortcomings, the division's soldiers not only had to fight in terrible weather without fire cover, but they also had to fight with virtually no food and insufficient ammunition. Every charge was repelled by heavy German fire. Many of the wounded died before they could be moved to the special collection points. Furthermore, the Germans operated loudspeakers over which people speaking Lithuanian called on the division's soldiers to quit their "pointless" fighting and come over to the German side.

After the failure of these assaults, and with the ranks of most units depleted by more than half, the division was moved back to the second line of defense, southwest of Alekseyevka, where thousands of its soldiers were buried.

In the wake of this debacle, the division was reorganized. Major-General F. Baltušis-Žemaitis was replaced as division commander by his deputy, Major-General V. Karvelis, and Colonel A. Urbšas was named chief of staff; both Karvelis and Urbšas had been professional officers in the Lithuanian army. The decimated units were restored to their full complements with Russian and other soldiers. Then, the division was placed on the alert for the tribulations which awaited it in the summer of 1943 in the Orel-Kursk salient on the central front.

When the Germans launched their large-scale offensive, "Operation Citadel," on the night of July 4, 1943, in the Orel-Kursk region, the Lithuanian Division was ready.[11] This time it repelled the enemy in the sector for which it was responsible, suffering its main losses in the Germans' preliminary air and artillery bombardment. Then, on July 23 the division participated in the great Red Army counteroffensive that eventually broke the German defense lines in the Orel-Kursk region. In a series of fierce battles the division captured fifty-six settlements, including a village significantly bearing the name Litva. Here the division concluded its fighting of the summer of 1943. Its outstanding performance earned it a letter of appreciation from the Red Army High Command, and 1,817 of its soldiers, including many Jews, were awarded medals.

In the offensive launched on Nevel by the Red Army's Third and Fourth Armies on October 6, 1943, the Lithuanian Division was assigned the task of capturing the strong German fortifications at Palkino, the key access to the Byelorussian towns of Gorodok and

Vitebsk, situated between two lakes. It took Palkino after a week of fierce fighting.

Because of the rainy weather of November and December 1943, because of the marshy and wooded terrain which served the Germans as natural defense belts in the Vitebsk-Gorodok-Polotsk sector, and because the front lines were not clearly demarcated there, the division devoted most of this period to staging deep penetrations into the enemy's rear, harassing its communications lines, and staging diversionary actions. Then, the division got a short respite. In the winter of 1944, it was shifted frequently to different places in the Polotsk region until Polotsk was liberated, and in the spring, it was allowed to rest and reorganize. It was preparing for the big summer offensive in the direction of the Baltic countries, in which the division was to take part in the liberation of Lithuania.

On July 13, 1944, the day Vilna was taken by the troops of the Third Byelorussian Front, the Lithuanian Division set out on a 312-mile foot march, crossing the Lithuanian border in the north and continuing to the outskirts of Shavli. It suffered heavy losses in the fierce fighting there, and was saved from a rout only by the help of the tanks. The division was then given more than a month to reorganize and to replenish its ranks with local volunteers and conscripts. Some of its veteran soldiers used the opportunity to make quick visits to their homes and seek out relatives who might still be alive. On October 5, the offensive on the First Baltic Front was renewed, with the aim of driving the Germans from the Samogitia region in northwestern Lithuania. The Lithuanian Division crossed the Dubysa River to the west and fought its way to the East Prussian border not far from Tilsit (Sovietsk). For this brilliant operation, the division was awarded the Red Flag Decoration on October 31, and ten of its soldiers, including four Jews, were awarded the Soviet Union's highest decoration for bravery, the "Hero of the Soviet Union" medal.

Except for the port of Klaipėda (Memel,) which was still under siege, all of Lithuania was now liberated. So the Division was sent on a trek one hundred miles northward to Courland Peninsula in Latvia, to participate in the assault on the thirty German divisions still entrenched there. When the Soviets decided to drive the the Germans out of Klaipėda at the end of January 1945, the division was rushed back to Lithuania to help eliminate the last vestiges of Nazi occupation from Lithuanian soil. The order recalling the division, emphasized the symbolic political and historical significance of its participation in the final sweep. The conquest of the mined city and port of Klaipėda lasted from January 27 to 30. Afterwards, the division was dubbed the "Klaipėda Division." Immediately after the conquest, the division returned to Courland, where for the next three months it continued its siege on the German concentration there.

Victory

On May 8, 1945, when the division's commander was personally directing the shelling of the enemy, the Germans raised white flags all along the front. By approval of the High Command, the division accepted the surrender of the German corps in its sector. It was also in charge of gathering and storing the arms of eight German divisions and of moving prisoners to collection points.

The Lithuanian Division's military task in World War II was thus accomplished, and there was no military reason why it should not return to the homeland.[12] However, this occasion, too, was to be exploited for political purposes: it was used to display power and to impress upon the Lithuanian people, who were cool, to say the least, to the Soviet regime, the part that the Soviet-backed Lithuanian Division had played in the liberation of their homeland. On July 13, 1945, about one year after it had entered the country alongside other Red Army units, the Lithuanian Division set out on a festive parade across a considerable part of the country. The victory parade culminated in Vilna on August 2, with a mass rally attended by senior government and Communist party leaders. The division's general staff then established itself in Vilna, from where it directed the activities of the battalions now serving as garrisons in a number of Lithuanian cities. It was not until the end of 1945 that the demobilization of the division's veterans and their replacement by fresh recruits began. Of the veterans, only the career officers remained.

ETHNIC COMPOSITION

Despite the division's official name, the origin of its senior officers, and the language of its entertainment troupe and newspaper, ethnic Lithuanians constituted less than half of its personnel, at least from the time it was set up until its victory march two and a half years later. This was emphasized in Soviet publications, which stressed the "solid fraternity of the Soviet peoples," as shown by the fact that shoulder-to-shoulder with Lithuanians in the division there fought "Russians, Ukrainians, Byelorussians, Jews, Poles, and others, all of them striving for the same objective."[13] The primary reason for this was that relatively few Lithuanians had reached the Soviet interior at the outbreak of the war.

On the other hand, Jewish historians writing about the Holocaust period, in their desire to emphasize the extent of Jewish participation in World War II to offset those who would minimize it, have tended to exaggerate the Jewish membership in the Lithuanian Division, by putting it as high as 85 percent.[14] The same applies to the division's Jewish veterans.

The following estimates, based on both Jewish and non-Jewish sources, seem to be closest to the truth about the division's ethnic composition in its initial period:

TABLE 2
Ethnic Composition of the Division of its Initial Stage

Ethnic origin	Estimated percentage
Jewish	45–50
Lithuanian (including those born or living in the Soviet Union)	25–30
Russian	20–25
Other	4–5

For a considerable time, then, the Jews were the division's largest ethnic group, numbering about 5,000, and many of its soldiers referred to it as the "Jewish Division."[15] But the war apparently took its greatest toll among the Jewish soldiers, and by the time the German army surrendered on May 8, 1945, the Jews probably constituted no more than 10 percent of the division, in spite of the fact that throughout its existence the division admitted fresh Jewish recruits, although in extremely limited numbers.[16]

Table 3 reflects the change in the composition of the division's personnel between January 1, 1943, and April 27, 1945:

TABLE 3
Change in the Ethnic Composition of the Lithuanian Division (January 1, 1943–April 27, 1945) (according to a Soviet source)

Date	4/27/45								7/1/44		8/15/44		10/1/44		1/1/45		4/27/45	
Rank	Private		Sergeant		Officer		Total		Total		Total		Total		Total		Total	
Ethnic Group	number	%	number	%	number	%	number	%	number	%	number	%	number	%	number	%	number	%
All	6,771	100.0	2,455	100.0	1,025	100.0		100.0	4,723	100.0	7,260	100.0	7,180	100.0	5,199	100.0	6,038	100.0
Lithuanians	2,219	32.8	1,006	40.9	492	48.0	3,717	36.3	1,477	31.2	3,549	48.9	3,644	50.8	2,906	55.9	4,132	68.4
Russians	1,960	28.9	794	32.4	307	23.9	3,061	29.9	1,795	38.0	2,069	28.5	1,974	27.5	1,336	25.7	1,182	19.6
Ukranians	94	1.4	55	2.3	43	4.2	192	1.9	108	2.2	103	1.4	141	1.9	102	1.9	110	1.8
Byelorussians	31	0.5	19	0.8	22	2.1	72	0.7	34	0.7	35	0.5	36	0.5	26	0.5	8	0.1
Jews	2,319	34.2	516	21.0	136	13.3	2,971	29.0	1,134	24.0	1,324	18.2	1,217	18.2	713	13.7	540	9.0
Other	148	2.2	65	2.6	25	2.5	238	2.2	175	3.9	180	2.5	168	2.5	116	2.3	66	1.1

Source: J. Dobrovolskas, *Lietuviai kariai Lietuvos Didžiojo Tėvynės Karo Frontuose* (Lithuanian Soldiers on the Frontlines of the Great Patriotic War), p. 49, table no. 2: p. 96, table no. 6.

CHAPTER 5
THE JEWISH SOLDIERS:
A SOCIAL CROSS-SECTION

DEMOGRAPHIC COMPOSITION

As NOTED, THE LITHUANIAN DIVISION DREW ITS RE-cruits from a disparate community of refugees whose flight, of course, had not been organized. This was reflected, among other things, in the demographic imbalance of the division. The age group between twenty and thirty-five comprised 80.2 percent of the division; the next largest group was between thirty-five and forty-five.[1] Only eighty-four (besides some senior officers) were over forty-five, and although several of these older recruits had served with distinction in combat units, generally speaking, finding tasks that they could perform, like internal transport, created some problems for the organization. The role played by those over 35, predominantly Lithuanian residents of Russia and Russians of the Gorki region, was relatively more important until the division entered Lithuania in 1944, and thousands of young Lithuanians joined it.

Relatively, few women were conscripted into the Red Army, and the division had only 171. Many of these were young Lithuanian Jews who were alone in the world after their brothers joined the division, and had no place to go, and Lithuanian girls who were lonely in the kolkhozes, principally because of the "language problem." Upon joining the division, the women underwent basic training, and, for the most part, further training in communications and paramedicine. Except for the few who were assigned to combat units as snipers and machinegunners, women became medical orderlies, dispensary nurses, radio and telephone operators, couriers, clerks, and service workers in the battalion laundries, kitchens, barbershops, and clothing-repair shops. During the first battle, when service people were rushed to the front, some women went along, and a few were killed or wounded. One of these was Bunia Glazer, who fell at Orel on March 4, 1943.

Because officers and their mistresses or wives were permitted to live together, some female soldiers, especially those who worked at the different commands and chose suitable partners, enjoyed staff privileges. For all practical purposes, such couples were considered married. Yet problems arose when women became pregnant and had to be removed to the rear, and when the war ended, most of these couples separated.

A study made of 1,000 Jewish soldiers in the Lithuanian Division, a representative sample of the division's 5,000 to 5,500 Jewish soldiers indicates that 97.8 percent were between sixteen and forty-six years old and that two-thirds of the total were between sixteen and twenty-five.[2] It also allows us to divide the group into the following categories, to provide a clearer profile of the Jewish soldiers in the division:

Category A: Those born between 1921 and 1925. With the exception of those born in the Vilna region, all of these were born in independent Lithuania and spoke Lithuanian fluently. Most had completed elementary school as required by the Compulsory Education Law of 1922, and many had also completed high school and even university. None had previously done any military service.

Category B: Those born between 1916 and 1920. Some were born in Lithuania, others in Russia, during World War I, the Revolution, or the Civil War. These were the children of refugees who had remained with their families in Russia and returned to Lithuania only after World War I. Despite their tender age, their brief stay in Russia had left its mark on them, at least in terms of a slight familiarity with the Russian language. Yet they were well integrated into Lithuanian life, including conscript military service before World War II, which explains the relatively large number of Lithuanian Division officers among them. Some of them had even attended the Infantry Officers School at Vilna, or served in the 29th Territorial Rifle Corps.

Category C: Those born between 1895 and 1915. These were all born when Lithuania was under Russian Czarist rule. In addition to at least a basic Jewish education, many of them also had learned the Russian language and absorbed Russian culture. All had observed, if not in some way been involved in, the political events that shook Russia in 1905 and after 1917. Some, namely, J. Broyer, V. Mitzelmakher, and D. Klibansky, had even served in the International Brigade in the Spanish Civil War. Most of the Lithuanian Division's Jewish political personnel came from this group.

At least two thirds of the division's Jewish soldiers, then, were relatively young, and most had received some systematic Hebrew and Yiddish education before World War II, within the framework of the Compulsory Education Law of 1922. Most of the remaining one third had performed conscript military service either in the Lithuanian or in the Polish army. In view of the group's young age and of marriage practices in Lithuania and Vilna province between the wars, it may be assumed that most of the division's Jewish soldiers were unmarried. Naturally, in the higher age brackets the marriage rate was higher.

The division's Jewish component also included a notably large number of family groups. Among the 1,000 Jews in the study, 116 (11.6 percent) were either brothers, sisters, fathers and their children, or married couples. The number is even higher if we include extended family ties—the in-laws and avuncular relations that are frequently mentioned in the testimonies of the division's Jewish veterans.

The division's non-Jewish component included Russian-born Lithuanians in addition to the few Lithuanian-born soldiers who had fled to Russia when the Germans invaded their country. Russian-born Lithuanian Jews, on the other hand, were not conscripted into the division. Therefore, the Jewish component, the first to volunteer, consisted only of citizens from Soviet Lithuania, Vilna-born soldiers, and a handful of Russian and Polish Jews. Only fifteen of the 1,000 Jews on whom there is data were not from areas within Lithuania's 1941 borders.

Although Lithuania's five major Jewish communities—Vilna, Kovno, Shavli, Ponevezh, and Alitte (Alytus)—comprised 52.8 percent of Lithuanian Jewry, former residents from these communities constituted only 40.8 percent of the division's Jewish component. The Jews from the smaller towns and hamlets, where 47.2 percent of Lithuanian Jewry lived, constituted 59.2 percent of the division's Jews. One of the reasons for this, of course, was the higher birth rate in the provincial areas. This analysis of the division's Jewish component certainly helps account for the solidarity which developed among them.

SOCIAL COMPOSITION

The only data on the economic backgrounds of Lithuanian Jewry come from the 1923 census,[3] which shows the following breakdown:

TABLE 4
Social Composition of Lithuanian Jewry

A. Private entrepreneurs and self-employed	50.1%
B. Families of private entrepreneurs	25.5%
C. Salaried workers	5.2%
D. Laborers	19.2%

These data can serve, however, only as a departure point and not as a basis for projections about the division's Jewish component as a whole, because the division's soldiers were truly representative of the population, and economic and political fluctuations characterized Lithuania in the years following the census and especially in the years before the division was established.

Furthermore, the social composition of the division's Jewish component was influenced to varying degrees, by the following factors:

1. More than one third of the division's Jewish soldiers were age twenty or younger. It may be assumed, therefore, that on the eve of their mobilization, they had been attending school and were not active in the economy. Those who were active in the economy certainly did not fall into category A of Table 4, but rather into categories B, C, or D. Even those between the ages of twenty-one and twenty-five who had had to perform compulsory military service, most likely had not had sufficient time before the war to establish themselves in category A. Therefore, category A includes principally people aged twenty-six and up, in rising proportions as the age increases, and even with respect to them, certain restrictions operated.

2. The vocational and class transformation that Lithuanian Jewry underwent during the period of Soviet rule between 1940 and 1941 following the nationalization of business and industry and other measures reduced the number of private entrepreneurs and self-employed. Furthermore, the wives or children of the latter, who had previously worked in family enterprises, were now integrated into the state artisans' and craftsmen's guilds, or preferred to work elsewhere as laborers or clerks.

3. The Soviet authorities' mass expulsions of people they defined as "unreliable elements" and "enemies of the people"—in 1939 in the Vilna province and in 1941 throughout Lithuania—also embraced a considerable number of shopkeepers, operators of industrial workshops, the self-employed, and other working classes and, usually, their families. As a result, the people of this class, with the exception of a few factory owners and their sons, were prevented from serving in the Lithuanian Division.

4. Many men of categories A and B who sought to enlist in the division were prevented from doing so, and some who were mobilized were then expelled, as a result of the "political" security checks conducted from the very beginning of the recruitment.

All these factors, then, kept to an absolute minimum the number of men in category A serving in the division, which consisted largely of laborers, white-collar workers, and servicemen. A reasonable estimate of the social composition of the division's Jewish component may be reached on the basis of the figures available on the division's privates, most of whom, as noted, were Jews. These figures are: laborers—53 percent; farmers—29 percent; others—18 percent.[4] The assumption is that "laborers" and "others" include artisans, craftsmen, mechanics, technicians, engineers, and other classes of industrial workers; students; and professional men and women." It may be assumed that the social uniformity imposed by the Soviet regime on managers, clerks, engineers, technicians, doctors, and so forth, penetrated to those involved, and was an important factor in creating solidarity among the soldiers and in reducing the tension among the ranks.

CULTURAL AND POLITICAL COMPOSITION

It is not our intention to analyze all aspects of cultural life in the Lithuanian Division. We wil treat only such aspects as the educational level, knowledge of languages, and national and religious tradition, which played an important part in the cultural life of the Jewish soldiers. These elements also played an important role in the Jewish soldiers' integration into certain units, their chances for advancement, their general status within the division, and the nature of their relationship with the non-Jewish soldiers.

Unlike the Lithuanian privates, whose general educational level was relatively low, most of the Jewish soldiers had had some schooling in their childhood, and many had studied, among other subjects, Jewish religious texts or some form of Hebrew reading and writing. As a result, there were almost no illiterates among them. In fact, a relatively high number were high school and university graduates.

Yiddish, the only language which all the Jewish soldiers knew, was their vernacular. Eighty percent also knew at least some Hebrew; 60 to 65 percent also knew Lithuanian; 30 to 40 percent Russian; 20 to 25 percent Polish; 15 to 20 percent German; and 10 to 15 percent English and/or French.

Of the three main political blocs among Lithuanian Jews between the wars, the Zionists—from the Left-Labor Zionists to the Orthodox Mizrachi and the right-wing Revisionists—had the largest membership, followed by the Orthodox non-Zionists. The Bundists, the Yiddishists, the Folkists, and the tiny handful of Communists, formed the smallest group. Since, on the eve of the German invasion, many Zionists had been arrested and exiled to Siberia, while members of the Communist Party or occupants of vital posts were assisted in moving to the Soviet interior when the Germans attacked, it might be assumed that the proportion of Communists in the Lithuanian Division was relatively higher. Nevertheless, from the available data it does not appear that the Communists, including Komsomol members, ever constituted more than one-fourth of the division's Jewish soldiers, and even many of these had previously been members of Zionist youth movements.

From the testimonies we have, we know that former members of the Zionist youth movements, including the right-wing Betar, were not deterred by their political background from seeking refuge in the Soviet Union. Moreover, their age, their disciplinary habits, their experience in organized excursions, and their group solidarity afforded them advantages that others, who had no youth-movement background did not have. It is thanks to their background that they remained together during their peregrinations.

It is reasonable to assume that former members of the Zionist youth movements in the division constituted at least 23 percent of the 21–30 age group, the same proportion as in the Lithuanian Jewish population as a whole. Furthermore, it should be borne in mind that in the division's 15–20 age group, and among the over-30s, there was a certain percentage who had at least briefly belonged to some Jewish youth movement and some who, upon reaching adulthood, had been active in a Zionist party, or had been among the 50,850 Lithuanian Jews who had bought a *shekel* entitling them to vote for delegates to the Nineteenth World Zionist Congress in 1935. If we add to these the larger number who had attended the Zionist-oriented, Hebrew-speaking schools, including those who went on to join the Komsomol, it would be no exaggeration to state that more than 50 percent of the division's Jewish soldiers had a Zionist background or were oriented towards Zionism.

The general tendency on the part of the Jewish soldiers, with the possible exception of the old-time Communists, was not to mention the political past, especially in their contacts with the military, political, and security institutions. Nevertheless, these institutions had sufficient information at least to assess the political history of the division's soldiers and also, to some extent, the prevailing political tendencies in the division. This information was based on personal data gathered systematically by the security services' usual means and on the prewar acquaintances that members of the security and the political section had with many of the soldiers. In spite of this, there were fewer purges in the division than might have been expected, for the following reasons: (1) there were almost no leading figures among the men of Zionist background, as a result of the expulsions implemented on the eve of the German invasion and because of the age breakdown; (2) methodical purges of all former Zionists would, because of their large number, have meant the expulsion of a substantial number of the division's combat soldiers and the demoralization of the others; (3) because it was a difficult period for the Soviet Union, the authorities were temporarily inclined to overlook some of those whom they had bitterly fought in the past; (4) Jewish solidarity, which grew as large numbers of Jews fell in battle and as news of the Holocaust reached them, caused some of the security personnel to avoid initiatives that might lead to "a Jew's burial."[5]

These factors, it seems, considerably reduced the extent of the security measures implemented in the division, in spite of political opposition. The security measures that were taken were largely preventive in nature and may be classified as follows, in order of severity:

1. *Expulsion from the division, combined with arrest, exile, or hard labor.* This seems to have been first applied to the division's Jewish soldiers in the latter part of 1942, before the division set out for the front. They were surprise actions, carried out quietly, and applied primarily to commissioned and noncommissioned officers known to have been active in any Zionist party,[6] or known to have been on the list of those slated for banishment to Siberia on the eve of the German invasion, such as the Socialist Zionist leader, D. Krivosheyev.[7] Even during the fighting, there were a few instances of expulsions from the division and detentions for ten-year terms. Altogether, dozens of Jews, and not all of them Zionists, were removed from the division under such circumstances.[8]

2. *House arrest.* A number of Jewish officers with Zionist backgrounds were removed from their posts when their units were sent to the front and were assigned to rear-line training jobs.

3. *Surveillance.* In addition to the routine surveillance to which all the soldiers of the division were subjected, special attention was paid to the Jewish soldiers for any expression of Zionist loyalty. For this purpose, the security agencies used both Jewish and non-Jewish in-

telligence agents, with the latter first undergoing special courses in Jewish internal politics to teach them to distinguish between Zionists and non-Zionists and between more and less "dangerous" expressions of Zionism.[9] The security agencies were especially on the lookout for enthusiastic expressions of interest in Eretz Yisrael, including the British army's Palestine Brigade (later the Jewish Brigade Group), which consisted entirely of Jewish soldiers. The Lithuanian Division's political section was especially sensitive on this score, because the discussions often ended invidiously for the Soviet Union, which did not permit the creation of a Jewish fighting unit.

4. *Persuasion.* A few instances are known of soldiers who came under suspicion of showing more than "tolerable" interest in Eretz Yisrael and Zionism. These soldiers were called in for interrogation by the division's political commissar, who told them that their active interest "verges on counter-revolution," for which the penalty was death.[10]

These measures had a quantitative effect, of course, but some of those who ostensibly renounced their Zionist interest and joined the Communist party or the Komsomol, did so not because they had been ideologically convinced, but simply out of prudence, regarding the party membership card as a *parnosseh bichl* ("livelihood booklet"); that is, a necessary evil. Furthermore, these measures were applied only to a relatively limited extent against people who had been active members of certain Zionist parties. This indicates that the measures were intended to be a deterrent to Zionist political activity, among this large concentration of soldiers of Zionist background, rather than a means of punishment or of settling accounts with rivals. We see, furthermore, that a large number of Zionists not only were not expelled from the division, but were even promoted to comparatively high ranks.

As we shall further see, the Jewish soldiers of the division were permitted to give some voice to their affinity with Eretz Yisrael and the Hebrew language. We shall also see that, despite the above measures, the Jewish soldiers continued to maintain the strong ties that they had formed in their respective prewar organizations and youth movements. These ties cut across lines of rank and were a powerful factor in strengthening group solidarity, which mounted as the division approached Lithuania. The return to ruined Lithuania and encounters with former comrades who had survived led to a renewal of organizational ties. At the same time, the gap between former members of the Zionist movements, and new and veteran Communists, gradually diminished; in fact, the number of Communists in the division decreased, as a result of their participation in the fighting.

CHAPTER 6
THE JEWISH SOLDIERS IN VARIOUS UNITS

ONCE THE ORDER HAD BEEN ISSUED FOR THE ESTABLISH-
ment of the Lithuanian Division, it was urgent that the tables of
organization be quickly filled for the infantry regiments, the 224th
Artillery Regiment, and the headquarters and service staffs. As a
result, on the banks of the Volga, people were assigned to units in a
haphazard manner. Most of the recruits at the reception center at the
time were Lithuanian Jews, whose personal data, although available
on the forms they had filled out, had not yet been studied. This
created many serious problems, only some of which were eventually
solved.

A study of the data shows that only the assignment of the following categories of people was done methodically: (1) Those with some
military experience were immediately appointed to relatively senior
command posts. Priority was given to those who had served in the
Lithuanian People's Army and the 29th Territorial Rifle Corps, but
those who had served in the Lithuanian "bourgeois" army were also
given preference. (2) Many of those with a record of Communist
party activity were assigned to political posts in the division's sub-
units, to the extent permitted by the unwritten law of "national proportions." Some party members were assigned to such special tasks
as the guarding of secret installations and security institutions, and to
the aforementioned Special Company. (3) People in vital professions
and trades—such as doctors, nurses, engineers, and technicians, of
which there were more among the Jews than the Lithuanian Division
could use—were scattered throughout the Red Army. Some of them
were placed at the disposal of the Lithuanian government, to serve
later as a nucleus of "cadres" for the reconstruction of Lithuania after

its liberation from Nazi rule. Engineers for whom there was no need in the Lithuanian Division, but who did not wish to leave the division, accepted other assignments. (4) People with special skills, like the many drivers and printers among the Jews were needed, as were those who knew Russian and Lithuanian fluently, who were made office and warehouse clerks. In addition, many mathematicians, technical college students, and high school graduates were assigned to artillery units to handle measuring instruments and ballistic calculations, while those who had degrees in the natural sciences were assigned to chemical units. Medical orderlies were chosen from among those with at least a high-school diploma, and people with suitable backgrounds were assigned to entertainment troupes.

The majority of the Jewish recruits, however, had almost no idea how they would be assigned. Except for those with military backgrounds, the army seemed to be a vast concentration of soldiers and officers enjoying a certain aura of glory and certain minimal, but guaranteed, living conditions. Only after they had been through the medical examinations and met the "oldtimers," those who had already been assigned to units, did they start learning to distinguish between different units and tasks. As a result, some of them sought to be assigned to "safer" units,[1] using various strategies and exploiting connections with senior officers, for a degree of protectionism did exist.[2] On the other hand, some made strenuous efforts to be assigned to patrol units, so that they might be the first to make contact with the enemy and avenge the death of their families. Most, however, left their assignments to chance.

Generally speaking, the Jews were integrated into the division without impediment. Many individuals, however, felt discriminated against and frustrated, and some experienced difficulties in standing up to the physical hardships of army life, particularly those with higher education, the "intellectuals" and the older men.

The intellectuals, as they were called by their fellow Jews in the division, actually included not only those who had a formal education, but also those who had not engaged in manual trades—actors, writers, clerks, managers, and even salesmen. Many of them were assigned according to their background, but, as mentioned, since there were too many of them to be thus assigned, the remainder had to be "ignored," or misassigned. In many instances, for example, a newspaper editor was assigned to wash floors and an engineer or theatrical director was assigned to cleaning stables.[3] This caused not only frustration but often much suffering. But there were, however, no grounds for a feeling of group discrimination, for such units as the medical corps, the engineering battalion, the divisional newspaper, and other professional and technical units were staffed almost exclusively with Jews.

Although there were relatively few of them in the division, men over forty—"oldsters," as their comrades called them—and boys aged sixteen to seventeen also suffered. The problem for the boys, fresh from their school benches and parental homes and now virtual waifs, was primarily their lack of education. This was resolved, to a great extent, by their rapid adjustment to the military framework. The problem of the "oldsters," however, was far more serious. Because they were physically weak and many were already suffering from the ailments of age, they could not withstand the rigors of training, and some of them could not even perform routine military tasks. Furthermore, it was much harder for them to adapt to the rigid discipline of the army. So the "oldsters," who did not find a common ground of understanding with their comrades and commanders and even those who were fortunate enough to have commanders who understood their problems, became objects of mockery and even harassment by their comrades, Jews and non-Jews alike.

It should be noted that there were other problem soldiers, too. There was D., for instance, who was finally executed on charges of chronic neglect and insubordination and for thrusting the barrel of his submachinegun into the ground. Arguing in his own defense, he said: "I don't have the strength and I don't have the will." However, most of the "oldsters," the very young, and the "intellectuals" tried their best to reach some understanding with their comrades and commanders, or to get assigned to tasks that they could perform, and manpower was fluid enough to render this possible. And one other factor must not be discounted: the solidarity displayed by Jews occupying key positions in the Lithuanian Division.

Apparently, possibilities for promotion were open equally to soldiers of all nationalities, with this exception: only Lithuanians could rise to the highest ranks, on the basis of the unwritten principle that the division's commander and his deputies had to be Lithuanians, partly because of the division's political role. Very few Jews, on the other hand, rose to the highest echelon. And yet, it should be borne in mind that the Jews who came into the division with a military background had been in the lower echelons, very few higher than lieutenants, while the Lithuanians had been colonels and generals. Furthermore, because a fairly large number of Jews rose to captain after entering the division as cadets or privates, it seems clear that there was little discrimination on ethnic grounds, with the possible exception of the highest echelons.

Promotion was based mainly on three factors: first, was the need for commanders of various ranks, either for immediate assignments or as reserves. Due to the mass desertion of officers of the 29th Territorial Rifle Corps, whose men had been an important component of the Lithuanian Division's command, the division was short of middle-rank officers. Therefore, many men were sent to officers' courses, even though only those with military experience were assigned to command positions, preference being given to men who had already held grades. The second factor was personal qualification. On the whole, the Jewish soldiers were eminently qualified for officers' courses, and especially for sergeants' courses. In spite of the Jewish component's political background, which in a few extreme cases did result in Jewish soldiers being transferred from the division, the high command generally prefered Jewish candidates for these courses, since they were certain that Jews would not desert to the enemy. They also felt that it was better for Jewish soldiers to have Jewish commanders, so the average Jewish soldier had ample opportunities, were he prepared to accept them. The third factor was motivation. When the division was first formed and many Jewish soldiers were discontented with their assignments, it might seem that they would have applied *en masse* for officers' courses, especially the "intellectuals" who found themselves infantry privates although they had the qualifications to be officers. This, however, was not the case. Some hesitated to seek promotion for fear that after the war, officers would not be released from the army, or might be required to remain in Russia.[4] Presumably, others hesitated to become officers, especially in the infantry, because officers lead their troops in battle, and their chances of being killed at least equaled those of the privates. Even so, in most instances, the division command compelled Jews to take the courses, and it is safe to assume that refusals were not common.

In time, prospects also improved for infantry soldiers, bearing the often wretched day-to-day burden of riflemen and lacking the necessary qualifications for promotion through the ranks or for officers' courses. Eventually, many of them were assigned to transport units, kitchen duties, the signal corps, the medical corps, or cultural and entertainment units. In addition, with the increase in casualties during the course of the fighting, more men were needed in the burial units. Men who were not in fighting form, including those who had been wounded in battle, were assigned to these units. Some of them were assigned the task of making tombstones for the fallen. Later, men who spoke German fluently were also needed—for propaganda broadcasting and for interrogating prisoners.[5] Numerous positions also opened up in recruiting after the division crossed into

Lithuania. As it happened, then, there was constant horizontal movement on the part of Jews, primarily self-generated and for personal
reasons. Privates and others from the ranks moved from rifle units to
auxiliary and service units, or to tasks requiring various kinds of
expertise. However, as the division became increasingly involved in
the fighting from 1943 on, the difference between frontline and rear
became blurred.

Although there is no precise unit-by-unit information on the Jews
of the Lithuanian Division, some general estimates can be made. In
the three infantry regiments that constituted the division's main
fighting force, the Jews initially formed an overwhelming majority.
Most of them were privates, but they included some noncommissioned and commissioned officers. In the period that followed, the
percentage of Jewish noncommissioned and commissioned officers
increased. This was especially true of the 167th Regiment, which
included the 6th Company, known as "the Jewish company." This
period was also characterized by horizontal mobility, with many Jews
being transferred to auxiliary units, mainly mortar and anti-tank
units, but also submachinegun and patrol units. At the same time,
the percentage of Jews in the service units, mainly hygiene, maintenance, and administrative, increased.[6] A number of Jews also served
in senior political posts.[7] During the third period, the number of Jews
in the rifle units dropped to an all-time low. The number of Jews in
the 224th Artillery Regiment had never been large, and it remained
stable, compared to those in the rifle units, during the second and
third periods, since the 224th suffered fewer casualties than the rifle
regiments. At the same time, promotion through the ranks in the
224th was much slower for the Jews; most remained in technical jobs
connected with the use and maintenance of optical instruments. The
situation was the same in the antitank and antiaircraft units. Undoubtedly, the medical unit had the highest concentration of Jews
throughout the history of the division: 90 percent of the doctors,
nurses, orderlies, and service workers of all ranks. Most of the engineering units' officers were Jews. In the special sappers' units, 80
percent of the officers were Jews. The quartermasters of the three
infantry regiments were Jews, and in the second and third periods,
Jewish officers and privates occupied additional key positions. The
overwhelming majority of the division's bakers were also Jews. A few
Jews were officers on the staffs of the adjutant-general, the chief
operations officer, and the chief ordinance officer.

Although many Jewish soldiers were qualfied for the political
units, which sought experienced and reliable people, political con-

siderations demanded that such posts be filled by Lithuanians, among whom few were qualified. This, however, did not prevent the Lithuanians from applying pressure to obtain these positions which, while the war was raging, were relatively safe, and which, when peace came, would serve them as springboards for civilian political careers. The inclusion of Jews in these units was, therefore, far more problematic, and was effected by means of compromise. Ultimately, the political section consisted of one-quarter to one-third Jews, while the security section, which included a counterespionage unit, had many Jewish officers, veteran Communists. There were also a number of Jews in key operational and administrative positions in the "Special Company," and several dozen Jewish parachutists who underwent special training before being parachuted into occupied Lithuania. Finally, as noted above, the divisional newspaper and the cultural and entertainment units also had many Jews.

CHAPTER 7
THE JEWISH SOLDIERS IN BATTLE

THE PERIOD OF ORGANIZATION AND PREPARATION, crammed with intensive daily training, also gave rise to a vibrant social life in the division. This, in turn, harmed military morale, for some people began to shirk training and to commit other disciplinary violations. The result was that the Jews "were not looked upon favorably" by the senior commanders. And, indeed, the division's baptism by fire, in the winter of 1943, was a disaster. But not because of the Jews, the mainstay of the infantry. The valiant effort of the thousands who were killed or wounded in the abortive head-on charge through the snow and against the fire of the fortified enemy pleasantly surprised the embittered commanders, who otherwise were depressed by the debacle. Said the astonished commander of the 167th Brigade, "In training, I couldn't get those Jews on their feet, but in battle, I couldn't get them down: they charged at the enemy with their heads held high."[1] As the division continued to fight, the Jews continued to acquit themselves well, gaining an excellent reputation among the division's senior commanders and the Lithuanian soldiers as well as among other units in the area, and earning a large number of medals and citations for bravery, resourcefulness, perseverance, and leadership. And in an appreciation of the medical staff, (90 percent of whom, as noted, were Jews) the division's commissar said, "After trudging thirty miles a day through the snow and arriving at the front in time, they saved the lives of the men not only by operations performed under the open sky and by their devoted care, but also by giving their own blood for transfusions."

Even before this battle, despite the generally unfavorable reputation, soldiers were awarded citations and were promoted for outstanding performance in training.[2] In the gloomy atmosphere prevailing after the debacle of the winter of 1943, the principal citations and awards went to soldiers whose excellence in battle was expressed by endurance, perseverance in pursuing their objectives, and fulfillment of their duties in the face of overwhelming enemy fire. Such citations were given, for example, to Sonia Danin and to Rachel Butler, a field nurse, whom the soldiers nicknamed "the fearless girl." The Jewish soldier L. Koriski was cited because "by replacing the mortar operator who had been hit, he assured the continued operation of the mortar." D. Channes, a medical orderly, was awarded a citation for bravery on March 1, 1943, for safely removing twelve wounded men from the battlefield. The battle successes of the summer of 1943 made it possible to express appreciation to many more soldiers for their daring in charges into enemy trenches and in face-to-face encounters with the enemy. For example, Private M. Ascher was cited for "leading his comrades into the enemy trenches and killing five German soldiers in a bayonet battle." And in November 1943, on the occasion of the twenty-sixth anniversary celebrations of the October Revolution, when the division was temporarily moved back from the front, many more Jewish soldiers were awarded citations and decorations, some of whose names and deeds were published in the Lithuanian press and in the Jewish press in the Soviet Union and Palestine.

Since the subsequent battles in Byelorussia, Lithuania, and Courland involved special tactics, such as outflanking the enemy and penetrating to his rear and the concentrated use of artillery against tanks, there was an even greater need for the expertise of infantry commanders and artillerymen. Now four Jewish soldiers were awarded the highest decoration, "Hero of the Soviet Union." They were Major V. Vilenski, Sergeant K. Shur, Lance-Corporal H. Uzhpol (Užpalis), and Private B. Zindel (Cindelis).[3] At the same time, it seems that the authorities took care to "balance" the number of citations and decorations that went to the three ethnic groups in the Lithuanian Division. Later, when the number of soldiers of the division deserving citations and decorations grew to considerable proportions, this balance was kept, it appears, only with respect to the highest awards, especially "Hero of the Soviet Union." Thus, the "Hero of the Soviet Union" award was also granted to four Lithuanians and four Russians. A fifth Jewish soldier, Major L. Buber, the commander of the 167th Regiment, was made a "Hero of the Soviet Union" for his valor in the Russo-Finnish War.[4]

The award of citations and decorations was not the only way that official appreciation for the fighting qualities of the Jewish soldiers was expressed. Their stories were also told in the press, in books, in the soldiers' discharge papers, and at public ceremonies, including those held by the Supreme Soviet of Soviet Lithuania.

Still, we might ask what motivated the Jewish soldiers to excel in battle, and what factors, if any, might have inhibited such meritorious conduct? Besides all the motives that incited them to enroll in the division in the first place, the relatively long training caused them to "itch for battle." Then, after the debacle of their first battle, especially at the village of Alekseyevka, which might have damped the enthusiasm of the survivors, they were eager to be victorious and "settle accounts," in the second assault on Alekseyevka the following summer. Furthermore, as the soldiers received news of the destruction of their home towns and the annihilation of their families, the desire for revenge intensified, and the best opportunities for revenge were in the countless face-to-face battles with the enemy.

This atmosphere, of course, simplified the work of the political section, which used every opportunity in both verbal and written propaganda to tell of the atrocities taking place in Lithuania and to spur the soldiers "to continue marching westward, homeward." There are many indications, including the letters of soldiers and the texts of speeches delivered by Jewish commissars, that in this respect the soldiers and the propagandists were one. The Jewish soldiers were further spurred, at least indirectly, by Jewish public opinion, which encouraged cooperation in the war effort and condemned shirkers.

And yet, fear, of the kind that can strike individual soldiers or entire groups in the heat of battle or immediately preceding it, was present in the Lithuanian Division, too, especially during the difficult fighting of 1943. In some instances, the soldiers overcame fear by their own efforts or with the help of their comrades. Jewish soldiers also kept up their morale by vowing to each other that if one fell in battle, the survivor would find the fallen man's family and bring them his last words. The effort that was always made to bury the fallen according to traditional Jewish practice also helped maintain the Jewish soldiers' spirits. In addition to fear, there was the phenomenon of open envy toward comrades who were no longer able to fight because of wounds to their arms or legs and who seemed sure to get out of this war with their "heads on their shoulders." There were also instances of soldiers wounding themselves with their own guns or spades in order to get sent to the rear. During the difficult fighting in the Orel region, when there was fear that self-maiming would become a mass phenomenon, the tendency was to execute offenders.[5] In less critical periods, offenders were sent for fixed terms to "penal battalions." On the whole, the Jewish soldiers frowned on self-maiming and branded it as a disgrace, and there was relatively little of it among them.

One of the main concerns of the Jewish soldiers was not to be captured by the Germans. From the bitter experience of Jews who had fallen into Nazi hands, there arose a kind of unspoken consensus that "a Jew cannot surrender." This concern was heightened when quite a few of their Lithuanian comrades deserted to the Germans and, during patrols and under other circumstances, compelled Jews to cross enemy lines with them.[6] The division's senior commanders were well aware of this phenomenon, but attempted to cover up by publicizing stories as to how the Germans had tortured Lithuanian captives to death.

At certain points, Jewish soldiers vowed to kill each other if they were about to be captured. Such a discussion was held at an emergency meeting of the high command of a battalion that was surrounded. The Lithuanians promised that if the battalion was captured, they would not betray their Jewish comrades.[7] But in spite of the determination of the Jews not to fall into German hands, a number of them were captured. In most of these instances, their Lithuanian comrades disclosed their identity and the Germans tortured them to death,[8] except when they managed to commit suicide first. Very few Jewish soldiers survived captivity. The few who did, if they could prove exemplary conduct during captivity, were decorated. Such was the case of Private Y. Levy of the 156th Regiment. Seriously wounded and barely conscious when he was found by German medical orderlies, he was taken to hospital in Tula with several other Soviet prisoners. The latter knew Levy's identity, although he had declared he was Ossip Ivan Ivanovich, a distinctly Russian name. But they did not betray him; some even helped by paying close attention to the laconic replies he gave when questioned by the Germans. When the Germans began retreating from Tula, Levy's Russian fellow prisoners hid him, and he soon returned to his unit in the Lithuanian Division. When the hospital staff, which included Soviet security agents, reported Levy's conduct to his superiors, he was not subjected to a security interrogation; he was awarded a medal for bravery.[9]

CHAPTER 8
THE STATUS OF THE JEWISH SOLDIERS

THE MEMBERS OF THE LITHUANIAN DIVISION'S HIGH COM-
mand had almost no direct contact with any of the troops, including
the Jews. Their attitude toward the Jews was largely a function of the
division's political and military aims and of the need to maintain a
balance among its three ethnic elements. Most of the Jewish soldiers'
complaints about the high command emanated from problems connected to this balance, often that the Lithuanian members of the
division were receiving favored treatment.

The Jews reconciled themselves to the fact that the higher command echelons were closed to them, but they would not accept at-
tribution of their bravery to the Lithuanians. Furthermore, the high
command had to be very careful about manifestations of anti-
Semitism. The division's political section and the Party dealt on a day-
to-day basis with this problem, which was termed "national
antagonism."

Both as subordinates and as officers of equal rank, the Jews were
in frequent contact with the middle-echelon officers, and in the
course of time, competition between them and their non-Jewish comrades of the lower and middle echelons grew. This, of course, lead to
tension between Jews and non-Jews. Another cause of tension at first
was the popular belief that Jews are not good fighters, but the Jews
soon proved their mettle. Occasionally, tension also arose over disciplinary problems. The Jews were especially embittered over the severe punishments (including execution by shooting) meted out for
insubordination, which were generally felt to be out of proportion.
For example, when a Lithuanian officer pulled out his revolver and
shot a nineteen-year-old Jewish boy named Becker for disobeying an
order, there was a considerable furor.

67

Sometimes, Lithuanian senior officers did order Jewish soldiers and junior officers to execute orders that clearly involved risk of life, because the Jews had complained about Lithuanian anti-Semitism or because the Jews had not been quick enough to supply them with vodka. There were also instances of Jews being falsely accused of signalling to the Germans or of trying to desert to them. And some incidents between Jewish soldiers and their non-Jewish officers broke out after the officers hurled anti-Semitic epithets at the soldiers, calling them "the Cossacks from Jerusalem," for instance. Since only a few officers dared to give open expression to their anti-Semitic tendencies, however, they were well known throughout the division, and, occasionally, they were assaulted. Complaints of this nature were handled on a day-to-day basis by the political commissars, headed by Division Commissar Macijauskas, who worked very ardently in this realm,[1] and in general, the commissars were quiet efficient. However, some of the commissars were suspected by the Jews of anti-Semitism. In such instances, field commanders of equal rank with the commissars dealt with the rare cases of open anti-Semitism, both of a major and of a minor nature, and even argued with the commissars involved.

The Communist party, a powerful apparatus for raising the soldiers' morale and preparing them politically for their tasks, conducted a systematic program of education among the troops. The topics dealt with included tolerance and cooperation between the division's different nationalities, and many discussions were devoted to the theme of anti-Semitism. Apparently, this helped a great deal to soften the impact of incidents that had already occurred and to keep recurrences to a minimum. Despite this, and despite the fact that Jews comprised a considerable part of the party machine, the Jewish soldiers were not always pleased with the way the party functioned. For example, party officials, and often, particularly the Jews among them, were on constant lookout for "chauvinistic" tendencies. Talking and singing publically in Yiddish were sometimes branded as such. On the other hand, the party encouraged the Jewish soldiers to participate in official rallies conducted in Yiddish. Party activists were also mobilized to prepare the Jewish soldiers for the effects of the Holocaust in Lithuania just before the division crossed into the country. This was especially important to prevent a widening of the rift between the Jewish soldiers and their Lithuanian comrades, and to prevent incidents between the Jewish soldiers and the Lithuanian populace. The party went to considerable trouble to recruit talented Jews. It should be noted, however, that in the end, Jews were actually admitted on the basis of nationality, so that there would not be more non-Lithuanians in the party than Lithuanians.

Because of the special character of the Lithuanian Division and the close links between it and the Lithuanian government-in-exile in Moscow, the government did influence the status of the Jewish soldiers. This was expressed primarily by the additional support given to the families of the division's soldiers, including the Jews, and to the maintenance of their children in institutions created specially for them. On the other hand, the Jewish soldiers were unhappy over reports that Lithuanian officials in Moscow gave favored treatment to Lithuanian war invalids with respect to technical arrangements and rehabilitation. More serious was "Operation Cadres," which the Jewish Communist, H. Eisen, among others, planned. This operation was launched at the end of 1943 in preparation for the division's entry into Lithuania. Most of the soldiers chosen for security and civilian tasks in liberated Lithuania were Lithuanians. Only a minority were Jews, in spite of repeated assurances from Lithuanian government leaders that all of the division's soldiers were fighting for a "common goal," and the survivors will enjoy "full national equality" in Soviet Lithuania. It would appear that, for political reasons, the Lithuanian government was inclined to diminish the role played by the Jews, by minimizing a Jewish soldier's origins, for example, when reporting his outstanding performance in battle. This was especially true of the writing in the many newspapers and journals published by Lithuanian institutions in the Soviet Union.

Before the end of 1943, the relatively few Lithuanian soldiers who came to the division from the 29th Territorial Corps were stunned by their new, and what seemed to them hostile, environment. At best, they regarded the large number of Jews in the division, who were then its most visible, in fact, only ethnic concentration, as "the least of all evils." The Lithuanians believed that the Jews enjoyed favored treatment by the Soviet authorities. On the other hand, the non-Russian-speaking Lithuanians could talk to the Jews in Lithuanian, a few in Yiddish, and some even found hometown acquaintances and former schoolmates among the Jews. In time, these Lithuanians came to regard their Jewish comrades as fellow countrymen-in-exile and brothers-in-fate. Moreover, this feeling was heightened by their common experience as soldiers, which required close teamwork. Many formed close friendships that continued after the war, and even the Jewish soldiers from the Vilna region, who were inclined to disdain other Lithuanians whose language they barely understood, came to regard them as "fine fellows."

The Lithuanians who had been active in government and party affairs did not experience the same insecurity that the soldiers of the 29th Territorial Rifle Corps felt, but by and large, they, too, formed a bond with the Jews, especially in view of their common background in the Communist party underground in "bourgeois" Lithuania and in the party and government organizations of 1940 and 1941.

This was not the case with Lithuanians who had been born or lived in the Soviet Union, however. Firmly established in key positions within the division, not only did they not feel any affinity with the Jews from a culture very different from their own, but, despite party orientation, they held many of the anti-Jewish prejudices then prevalent within the Soviet populace. As a result, these Lithuanians tended to give vent to their prejudices more than the others, as attested by the many incidents between them and the Jewish soldiers.

The relationship between Jewish and non-Jewish soldiers in the division became even more complicated after the division entered Lithuania. When the ranks were filled by thousands of Lithuanian recruits whose anti-Semitism had been fortified by three years of close collaboration with the Nazis and participation in the massacre of Jews, the Jewish soldiers' position in the division became no less dangerous than that on the battlefront. In fact, they dubbed this situation "the second front." Although the Jewish soldiers were careful to distinguish between fresh recruits and veterans in the division with whom after three years of living and fighting together, they felt close camaraderie, the shock of the Holocaust and the knowledge that Lithuanians had actively collaborated in the massacre of the Jews generated a crisis that caused the Jews to manifest hatred of all Lithuanians.

To make matters worse, the arrival of the Russians compounded the anti-Semitism of the Lithuanians, or at least helped to bring it out into the open. When they first joined the division, the Russian reserves found a concentration of Jews whose mentality and culture were very different from those of the Soviet Jews with whom they were acquainted. The Russians were not even accustomed to hearing Jews converse in Yiddish, at least not in their presence. And although the Jews, many of whom knew Russian, were more open to contact with the Russians than the Lithuanians were and friendships between individual Russian and Jewish soldiers often developed, most Russians made no attempt to conceal their attitude toward the Jews as a whole. They were especially fond of anti-Jewish generalizations and jokes, particularly about "the Jewish defenders of Tashkent."[2] Even though there were few public incidents—or perhaps because there were only a few—they stood out against the background of relative tolerance prevalent among the division's other ethnic groups.[3]

For all the complexity of the nationality problem, the Jews of the division in general did not lack self-confidence, and sometimes their attitude even verged on over-confidence. This stemmed from four main factors. First, there was a general feeling that the Lithuanian Division was, in fact, a "Jewish division," largely because in its formative period and for a little while afterwards, the Jews were in the majority, and some units consisted exclusively of Jews. Second, the Jewish soldiers felt at home for quite a while, for upon arrival at Balakhna, many of them met brothers, sisters, fathers, cousins, uncles, friends, and acquaintances, as though it were a family gathering or a hometown reunion.[4] The feeling was fortified afterwards by their life together in a more-or-less Jewish vein, by the natural solidarity between them, and by the common concern for families left behind in Lithuania. The feeling that "we Jews have done more than our share"[5] that developed in the course of the fighting, in view of the large number of Jewish soldiers who fell and of the large number of Jews who won decorations and citations was the third factor. The fourth element stemmed from the singularity of their experiences in military hospitals or in other Red Army units and the need to defend their positions. A Jewish captain from the Lithuanian Division described his experience in another unit: "There weren't so many Jews there, and those few didn't know Yiddish at all."[6] Wounded Jewish soldiers from the division in military hospitals would often hear Russian soldiers say that "the Jews don't fight." Such experiences heightened the feeling of the division's Jewish soldiers that they enjoyed an especially favorable situation as members of the division. This sentiment was further heightened by the reaction of Jews from other units who came to visit people in the Lithuanian Division, who could not get over "the Jewish atmosphere" prevailing there. As a result, some of them requested and were granted transfers to the division.

Even the deterioration of their position that began in 1944 did not undermine the feeling that the division was "theirs." This feeling indirectly served to strengthen their position in at least two ways: First, they were highly motivated to remain in the division or to return to it after recovering from wounds in the hospital or upon being transferred to another unit, despite the difficulties involved in getting reassigned. Many wounded men tried very hard to pass themselves off as fully recuperated . . . because "nobody wanted to be sent to another unit."[7] Second, they often overlooked outbursts of anti-Semitism, or at least did not make a public issue of them.

CHAPTER 9
NATIONAL MOTIFS OF THE JEWISH SOLDIERS

LANGUAGE AND LEISURE ACTIVITY

Most of the Jewish sources treating the Lithuanian Division point to a central phenomenon that was present from the first day of the division's existence—the almost total dominance of Yiddish as the daily language of the Jewish soldiers. They spoke to each other in Yiddish publicly, without embarrassment. In fact, there was an unwritten agreement that applied to people of all ranks and jobs, from the Jewish carter, who even directed his horses in Yiddish, to the dentist treating his patients, that Yiddish was the only language to be used among Jews. In the heat of battle, Jewish soldiers spurred each other on, by shouting in Yiddish: *"Far unsere tattes un mammes"* ("for our fathers and mothers").[1] There were two reasons for this. First, almost all the Jewish soldiers understood and spoke Yiddish before entering the division. Secondly, unlike the Polish Jews, who had joined the Red Army or the Polish army of General Anders two or more years after leaving home, the Lithuanian Jews had been away from home only six months when they joined the division.

By and large, the non-Jewish soldiers, especially the Lithuanians, accepted hearing Yiddish spoken in their presence. Sometimes, even drill orders were given in Yiddish, as were orders given in less formal situations.[2] The division's high command generally ignored this, although in certain instances they did make a special point of asking that Yiddish be used at official assemblies. For example, Jewish soldiers were encouraged to deliver speeches in Yiddish at rallies held before the division went to the front, and a Jewish officer from Vilna describes a rally held in the 249th Regiment as follows:

Before we left Yasnaya Polyana, a meeting of Jews was held at the big clubhouse in which all the Jewish soldiers participated. A special order had been issued. . . . The head of the brigade's political section spoke in Russian, but Yiddish was also spoken. Yosadeh and Beilis (Yiddish writers from Vilna) were there, but some of our soldiers also spoke. . . . I recited Itzik Feffer's *Di Shvue* ("The Vow"). It went on all evening and was good for morale. . . . It was intended to encourage us and to remind us what the war was all about and what our role in it was. Of course, it was a good experience: we saw that this rally had been organized especially for us. . . . Everything was addressed just to us.[3]

To the Jewish soldiers, the use of Yiddish was so natural that at first they were not even self-conscious about it, and certainly they did not view it as special, since there were so many of them in the division, and so many of them were relatives, old friends, and former fellow townsmen. However, as a result of their contact with Jewish soldiers from other Red Army units who did not conceal their astonishment at this mass use of Yiddish, and from a few, albeit minor, incidents within the division over this phenomenon, the division's Jewish soldiers began to realize that they enjoyed an advantage over the Jewish soldiers in other units of the Red Army. Furthermore, in addition to having to know Yiddish in order not to stand out in their daily relations with fellow Jews, Jewish officers' attitude toward the use of the language became a symbol of their attitude to their Jewish identity. Yiddish was also important for communications, both verbal and written, with Jews outside the division and was especially useful in establishing contact with Jewish survivors in liberated areas.

Compared to Yiddish, Hebrew was rarely used, although a considerable number of the division's Jewish soldiers were fluent in it. Generally speaking, except for the singing of Hebrew songs, spontaneous even at public mass gatherings, the use of Hebrew was restricted to the writing of diaries and letters and to personal conversations. The Jewish soldiers' leisure time had a character of its own. Like their non-Jewish comrades, most Jewish soldiers went to the cinema, but drinking was less widespread among them, and many exchanged their official vodka rations for other commodities or gave them away. Singing, for instance, was far more prevalent.

On the long train ride from Central Asia to Balakhna, the Jewish soldiers became known for their communal singing in Yiddish. In the first period in the division, they also sang while marching, so the people of Balakhna and Tula were frequently treated to the sight of the division's units marching through the streets, singing Yiddish marching songs. From time to time, the division's entertainment

troupe would offer a song or two in Yiddish or Hebrew, and occasionally, on the initiative of Jewish singers or instrumentalists, would treat
its audience to Yiddish theatrical songs or Hassidic singing and danc-
ing.[4] Especially impressive were the evenings of spontaneous community singing in the "Jewish barracks," where the younger and
older men together would sing the whole range of songs from the
Yiddish and Hebrew repertoire. Frequently such evenings would cul-
minate with energetic *horas,* the Jewish circle dance. One soldier described such a hora as follows:

> Around the campfire we started singing Yiddish songs. Soon we went
> over to Hebrew, and someone called out: "Fellows, we're going to the
> front. Who knows if we'll get back alive? Let's do a hora! What's there to
> be afraid of?" "Hora! Hora!" came shouts from every direction. And the
> circle immediately formed and rapidly grew. Even those who hesitated
> at first soon joined in. Anyone who didn't see that hora can't imagine
> the ecstasy that overcame our men as they chanted: "Who are we? Is-ra-
> el!" Even the few Lithuanians who were with us joined the circle, even
> though they had no idea what was going on.[5]

There was even a distinctly Jewish tone to the soldiers' small talk,
which on the surface concerned such banal matters as the outcome of
battles and problems of food and clothing. But it also had its nostalgic
moments, so that when officers joined privates in these "bull sessions," all distinctions of rank temporarily fell away. In fact, in addition to the "Jewish barracks" and the battle-area bunkers where these
"bull sessions" generally took place, the Jewish soldiers developed
special places to meet whenever they had a free moment, to exchange
"racy jokes" in Yiddish and sing Yiddish songs over a glass of Vodka.
But the conversations would usually change to reminiscences about
Jewish life in prewar Lithuania and concern over the current situation. As the news started trickling in about the Holocaust, various
battle fronts, and the world in general, the intimate conversations
turned more and more to the fate and the future of the Jewish people.
There were many heated debates on the subject of *Eretz Israel.* One
Jewish soldier recorded in his diary a conversation with a comrade:
"We had a long discussion about our people's future in the Socialist
world. We came to the conclusion that the future of the Jews lay in a
Socialist Jewish state." He also reports:

> Last night I had a heated argument with S.G. about the future of the
> Jewish people. . . . He wanted to know why he should go to Palestine,
> where workers are oppressed just as they are in Poland. "Now

America—that's another matter," he said. But that was only for people whose pockets were filled with gold. However, that was his privilege as a human being. I said that he wasn't a human being or a Jew, but just a creature who wants a full stomach, a change of clothes, and a good job.

In a discussion between a soldier and a commissar in a trench in the snow, one of them said wistfully: "Wouldn't it be better if both of us were now in Palestine fighting for a Jewish state?"[6] These discussions encouraged some soldiers to start spinning dreams and plans about going to Palestine, some of which materialized after the division entered Lithuania.

Because of their hasty departure from Lithuania and because, in the period immediately prior to joining the division, the Jewish refugees had not lived in Jewish centers, Yiddish books were rare and Hebrew books ever rarer, except for the few prayer books, or photo albums with Hebrew inscriptions that some had brought along. When in the division itself, a Yiddish book was found now and then, it was passed along as soon as one person finished reading it. A few got the Yiddish newspaper, *Einikayt,* and other publications of the Jewish Anti-Fascist Committee in Moscow.

Some soldiers kept abreast of developments in the Jewish world, from letters from abroad and from the Jewish and non-Jewish newspapers. But rumors were also rife. There was, for example, one about a meeting between Ben-Gurion and Stalin concerning the imminent establishment of a Jewish state and another about a meeting between Dr. Weizmann and the Soviet Yiddish writers Itzik Feffer and Shlomo Mikhoels.

The Jewish soldiers also managed to do quite a lot of writing. Many corresponded in Yiddish or Hebrew, mainly with relatives and friends in the Soviet Union and elsewhere, which the political sections encouraged, at least for a time. Despite various difficulties, many Jewish soldiers found the time and means to jot down their impressions and experiences in diaries, in the margins of newspapers, or in anything else available, "lest nobody know what we went through."[7] A number of prose writers, poets, and painters, including Y. Yosadeh, Y. Zhilin, Tamsheh, G. Yocheles, and M. Gluch, continued to create during the fighting. All were killed in battle, except Yosadeh. Eventually the high command made special provisions for Yosadeh, along with the Lithuanian authors, to devote time to writing. Much of the work of the veteran writers, and of those who started writing in the division, was devoted to Jewish themes. Their creations, however, were not generally known to the others while they were in service.

At the same time, a rich folklore was created in the form of sayings, nicknames, code-words, and limericks pertaining to the life of the Jewish soldiers in the division.[8] For example, a rifle was known as a pointer (referring to the pointer used by the Torah reader to show the place in the Torah Scroll); battle-dress was described as *"tachrichim"* (the Hebrew word for shrouds); a softening-up operation before a charge was called *"a huppa"* (the Hebrew word for bridal canopy), and the charge itself was called *"a chasseneh"* (the wedding.) The party membership booklet was called *"the parnosseh-bikhl"* (which is Hebrew-Yiddish for livelihood-booklet). Jews would identify themselves to each other with the Hebrew word *"amcho"* (meaning your people). What is more, the use of place-names from Palestine, like "Galilee" and "Negev," became so widespread as code-words among Jewish radio and telephone operators that some of them were officially adopted.

RELIGION AND SOLIDARITY

The fact that a considerable part of Lithuanian Jewry had grown up in religious homes was felt in the division. Even many soldiers who had not been observant began taking an interest in religious observance and tradition. This was especially true with respect to burial rites for fallen soldiers. "The men insisted—and no one could object to this—that the grave be dug so that the fallen man's head be in the direction of Jerusalem."[9] Many mortally wounded men managed to say the traditional Jewish prayer of confession or at least to recite the six-word verse *(Shema Yisrael)* "Hear, O Israel" before they died, and often a fallen man's comrades would recite the *Kaddish* (mourner's prayer) at a comrade's burial.[10] During quiet periods, especially after the division entered Lithuania, the soldiers would celebrate the Sabbath and festivals in traditional fashion. They had three ways of keeping track of the Sabbath and other holy days: first, a few men had brought Jewish calendars with them, or were sent calendars from Palestine, or hand-copied calendars from printed ones that some comrade had; second, relatives and friends would write when some Jewish holy day was approaching, and finally, some of the men, especially the older ones, tried to keep track of the Jewish date by their own calculations. Of course, sometimes they erred, and in at least one instance a medical unit fasted twice because of a wrong calculation of Yom Kippur (the Day of Atonement).

Although at the front few people came to prayer services on weekdays or on the Sabbath, on the High Holy Days, especially for the *"Kol Nidre"* service of Yom Kippur Eve, they showed up *en masse.* Many fasted on Yom Kippur and ate the Yom Kippur Eve prefast meal in the traditional manner. In addition to the soldiers who participated as regularly as possible in the prayer services, some observed certain religious precepts even though they were not religious, and all displayed tolerance towards and even admiration for their comrades who tried to observe the precepts under field conditions.

Since the Soviet authorities had called a temporary halt to their war against religion, and moreover, since they considered the Lithuanian Division so important politically, the higher command echelons, and even more so the middle and lower echelons, treated the matter liberally, as shown by the fact that they freed the Jewish soldiers from training on Rosh Hashana and Yom Kippur so that they might attend prayer services. The men of the 249th Regiment's Second Company, while they were in Tula, were even marched off every Saturday morning by a Jewish sergeant, M.B., to the synagogue in town. Even more remarkably, in the 167th Regiment's Sixth Company, a former *Yeshivah* (rabbinical academy) student was given time off for daily morning and evening prayers because his commander regarded him as a kind of holy man "praying against the Germans." This soldier even helped the command to persuade Lithuanian Baptists that it was not against their religion to kill Germans. One man, who had with him his rabbinical ordination from the Slobodka Yeshiva and a ten-year Jewish calendar, got help from the commander of the 167th Regiment in observing the religious precepts, and his Russian company commander helped him to get special food for his Yom Kippur Eve prefast meal.[11]

In this general atmosphere, even the Jewish Communists did not wish, or were unable, to interfere with religious observance. Furthermore, the concept of "tradition" served some party members as a pretext for tolerance and even for their own participation in religious ceremonies. On the other hand, some soldiers were not prepared to observe religious precepts or thought it impossible under the circumstances. For example, a political commissar in the 249th Regiment, on learning that his parents had perished in the Holocaust, wrote to his brother in Palestine: "Say *Kaddish* for papa, mama, and our sister, and go to synagogue and give charity in their memory—they deserve it! I don't have time for it."[12] Religion also served to bring the Jews of the division closer together and helped them to establish closer ties with Soviet Jews.

Upon arriving in the division, the soldiers spent as much time as possible looking for relatives, old friends, and acquaintances. Many of them eagerly awaited the arrival of newcomers, in hope of finding relatives or friends among them or of hearing some news. Some men thus found wives whom they had thought dead, as well as sons, parents, brothers, and uncles. Some, learning that relatives or friends were in other units, made strenuous efforts to be transferred. When that failed, they used every free moment for reciprocal visits, or at least found people through whom they could send personal reports.

In the course of time, "communications nerve centers" spontaneously developed among the Jewish soldiers, through which it was possible to obtain addresses, personal regards from friends and relatives, or news of general Jewish interest. Furthermore, friendships that developed among the early arrivals developed into lasting relationships, and embraced entire units, which became substitute families. In this atmosphere, each "family" tried to deal with the small daily problems of its members, problems like job assignments, relations with commanders, shortages of food or tobacco etc. And if people could not help each other, they at least consoled and encouraged one another. Sometimes, this help and mutual encouragement even involved collusion in breaches of regulations, such as concealing the fact that a comrade had lost his weapon or some other equipment.[13] Only in rare instances, however, did Jewish officers or their soldiers breach rules of discipline or order.

Gradually, this sense of solidarity grew to embrace not only the members of a particular "family" but all the Jewish soldiers of the division. Even if they had not know each other previously, or did not come to know each other particularly well, they all knew that, as Jews, they shared a common fate. The urge to help each other became all the more intense during the difficult fighting in the Orel region, when they sensed that it was now their duty to do everything possible "to save the few survivors." This feeling spurred officers and others in key positions to help fellow Jews not only in their own units but also in other units, and emboldened Jewish soldiers to appeal to Jewish officers, even those they did not know personally, for help for themselves or for their comrades. The Jewish soldiers, therefore, generally preferred to serve under Jewish commanders. And in general, they were not disappointed.

As a rule, the Jewish officers were not compromised. The Jewish soldiers displayed understanding for the delicate situation of the Jewish officers, especially in situations involving a clear contradiction between military regulations and Jewish consciousness. Except in certain grave instances, which the soldiers thought to involve sadism, degradation, and exploitation, they obeyed orders from their Jewish officers without demur, for in general they viewed the latter as father figures. They did, however, condemn and resist Jewish officers and political activists who turned their backs on their Jewishness and tried to prevent manifestations of a national spirit among the Jewish soldiers. Jewish soldiers came to identify the Jewish solidarity of Jewish officers by their use of Yiddish and by their participation in Yiddish community singing, entertainment evenings, comradely "bull session," joke sessions, and so forth. The Jewish soldiers reacted very strongly, in various ways, to Jewish officers who mistreated them.

In a number of areas, Jewish public opinion in the division coincided with the declared aims of the high command even more than that of the Lithuanian soldiers. Prominent among these were the character of the war against the Germans and the determination not to be taken prisoner. Even though the high command and its political institutions did not officially recognize the Jews as a separate, distinctive group, they did take it into consideration in their propaganda efforts.

CHAPTER 10
THE JEWISH SOLDIERS AND OTHER JEWS

CONTACTS WITH JEWS IN OTHER UNITS AND WITH CIVILIANS

ALL OF THE SOLDIERS IN THE LITHUANIAN DIVISION KEPT in touch with old friends in other units through letters and through common acquaintances. But the Jewish soldiers made special efforts to meet and form continuing ties with Jews from other units whom they met at the front. Moreover, as the division moved westward the Jewish soldiers undertook searches for Jewish survivors in the liberated areas, and when they met people who emerged from their hiding places in villages or in the forests, they took a special interest in them.

With few leaves being given, little transportation, and great distances to travel, few of the division's soldiers, with the major exception of wounded men, were able to visit their families in the rear. Contact was therefore maintained by correspondence (of which there was a great deal among the Jews) and by sending money and packages. Many soldiers exchanged names and addresses with one another and vowed that if anything happened to one of them, the other would inform his family. Hence, Zvi Rosenzvaig wrote on April 13, 1943, to the sister of Z. Telem, a comrade who had fallen in battle two months earlier:

> Unknown but none the less dear friend Telem, you are dear to me because you are a daughter of our suffering people, one of the numerous sisters sent wandering from home by the murderous Hitler. Like all the rest of us, you must take consolation from the thought that your brother did not die in vain—not as a helpless victim of a pogrom by the Czar's bandits, but in battle against the German fascists, with the murderers

who drove you from your home, and for a better future for all of us.

Frequently, wounded men in hospitals at the rear encountered Jewish staff members who discussed Jewish matters with them and gave them special treatment. When they received recuperation leaves, the wounded occasionally were able to meet local Jewish families in various parts of Russia. Some met relatives who had been living in the Soviet Union for a long time, who admired the Jews in the division, as soldiers and as Jews, but who also hesitated to approach these "Western Jews." When Jewish soldiers of the division marched through the streets of Tula singing in Yiddish, the local Jews followed them for a long while "with mute glances and tear-filled eyes."[1] Some soldiers also visited the Jewish institutions in the Soviet Union such as the Moscow Yiddish Theater and kept in touch with members of the Jewish Anti-Fascist Committee such as Ilya Ehrenburg, Shlomo Mikhoels, Itzik Feffer, Peretz Markish, Leib Kvitko, and David Bergelson.

CORRESPONDENCE WITH PEOPLE ABROAD

Jewish members of the division started writing to relatives and friends abroad very early on, and, some received answers. For instance, before joining the division, N. Skurkovitz of Vilna wrote one or two letters to Kibbutz Degania, in Palestine, asking that his uncle in Jerusalem be informed that he was alive and was going to the front to fight the Germans. Some time later, when he was already in the division, he received a cable saying that his request had been fulfilled. He expressed delight that "someone outside was thinking of him and knew about him." A few soldiers were able to continue corresponding with their relatives in Palestine and elsewhere after joining the division, some writing in Hebrew.

Then in April 1942, when the Soviet Union launched a campaign to open a second front by the Western Allies, correspondence increased dramatically. The political commissar of the Second Army, to which the Lithuanian Division was then subordinate, instructed the political staff to master the subject of the second front and to advise the soldiers to tell their relatives abroad how vital it was, not only for the Soviet Union but for "all free nations," while emphasizing the heroism of the Red Army. The soldiers were told to write not only to relatives but "also to friends and even to ordinary acquaintances."

The political workers even supplied writing materials, for in general there was a paper shortage and people had to write in the margins and between the lines of newspapers. And if the soldiers did not know the exact addresses of their contacts in America, the Soviet embassy in Washington located them.

The thrust of this campaign was directed at England, "which is already in real danger from Fascism, and to some extent also to the United States, which is also in danger if Fascism is not halted." After a struggle between the Jewish soldiers and some of the political officials, however, Palestine was also included, on the grounds that "for the time being, Palestine belongs to England."[2]

The correspondence with friends and relatives overseas was mainly of personal significance, but the letters and packages from Palestine were more symbolic. The packages often contained *matzot* for Passover, Jewish calendars, and other useful items, while stamps with the Hebrew imprint evoked special interest. Many soldiers, who did not know the addresses of their relatives and friends in Palestine, found them by writing to the newspapers there, which published their inquiries.[3]

"Operation Correspondence," which was restricted almost exclusively to the Lithuanian Division, officially lasted from April to August 17, the day the division went on front-line alert. Unofficially, however, the Jewish soldiers continued the correspondence, which tended to be more significant to them than it was for the Lithuanians or Russians, because more of their correspondents lived abroad. Conversely, for many abroad, these soldiers were an important source of information concerning the fate of their families in Lithuania.

ENCOUNTERS WITH SURVIVORS OF THE HOLOCAUST

The concern for relatives and friends in Nazi-occupied Lithuania preoccupied the division's Jewish soldiers from the day they left Lithuania, and, of course, was a frequent topic of conversation. But many refused at first to believe the truncated reports that appeared in the division's newspaper from time to time regarding Nazi atrocities against the Jews; they regarded the reports as propaganda.[4] For a long time some even entertained dreams of returning to rousing welcomes and the smothering love of their families and townsmen. Even the relatively detailed official reports that they heard from the people of the political section in the autumn of 1942, as they were preparing to move to the battle front, did not extinguish their hopes. They began to believe the reports only when they started hearing confirming reports from isolated survivors in Byelorussia and from Jewish and non-Jewish partisans sent from Lithuania to the Soviet Union to survey the tragedy. One of these was the Yiddish poet, Abraham Sutzkever, who had been flown to Moscow from the forests on the Lithuanian border. His accounts shocked them.

They braced themselves, but what they heard then "was nothing" compared to what they actually saw and heard on their march through northern Lithuania to Panevežys and Shavli, through "towns that had been full of Jewish inhabitants."[5] "The first person I met," one soldier said of his entry into what had been a Jewish hamlet, "was a Karaite. His account of the things that the Germans had done to the Jews brought tears to my eyes. In the evening, I went to the pit in which our fellow Jews had been buried. Christian women explained that the Jews had been buried alive."[6] After a few such reports, which were confirmed by the Jewish survivors they met, mainly in Ponevezh (Panevežys) and Shavli, the Jewish soldiers made every effort to reach their home towns somehow or at least to send letters. For most who reached their prewar homes, the visits were conclusive proof that there was no hope of their ever seeing their loved ones alive again. A Jewish sergeant—one of the many Lithuanian Jews to receive a thirty-six hour leave to search for relatives—described his visit to his native town as follows:

> The streets of the town did not greet me; they were strangers to me. The few passersby threw me hateful glances and kept their distance. Silently I walked step after step, one hand on my heart and the other on my revolver—a queer feeling. . . . Empty sidewalks, empty roadways, hostile houses; not a single Jew, not even a half-Jew. . . . The eternal Gentile, witness and partner to the destruction, won't say a word. All I can get out of him is that no Jews remain.[7]

Some Jewish soldiers found last wills and testaments left by their families in the ghettos where the Germans had incarcerated them before murdering them. One found a letter that Yitzhak and Shulamit Rabinovitz had written in the Kovno ghetto to their sons Amos and Benjamin in Palestine. An officer, Zedak (Zadok), discovered in a bunker in the ruins of the Kovno ghetto, where the house in which his brother had lived once had stood, a note that his brother had written, apparently in his final moments just before the liquidation of the ghetto (on July 15, 1944) describing the ghetto's last days: "They hunted us like animals. For seven days we hid in a hot, stuffy attic without water. Then they hurled hand grenades at us and set fire to the house on all sides. . . . We're the last ones alive. . . . Let revenge for us be your life's goal."[8]

The shock of these revelations, and the fact that most of the murders had been committed by Lithuanians, had five primary effects on the Jewish soldiers: (1) they became more savage fighters than ever, sometimes even taking unnecessary risks; (2) they became more violent toward German prisoners and even stopped taking prisoners. One soldier reported that whereas once he had even fed German prisoners, "after hearing about all those atrocities, I wouldn't even leave them alive. . . . Afterwards, we always tried to wind up the battle in such a way that no German would remain to be taken prisoner."[9] (3) they began actively hating the local Lithuanian civilians and became aggressive toward them. "What made our blood boil," one Jewish soldier testified, "was the fact that the Lithuanians had turned out to be no better than the Germans. . . . Some of our own boys with submachineguns went wild with the Lithuanians." The Jewish soldiers were also infuriated by the hostile reception the division received at the hands of the local populace, and by some of their remarks such as "So many Jews still alive." As a result, they frequently set upon Lithuanian civilians in the streets and other places.[10] Besides personal acts of vengeance that Jewish soldiers committed against Lithuanian civilians,[11] some of them joined the army's special security services—as interrogators, interpreters, and field operatives—as a means of taking revenge. (4) the Jewish soldiers' hostility became generalized and turned them against even the division's Lithuanian veterans, with whom they had fought side by side, in spite of the fact that some of the Lithuanian soldiers told them that they were ashamed of their fellow countrymen and what they had done to the Jews. What tipped the scales for the Jews was that the Lithuanians found their relatives alive and marched through the country singing. (5) a general depression overcame the Jewish soldiers, many of whom withdrew into themselves, or displayed symptoms of hysteria. A Jewish officer reported that "the fighting capacity of the Jewish soldiers plummeted. They lost all their fighting spirit and thought that the whole struggle had become pointless, that we had lost everything." A female Jewish soldier told of the reaction among the women when they heard that all the Jews had been killed. She said: "Broken, we lay in our beds and cried. Then I remember one girl getting up and saying: 'Girls, if the war ever ends and we're still alive, each of us will have to have ten children in order to make up for what they did to us.' "[12]

To counteract these effects, especially the last three, the division's high command, with the help of several commissars from the political section, took the following measures: First, they placed greater emphasis on the role of the Germans in the atrocities and attempted to show that Lithuanians had suffered from German fascism no less than Jews. Second, they organized mass educational meetings, intended especially for the Jewish soldiers to stress the theme that "we have come to Lithuania not as conquerors but as liberators," which required the people of the division to treat "the Lithuanians as brothers and sisters who have been liberated from the German yoke."[13] Therefore, the soldiers were advised not to take matters into their own hands and not to help themselves to any objects in the possession of Lithuanians, even if they knew that these objects had belonged to Jews. Third, they forbade the public singing of moody songs, which were apt to deepen the depression of the Jewish soldiers.[14] The high command also tried to discourage the public reading of the letters that had been found in the ruins of the Kovno ghetto, and finally, they took stern measures against acts of vengeance. For example, a Jewish soldier who shot a Lithuanian after he learned that the latter had been responsible for the death of his family was sentenced to ten years' imprisonment, and a highly decorated Jewish officer was demoted for killing prisoners.[15]

In the wake of these measures, the division went into battle again—this time in western Lithuania and in Latvia's Courland province—and the situation grew calmer. Meanwhile, the Jews of the division became more preoccupied with the Lithuanian Jews who had survived.

The Holocaust survivors, who looked to the soldiers "like ghosts, not human beings,"[16] gave stark confirmation to the reports the soldiers had heard and had refused to believe about the extent of the Holocaust. At the same time, the survivors also roused the soldiers' sense of solidarity and their desire to do everything they could to help and console their suffering kinsmen. Reports from soldiers and survivors alike testify to this. One of the survivors, for example, testified that the help given by the soldiers of the Lithuanian Division in the days immediately following the liberation of Shavli saved them from starvation.

In addition, before a military government was properly organized, the Jewish soldiers organized the evacuation of the survivors to the rear. Frequently, the soldiers came to the aid of the survivors when the military authorities were too strict with them, or when they were harassed by the local population. Thus, for example, a Jewish soldier pointed his submachinegun at a grocer who refused to sell food to a Jewish girl whose father was ill.

As the battlefront moved westward and the administrative situation in central Lithuania stabilized, the survivors no longer needed special help from the soldiers. More normal, reciprocal social relations began to develop between the two groups. Increasingly, the soldiers joined in the activities of the Jewish political groups that had come to life again. At the forefront were the prewar Zionist youth movements, which no longer waited for official permits to resume their activities.

CHAPTER 11
JEWISH SOLDIERS IN OTHER MILITARY UNITS

MANY LITHUANIAN JEWS SERVED IN OTHER REGULAR military units before or after they served in the Lithuanian Division. But we also know of numerous Jews who served exclusively in other units. However, whereas in the division they formed a considerable concentration, in the other units, they were for the most part solitary individuals. As a result, the Jews in other units tended to hide their nationality, often because of widespread anti-Semitism.

Because of this, and because those Jews were scattered in hundreds of units throughout the Soviet Union, it is difficult to estimate their number; there is no doubt, however, that at least several thousand were involved.[1] Most of them served in the land forces of the Red Army and the balance in the Polish units that were formed on Soviet soil.

The first Lithuanian Jews to join the Red Army after the outbreak of World War II were some of the several hundred young men from Vilna who went to the Soviet Union just before the city was handed over to Lithuania in October 1939. When the Germans launched their invasion in June 1941, the Soviet authorities were at first reluctant to accept people from Russia's western border into their military units, and especially into their fighting units. Nevertheless, some of the young Vilna Jews were accepted into the ranks of the Red Army, where they served until they were wounded, taken prisoner, or assigned to the rear. Others fought until the end of the war against both the Germans and the Japanese, and remained in service after the war.[2]

Many Jews who fled to the Soviet Union after the Germans invaded Lithuania also succeeded in getting accepted into the Red Army. A considerable number participated in the defense of Moscow at the end of 1941, after being co-opted into the 122nd Regiment of the 201st Latvian Infantry Division, and many were wounded or killed in the attack near Naro-Fominsk. Others, who followed retreating Soviet units out of Lithuania in June 1941, were incorporated into the units on the road and were officially sworn in when these units reached collection points.[3]

Jewish doctors from Lithuania who were not needed by the Lithuanian Division were sent to other Red Army units. Many of the boys who did not reach military age until 1943 and 1944, along with able-bodied survivors from the liberated areas, were not assigned to the division, but to other army and police units operating mainly in the framework of the Forty-eighth and Forty-ninth Armies, which fought in East Prussia, the Danzig region, Western Poland, and Berlin.[4]

Most of the two thousand Vilna Jews who had been mobilized into the Polish army when the Germans invaded Poland in September 1939 survived and, after many vicissitudes, including being taken prisoner by the Germans, returned home.[5] But some of the Jewish soldiers and officers among them, mostly doctors, were arrested by the Soviet authorities on their way home and detained in special camps in the Soviet Union together with thousands of Polish officers and soldiers. Most of them remained in detention even after Vilna and the rest of Lithuania became Soviet on August 3, 1940. Only a handful were permitted to return home. Then, after the Soviets and the Polish government-in-exile signed an agreement making it possible for Polish subjects in the Soviet Union (refugees and people in detention) to enlist in the Polish army there under the command of General W. Anders, Vilna Jews attempted to do so. But many were rejected on various pretexts, because the Soviet authorities put obstacles in the way of the Polish volunteers in general and the Jews in particular, but also because the Polish authorities refused to accept more than a limited number of Jews.[6] Despite this, and despite the anti-Semitism that prevailed in General Anders's army, the Jews returned again and again to the Polish reception centers at Buzoluk and Guzari to enlist. They even intensified their efforts when they learned that General Anders's army was going to leave the Soviet Union. A number of Vilna Jews, however, were among the thousands of Jews who finally succeeded in being admitted to General Anders's army.[7] Most had served in the Polish army, and some were former officers. When the army was transferred to the Middle East, some of these Jews were permitted to take along Jewish civilians as family members.[8] Some Vilna Jews were also among the hundreds who, with the

encouragement and help of Jewish institutions, deserted when General Anders's army reached Palestine (some units in 1942 and others in 1943). Some went to *kibbutzim* and elsewhere; others enlisted in the Palestinian units of the British army or in the Mandatory Police. Those who remained in General Anders's army fought with it in the difficult battle at Monte Casino, Italy, and in other battles.

In May 1943, the Kosciuszko Division, the first of the three divisions which eventually would comprise the Polish People's Army, was formed in the Soviet Union under General Z. Berling's command. At its formation, the Polish recruitment offices began to recruit Poles and inhabitants of Western Ukraine and Western Byelorussia "who consider themselves Poles."[9] Furthermore, known Poles, who had been leftist leaders in Vilna and had occupied responsible posts in the Lithuanian Division, were transferred to the Polish People's Army. In order to preserve the Polish character of this unit, however, and because of certain other political considerations, admission of Jews was severely restricted. Nevertheless, national origins inscribed on the personal documents of recruits were not closely checked. As a result, not only Jews from the Vilna region were accepted, but also Jews from other parts of Lithuania who knew some Polish.[10] Many of the Vilna Jews who had not been accepted into General Anders's army hoped to rejoin their families this way. There were also instances of Lithuanian Jews from the Lithuanian Division and other Soviet units officially applying for transfer to the Polish People's Army. It seems, however, that only a few hundred of them were finally admitted.

PART III
IN THE GHETTOS AND LABOR CAMPS

CHAPTER 12
THE BACKGROUND AND DEVELOPMENT

LITHUANIAN VIOLENCE AND THE GERMAN *EINSATZGRUPPE*

THE COLLAPSE OF THE SOVIET REGIME IN LITHUANIA AT the end of June 1941 removed the last obstacle to the increasing hostility against the Jewish minority in Lithuania. This hostility, abetted both covertly and overtly by nationalist groups as well as by sectors of the anti-Soviet underground and people in key positions, took the form of murderous pogroms in various parts of Lithuania well before the entry of the Germany army.[1] On the night of June 25th in the well-known Kovno suburb of Slobodka, about 1,200 men, women, and children were brutally massacred by armed Lithuanians calling themselves "partisans," and about sixty houses were demolished and burned. During the following nights, 2,300 more Jews were killed. Jews were also kidnapped by Lithuanians belonging to paramilitary squads in Kovno and elsewhere, and mass arrests were made in Vilna, Shavli, and other places. The majority of the prisoners were assembled in prisons and concentration sites which were later to serve as mass extermination sites, such as Ponary (Paneriai) near Vilna, the Kužiai woods near Shavli, and "Fort Nine" at Kovno.

Then with the arrival of the German army, the wave of murders swelled, partly as a result of secret activity on the part of its vanguard, the *Einsatzgruppe* (or mobile killing unit). The *Einsatzgruppe* was sent ahead because, in the words of one of its commanders, "It was desirable that it appear as though the local population initiated the first incidents, as a natural reaction against the oppression suffered at the hands of the Jews for decades."[2] Ironically, as supervision and implementation of anti-Jewish activity grew more methodical, pillage and violence by bands of avenging Lithuanians decreased. Lithuanians were, however, soon accepted within the ranks of the secondary units, particularly in the *Einsatzgruppen.* Among them were a substantial number whose relatives or families had been murdered or exiled by the Soviets.

Acting upon the theory that "the Jewish problem would be solved only by means of pogroms," the secondary units of *Einsatzkommando* started a *3a* liquidation program in the cities and forests exactly according to their timetable, on July 3, 1941.[3] Upon arrival at their destination, the liquidation units seized the Jews, who had already been plundered by the spontaneous wave of riots, and marshalled them into synagogues, marketplaces, or various estates. From there, the units brutally transported them, in groups of five hundred, 2½ to 3 miles to sites especially selected for the massacres. The Jews were then herded into prepared ditches, sometimes forced to undress, and then liquidated by firing squads using light or medium firearms and sometimes incendiary bullets. When their work was finished, the executioners were driven to other destinations to implement similar operations.

Thus, the majority of provincial Jews were murdered in July and August. Most of the Jews in the large cities, who in the meantime had been forced into ghettos, were liquidated in a series of similar *Aktionen* between September and November. So by the end of December 1941, about 180,000 (approximately 72 percent of the Jews of Lithuania had been annihilated by various means; only some 40,000 remained, most of whom were concentrated in the large ghettos: Kovno (16,000); Vilna (17,000); Shavli (4,700); and Svencian (2,000).[4] Several months earlier Lithuania became *Generalkommissariat Litauen,* subordinate to the *Reichskommisar* in Ostland (Lithuania, Latvia, and Estonia). (See map 3.)

THE RESPONSE OF THE JEWISH AUTHORITIES IN THE GHETTOS

The Jewish authorities had almost unlimited power in the management of internal affairs in the ghettos, hence, the Council of Elders *(Ältestenrat)* and the Jewish police became powerful and well-organized forces. Their authority ranged from the supply of basic municipal services for the distribution of food and the settlement of private disputes to decisions on crucial questions such as the execution of death sentences, deportation, and the surrender of Jews to the Germans. Thus, one writer comments, after describing how the Jewish court of the Shavli ghetto condemned three Jewish profiteers to

"corporal punishment and imprisonment," and a fourth to being handed over to the Security Police, "That's not how you, great Dubnow, pictured Jewish autonomy!"[5] Similarly, in June 1942, the court in the Vilna ghetto condemned to death by hanging six Jews who had been found guilty of murdering and collaborating in the murder of Jews.

The Jewish authorities in the ghettos exercised great care in fulfilling the Germans' demands for labor because they realized that the existence of the ghettos depended upon their compliance, and the Jewish police helped enforce these quotas.[6] Nevertheless, they also

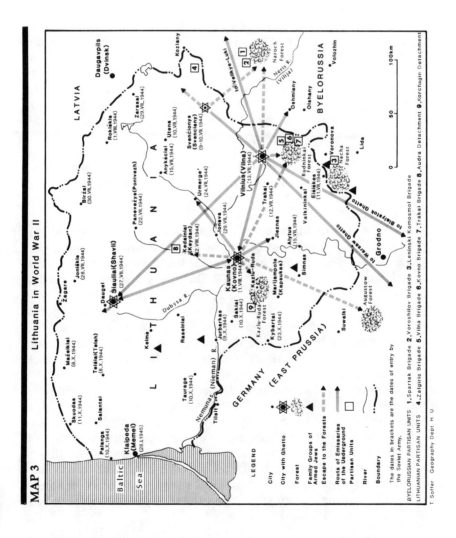

MAP 3   Lithuania in World War II

worked hard to safeguard the physical and mental health of the ghetto inhabitants. To this end, scores of services and institutions were established, from kitchens and clinics to a school and theater. The party organizations, including the Communist party, were likewise reconstituted. This activity flourished particularly during the period of "relative calm" from 1942 to the fall of 1943, supported both by political parties and by the ghettos' cultural, educational, and welfare institutions.

Because non-Jewish neighborhoods were included within the ghetto boundaries when the Jews were first enclosed at the end of the summer of 1941, the ghettos were bisected by a non-Jewish area. Therefore, when the population of the ghettos shrunk as a result of the *Aktionen* from the end of 1941 onwards, so did the size of the ghetto, for not only streets but whole districts were taken over by the non-Jewish neighborhoods. At the same time, a number of permanent and temporary labor camps where Jews from various ghettos were employed were added to the jurisdiction of the ghetto authorities. In September 1942, a number of small ghettos from the Vilna area, such as Oshmyany (Oszmiana) and Svencian were incorporated into the domain administered by the Vilna ghetto. A few months later, however, in the spring and summer of 1943, these ghettos were liquidated, with the active assistance of the Jewish police of the Vilna ghetto, an event which marked the end of the period of "relative calm."

At the end of the summer of 1943, the administration of the ghettos slipped entirely out of the hands of the civil authorities, and was transferred finally to the SS, in accordance with an explicit order from Himmler dated June 21, 1943. This order also incorporated a crucial decision concerning the continued survival of the Jews still remaining in the ghettos of Lithuania who were "to be concentrated in concentration camps." It was likewise forbidden, as of August 1, 1943, to employ Jews outside the framework of the concentration camps, "while all nonessential elements in the ghettos were to be evacuated to the East."

"In order that the feeling of desperation among the Jews should not mount too high and provoke resistance and mass flight,"[7] the highest echelons of the Security Service in Lithuania decided to execute a new program, beginning with the Vilna ghetto. First the ghetto Jewish workers were dismissed from the seventy-two different places of employment, which included both military and civilian jobs. Then thousands of Jews were deported to concentration camps in Estonia, beginning on August 6, 1943. The transports continued against fierce opposition until September 23, 1943. With the termination of the deportations, the Vilna ghetto was to all intents and purposes liquidated, and only three thousand Jews remained in the Heeres Kraftfahr Kompanie (HKP), Kailis, and Kriegslazarett camps.

The majority of the Jews in the Kovno ghetto were evacuated to Estonia and to five concentration camps in the Kovno area between October and December 1943. Devolving around the workshops, the Kovno ghetto, which had been reduced to half its size, became a central camp called *Konzentrationslager Kauen* (Kovno concentration camp). On March 27 and 28, 1944, an *Aktion* was carried out in this camp and its branches, in which some two thousand children, elderly Jews, and invalids were killed. With the Red Army's approach during the week of July 8, 1944, almost all the inhabitants (approximately eight thousand persons) were evacuated to camps in Germany, except for some two thousand who were killed while resisting, and several hundred who found refuge among non-Jews or who escaped.

In the Shavli ghetto, deportation to various camps was implemented in a similar manner in September 1943. An *Aktion* in which some eight hundred children, elderly persons, and invalids were exterminated was carried out there on November 5, 1943. Despite pressure from the advance of the Red Army, by June 22, 1944, the Germans had succeeded in evacuating the vast majority of the Jews (some four thousand persons) in the central camp and its branches to camps in Germany. Both the Shavli and Kovno ghetto sites were set on fire by the Germans during their retreat from Lithuania.

FORMS OF RETALIATION

After recovering from the initial shock of the first unexpected wave of murders, the Jews adopted various forms of retaliation before the final liquidation of the ghettos in Lithuania. These reactions, the majority of which were not violent, were, consciously or unconsciously, attempts to oppose the murder, starvation, and many other forms of destruction around them. All of these acts were impressive, some were even effective, and they ranged from the Jew who dipped his finger in his blood as it flowed and wrote "VENGEANCE" in blood on the wall, to the Jews who, on the brink of the pits, tore their money to shreds instead of surrendering it to the Germans.

A considerable proportion of the resistance took place within the framework of daily life, and in particular in the supply of essential requirements and services. For instance, since the official diet for ghetto inhabitants did not even provide enough to insure existence at the starvation level (adult rations included 3½ ounces of bread daily; 4 ounces of wheat flour per week; 3½ ounces of groats per week; 4¼ ounces of meat per week; tea or coffee substitute; a little jam; beans and salt), the Jews were forced from the first day to wage an active battle for survival, both to obtain food and to smuggle it into the ghetto—whether through the gate under the watchful eyes of the guards or through the fence. For this purpose, they employed a number of methods, most of them illegal. Having learned from these experiences, the arms purchasers would later use the same techniques and continue the smuggling, which, either directly or indirectly involved the majority of the ghetto inhabitants, despite the danger and severe punishments that such activities incurred. Furthermore, the majority of the spiritual and intellectual prohibitions imposed upon the ghetto inhabitants—against keeping books, establishing schools or synagogues, and similar interdictions intended to destroy morale still further—were not only disobeyed, but, on the contrary, protested with spontaneous demonstrations from the community.[8] This cultural and spiritual activity, in time, became an inseparable part of the underground cadres and sometimes even formed the essence of their activities. Contrary to the order by the German authorities to report every case of infectious disease (such as typhus and typhoid fever), the Jewish doctors concealed these incidents at great personal risk. They also frequently ignored the prohibition against births, despite the death penalty that threatened mothers and doctors who assisted at births, as well as those who cared for the "illegal" infants.[9]

Another major form of protest was flight, first exercised in the face of the Nazi invasion in the summer of 1941. However, the circumstances of the occupation and conditions in the ghettos made it possible only for small groups and individuals to get away. Later, in the brief pauses between *Aktionen* many others fled the city. Some of these were betrayed and perished; others continued to wander about in the towns and villages; some found refuge with peasants or on farms and in monasteries. Many Jews from the Vilna ghetto and surrounding villages escaped to Byelorussia, thinking that what had happened in Lithuania would not take place there. In fact, in some towns, the community leaders preached escape from the synagogue pulpit: "The fire blazes high, and we must all flee: whoever can, should flee to Byelorussia." Then, when the massacres began in the Byelorussian ghettos as well, many of these same people returned to Lithuania, some joining partisan units as early as May 1942.

The escape movement gained impetus again at the end of the period of "relative calm," with the renewal of the deportations and the liquidation of the remaining Jewish settlements in the Vilna area. Fugitives even turned to their non-Jewish acquaintances in the towns or villages in the hope that they would hide them in exchange for money or valuables, and the movement to rescue the children reached its peak. At great risk and sacrifice, desperate parents labored to save their children, using all means imaginable to place them with families or in institutions outside the ghetto. In the Kovno ghetto, where the *Aktion* against children was carried out later than in Vilna or Shavli, and therefore left more time for preparation, the underground and ghetto institutions lent their support. Women in the underground were particularly active in this area, reconnoitering outside the ghetto, finding ways to teach the children Lithuanian and even the fundamentals of the Catholic faith, and furnishing them with documents and suitable clothes. In the Kovno area, more than four hundred children were placed, but due to betrayals and exposures, or because of nonassimilation, only a fraction of the hundreds of children and adults smuggled out of the ghetto actually survived.[10]

Concurrently, more and more Jews began privately acquiring weapons and seeking refuge in the houses of peasants or among "armed gangs," which, according to rumor, were roaming the forests. An unknown number of them disappeared without trace; only a few succeeded in overcoming the innumerable hardships and managed to join family groups or full-fledged partisan units.

A further wave of spontaneous escapes took place when the Lithuanian ghettos were liquidated, and when the Jews of Vilna were evacuated to Estonia, we are told "some hundreds of Jews tried to escape; some of them were shot together with their families, others returned of their own volition. Nevertheless, some thirty of forty Jews succeeded in slipping away."[11] During the liquidation of the Kovno ghetto, however, many of the Jews who tried to break through the fence were shot by the guards. Others tried to flee while boarding the trains during the transport to Germany, and a great many people escaped from moving railway cars, and some even succeeded in returning to Kovno.

A particularly daring feat was accomplished by a group of "corpse burners" who were transferred to Ponary in chains, under the strict supervision of a special SS guard unit. The group of seventy men, which included some Soviet prisoners, dug a tunnel 130 feet long, using spoons and their bare hands, in the space of some two and a half months. On March 15, 1944, twenty of these men—thirteen

Jews and seven Soviet prisoners—slipped out through the tunnel under lethal fire from the guards. Most perished in the subsequent manhunt, but a few made it to partisan units in the Rudninkai forests.[12] A similar escape was also effected by the "corpse burners" at Fort Nine in Kovno.[13]

Hiding underground, however, was rather simpler to accomplish than escape, which usually depended upon a non-Jewish appearance, good connections, and great courage. Hiding, therefore, was more popular with the people of the ghetto. In Vilna, and especially in the suburb of Novogrudok, the Jews hid in *malines,* or bunkers, during the first pogroms. In the Kovno ghetto after the "Estonia *Aktion*" (October 26, 1943), which seemed to prove that "whoever hides is saved,"[14] building *malines* became particularly widespread. In the Shavli ghetto, however, *malines* and specially constructed hideouts were used much less.

At first, the *malines* were designed as temporary hiding places during roundups or *Aktionen:* people hid in cellars, attics, and storage rooms. When building methods were perfected and considerable advances made, however, people were able to survive in the *malines* for months. Occasionally, weapons were also prepared in *malines,* although that was not their original purpose, and their discovery led on more than one occasion to fights and violent resistance.

Such was the case in the *malines* of Kovno, which concealed many Jews during the ghetto's liquidation. SS and Gestapo men approached every building that looked suspicious and announced over a loudspeaker that they were about to blow it up; whoever came out, they said, would not be killed. When many of those in hiding refused to come out, the Germans threw hand grenades into them and set the buildings on fire. Consequently, two thousand Jews died a horrible death. At least one case is recorded of resistance when the Jews burst forth from a burning *maline* and encountered Germans. "Someone by the name of Chaim Schneider attacked a German and fought with him until he had strangled him."[15] Hundreds of hiding-places were discovered, demolished, and burned, together with their inhabitants. By the time the Red Army entered Kovno (August 1, 1944), only a few *malines* were still intact, with approximately ninety survivors in them.

Within the underground movement, attitudes toward the use of bunkers as a method of escape varied. While some underground groups in the Kovno ghetto, particularly Irgun Brit Zion (IBZ) regarded the *malines* as one of the principal ways of saving their members, the Fareynigte Partizaner Organizatsie (FPO), the United Partisans Organization in the Vilna ghetto, once said that "the flight of an FPO member to a *maline* under any and all circumstances will be considered like flight from the battlefield during an engagement: namely, as treachery."[16] On the other hand, the underground movement in the Kovno ghetto used *malines* to store and repair weapons, for shooting practice, and as temporary refuge for any members "who are being pursued for any reason, and in order to hide from the Germans during manhunts for workers."[17]

As early as 1941, during the riots and mass murders, Jews in a number of remarkable cases were already using force to resist their attackers. Although it is difficult to generalize, because the majority of cases were spontaneous, it seems that the use of force usually was limited to situations in which clearly "all was lost;" that is, when the principle of mutual responsibility on the one hand, and "internal responsibility" on the other, were immaterial.[18] Such was the case on June 29, 1941, when the Jews in the town of Shkud (Škuodas) were being taken in groups of fifty to be killed in prepared trenches. That was the day Yitzchak Malkenson, the strongest man in the town, attacked one of the executioners and "strangled him with his bare hands, before his [own] head was pierced by a German bullet."[19] A similar occurrence took place in the extermination sites near Kedainiai when Zadok Shlapobersky "dragged the German commander with him to the trench and bit the throat of one of the Lithuanian executioners."[20] And a twenty-four-year-old agricultural worker, J. Pastor, cut off the head of a Lithuanian policeman with a spade during the slaughter of the Jews of Pabrade on September 24, 1941, for which he was immediately shot. There were other acts of individual resistance in Kovno on the night of the Slobodka pogroms, at the mass extermination sites, and at Fort Seven. In the town of Jonava, seven strong Jews tried with their bare hands to wrestle with the armed soldiers. On December 20, 1941, two Jews in the Vilna ghetto, M. Haus and Goldstein, fell with a knife and an axe upon the Germans who came to take them to be killed. Both were shot on the spot, but on the following day during their funeral, anonymous notices of mourning were posted throughout the ghetto.

There are also many reports of resistance from the last two years of German occupation. On August 6, 1943, when the first Jews were being deported from the Vilna ghetto to Estonia, a Jew named Kossoy attacked two Estonian soldiers with a bottle and wounded them; during the ensuing confusion, he and scores of other Jews escaped. During the liquidation of the HKP camp near Vilna in June 1944, an old Jewish blacksmith, R. Baruch, was hit by an SS man with the butt of his rifle. In a flash, he snatched the rifle out of the German's hand

and, as though he were wielding a big hammer in the smithy, he brought the rifle butt down, with a well-aimed swing, on the head of the SS man. In the same locale, a Jewish policeman called Shukstulski, sensing that he was making his last journey, tore into an SS man with a knife. The manager of the camp's carpentry shop, Feldman, also did not hesitate when he saw that the shop was surrounded by SS men; he shot at them. Within a few minutes, he was riddled with bullet holes.

There were also spontaneous mass revolts, some of which are recorded only in German sources. For example, during a rebellion in the extermination site near the town of Žagarė (Zager) on October 2, 1941 "many Jews who had not been thoroughly searched drew pistols and amid shouts of 'Down with Hitler' attacked the police and wounded seven of them."[21] When the Jews of Valkininkai (Olkeniki) were taken away to be murdered on September 24, 1941, a number of Jews stunned the Lithuanian executioners with their assault and fled the city over their bodies by way of courtyards and backstreets.

The violent and unexpected resistance of the Vilna Jews of the small towns on their way to Ponary on April 5, 1943, led to a large-scale revolt. The Jews attacked the Lithuanian guards with pistols, knives, and even with their teeth. After this clash, some six hundred bodies were left on the track, but a few Jews succeeded in escaping and reaching the Vilna ghetto. Those who remained resisted bitterly, even on the brink of the extermination site in Ponary, where they wounded a number of Germans and Lithuanians. These facts, which are confirmed by German documents, were also mentioned in a popular song which circulated at the time in the Vilna ghetto.[22] When Jewish workers were brought from the Porubanek work-center near Vilna to the railway station to be deported to Estonia, they were afraid that they, too, were going to be taken to Ponary. Amid desperate cries of "There is nothing to lose in any case; let's scatter and escape!" they attacked the cordon of soldiers with their fists and breached a path leading outside the ghetto. Another armed rebellion by a group of Jews in the HKP camp took place at the end of July 1944, on the eve of the German retreat.

EXTERNAL FACTORS AFFECTING RESISTANCE

It is apparent from German documents that the site of the Kovno ghetto was chosen, *inter alia*, for clear-cut strategic and military reasons: namely, that, if necessary, it would be easy to besiege it. This was also the case of the Shavli ghetto, bordered on the north by a large pool, on the east, by a block of buildings belonging to a tanning factory, and on the southwest, by a municipal prison. In addition, most of the houses in both these ghettos were small and made of wood. The Vilna ghetto, on the other hand, not only was situated in the center of the city, but most of its buildings were mansions two or three stories high. And although the area over which it extended was relatively small (seven side streets), which hampered the possibilities of tactical maneuvers, the Vilna ghetto was still the most suitable of all the Lithuanian ghettos for street fighting. Its proximity to dense forests gave the Vilna ghetto another considerable advantage over the other two ghettos; the forests in Lithuania become larger from west (the Baltic Sea coast) to east, where the Rudninkai forests converge with the Nacza, Belowiez, Naliboki, and Lipszan forests of Byelorussia and Poland and thus offered the possibility of a quick breakaway. (See map 3.) The Kovno ghetto was considerably less well situated, since it was surrounded by small forests, while in the Shavli vicinity, there were only copses, and even these were scarce.

In every plan of escape from the ghetto—be it in the organized framework of the underground or by individuals—the possibility of assistance from other national minorities no matter how limited was crucial. Lithuanians, for example, were considered more than likely to hand Jews over to the Germans. Since the population in the Vilna district was ethnically the most heterogeneous, consisting of a considerable number of Poles, Byelorussians, Lithuanians, Russians, Tartars, and Karaites, the Jews of the Vilna ghetto and the surrounding small towns were in a much better position than those of the Kovno ghetto, where the number of Poles and Russians was extremely small. There were hardly any foreigners at all in the Shavli ghetto and the surrounding area.

In contrast to the Polish Jews, who had a breathing space of two or three years between the German occupation of their country in 1939 and the era of mass exterminations, Lithuanian Jewry became acquainted with extermination techniques from the first days of occupation in 1941. The length of time between the occupation and the final liquidation, which varied from ghetto to ghetto, also affected their ability to organize resistance. In the Vilna and Svencian ghettos, they had about one and a half years, as compared to two and a half years in the ghettos of Kovno and Shavli. During this period, two major events outside Lithuania had tremendous influence on the activities of the resistance movements in all the ghettos: the German defeat at Stalingrad and the Warsaw ghetto uprising.

With the exception of the Communists, however, neither the non-Jewish political underground movements nor the legal organizations extended aid to organized Jewish resistance activities. While the Polish underground, *Armia Krajowa* (AK), in Vilna did not hesitate to enlist individual Jews, it purposely procrastinated in negotiations with the Jewish underground in Vilna, which requested weapons. The answers were generally evasive: on one occasion, the ground was frozen and they were unable to dig out the weapons; on another, it was dangerous to go near the hiding place. Finally, it seems that a negative answer was tendered by AK headquarters in Warsaw. The Polish Socialists (PPS) in Vilna to whom their Jewish comrades, the members of the *Bund*, turned with a suggestion for joint action, likewise answered hesitantly, asking: "How can you help us?" Legal and semilegal Lithuanian organizations did not cease to claim from the Germans what remained of Jewish property, while they advocated employing the surviving Jews as work forces to restore the ruins of Russia and Byelorussia. There was, naturally, no basis for negotiation with these parties, nor any real prospect of help or cooperation from them. The sole ally from whom concrete assistance could be expected was the Communist underground, but the latter was scarcely in existence when the Jewish resistance movement in Lithuania was developing at the beginning of 1942. However, even when the Communist party was strengthened by emissaries parachuted from Moscow, the Soviet political line did not always correspond to the aims of the Jewish resistance movements.

INTERNAL FACTORS AFFECTING RESISTANCE

One of the principal problems of the Jewish struggle in Lithuania was that, even when the Lithuanian Jewish community still numbered nearly a quarter of a million persons, it had no real opportunity to fight and no allies. By the time prospects began to brighten in 1942, there was almost no Jewish community left.

From a demographic point of view, the forty thousand Jews who remained in Lithuania at the beginning of 1942 was a totally different population from the prewar Jewish population. It lacked young people and men of military age, for most of these had escaped to Russia or had died en route, and the *Aktionen* of fall 1941 had hit families with a conspicuous number of children or elders, who could not be exploited for forced labor, particularly hard. As a result of frequent Aktionen and selections, the majority of the ghetto population were women who were in the military conscription age group (18–55).[23] Therefore, when the vital interests of the resistance movement demanded maximum utilization of the remnants of Lithuanian Jewry in 1942, women were included as potential fighters, despite the problems this decision engendered.[24]

In addition to Jewish refugees from Poland, many refugees from the small towns in Lithuania who had escaped during the massacres were absorbed into the ghettos. With their familiarity with the villages and forests in the neighborhood, their experience in fieldcraft and forest life, and their mobility, they became extremely important to underground and partisan activities.

The constant movement within the ghettos; the chance intimacy in crowded conditions (up to eight families to a room) of people who before the war were far removed from one another culturally, economically, and socially; the economic situation which had transformed the social hierarchy and class system of prewar Jewry; and, above all, the feeling of common danger, all increased the tendency toward egalitarianism in the ghettos. Furthermore, because the Soviets had expelled hundreds of public figures and Zionist leaders during the last week before the Nazi invasion, and because the German massacres and *Aktionen* were often aimed at the Jewish elite, Lithuanian Jewry remained virtually without any communal or political leadership in 1942. Communist leaders were also lacking, as many had been evacuated to the Soviet Union. The party leaders and communal figures who remained were not popular with the Soviets.[25] The unavoidable necessity for cooperating with Soviet representatives, however, raised the level of leadership among those who became, along with the ghetto police, the nucleus of a popular movement.

During the thirty years which had elapsed since their active participation in the ranks of the Czarist army during World War I and in the Lithuanian war of Independence, the Lithuanian Jews of Kovno or Shavli had had almost no military experience or practice in self-defense.[26]

This was not the case with the Jews of Vilna and the surrounding area. In September 1939, thousands of them participated actively in the war against the Germans on various fronts in Poland. They also had gained experience in organizing popular self-defense during the student riots in the 1930s[27] and the pogroms, which broke out at almost regular intervals during the frequent changes of government between the German defeat of 1915 and the entry of the Lithuanian army in October 1939. Some of the Jews of Vilna grew up in an atmosphere of revolutionary activity, and in accordance with a tradition of bloody conflicts with the Czarist government that spanned several decades. They were, generally speaking, more aware of the concept of self-defense and more skilled in the use of arms than other Jewish communities in Lithuania.[28] In certain circles of Vilna Jewry, private individuals built up quite an extensive cache of arms between the wars. These facts proved very important during the Nazi occupation. The use of cold steel and firearms and trading in arms were more widespread among the Jews of Vilna than among the Jews of Kovno and Shavli.

The most experienced group within Lithuania's Jewish community from the point of view of organizational and underground work, however, was the Communist party, which, for twenty years, had illegally organized a wide range of political activities. Yet, most of the Communist party or Komsomol members who remained in the ghettos were young people who had joined the party as recently as 1940 or 1941, for the vast majority of veteran party members and those with underground experience had succeeded in fleeing to the Soviet Union at the outbreak of the war, or had been arrested by the police, who were already acquainted with them.

Members of Zionist groups and former pupils in Hebrew high schools, who had organized illegal activities, particularly in the fields of culture and education, during the Soviet regime, did have some underground experience, and the range and intensity of their activities were evenly distributed in Vilna, Kovno, and Shavli.

The tradition of family and community ties continued to exist even under ghetto conditions. Every popular resistance movement was obliged to consider the risk to the ghetto as a whole. This factor, knowingly or unknowingly, shaped the principal aims of these movements, and could be expected to have, at the very least, indirect results on the relationship between the resistance movements and the Jewish authorities in the ghetto, on the one hand, and between the Soviet and Lithuanian partisan movements, on the other.

CHAPTER 13
IN THE LARGE GHETTOS—VILNA AND KOVNO

THE VILNA GHETTO

ORGANIZED UNDERGROUND ACTIVITY IN THE VILNA ghetto during the *Aktionen* of autumn 1941—chiefly the work of the parties and youth movements—was focused on locating surviving members, establishing contact with them, and insuring their security.

At first, the youth movements worked separately. A small group of *Hashomer Hatza'ir* activists was organized in a Benedictine monastery, while a number of girls were sent to the Aryan side as liaison officers. The activists met in a one-room flat at 15 Strashun (Starszüna) Street, where they attempted to forge identity cards. Despite the repeated assertion that this measure was not for personal security, but to insure the existence of an activist nucleus, some felt that there was no purpose in such activity. Division among the activists grew when some members of the Coordinating Committee (representing *Hehalutz, Hashomer Hatza'ir,* and *Hanoar Haziyoni*), argued that instead they should use their connections with Sergeant Anton Schmidt of the German army and plan to transport large groups to Bialystok, where, as yet, there had been no large-scale massacres.[1] The two opposing factions in the Coordinating Committee eventually crystallized as follows: On the one hand there were some twenty-eight men, the majority of whom were from *Hehalutz, Hehalutz-Hatza'ir-Deror,* their leader, Mordechai Tenenbaum, plus three or four members of *Hashomer Hatza'ir,* who actually went to Bialystok. On the other hand there were 150 members of youth movements, who approved the proclamation, "Let us not go like sheep to a slaughter. . . ," written by Abba Kovner and read aloud in Hebrew and Yiddish at a meeting planned by *Hashomer Hatza'ir* and held in the *Hehalutz* kitchen on January 1, 1942. The proclamation warned "whoever goes out of the gates of the ghetto will never return. . . . Ponary is not a concentration camp—everyone is shot there." It ended with a call for armed resistance "until our last breath."[2]

Political frameworks in various stages of organization were also in existence at that time in the Vilna ghetto. They included the Communists, the *Bund*, and four parties under the aegis of the Zionists: *Póalei Ziyon–ZS–Hitahdut*, General Zionists, *Mizrachi*, and the Revisionists, including *Betar*. Of all these political bodies, the Communists and the Revisionists were the first to whom *Hashomer Hatza'ir* turned after the above proclamation was read, with a proposal to establish a united, armed underground. Negotiations were also undertaken with other groups, but to no avail.

On January 21, 1942, however, all the representatives who had brought the negotiations to a successful completion met in the room of Joseph Glazman, the *Betar* representative in Lithuania (and formerly the Revisionist representative in the Zionist umbrella organization). Itzik (Yitzchak) Wittenberg and Chiena Borovska (Communists), Abba Kovner *(Hashomer Hatza'ir)*, and Nissan Reznik (Hano'ar Haziyoni—Zionist Youth), as well as Captain Isidore Frucht, a former soldier, participated in the meeting. They resolved:

> (1) to establish an armed fighting organization that would operate clandestinely in the Vilna ghetto and include representatives from each body in the hope of unifying all of the organized forces in the ghetto; (2) to make preparations for mass armed resistance in the face of any attempt to liquidate the ghetto their fundamental aim; (3) to see defense as a national undertaking, a fight for its honor; (4) to carry out acts of sabotage and destruction in the enemy's rearguard; (5) to join the ranks of the partisans fighting in the rear guard and help the Red Army in the collective battle against the Nazi invader; (6) to inculcate the other ghettos with the ideal of self-defense and to establish a link with fighting forces outside the ghetto; (7) to elect a command consisting of Joseph Glazman, Yitzchak Wittenberg, and Abba Kovner. Yitzchak Wittenberg was elected commander-in-chief.[3] The organization was called the FPO, *Fareynigte Partizaner Organizatsie* (United Partisan Organization).[4]

After further negotiations, a considerable proportion of the *Bund* (in particular, the youth) joined the FPO in the spring of 1942. Their representative, A. Chwojnik, as well as the representative of the Hano'ar Haziyoni, N. Reznik, became members of the command. Despite attempts at negotiations with *Póalei Ziyon–ZS–Hitahdut, Mizrachi*, and, to a certain extent, with *Hehalutz*, these movements remained outside the FPO, with the exception of members who joined the organization individually such as A. Sheftel, L. Tarashinski, and Y. Kaufman.

Once the FPO was established, most of the groups organized outside the ghetto returned and joined the FPO. Despite the extreme strictness with which candidates for its ranks were selected, during its one and a half years, the membership of the FPO grew to three hundred, supplemented by as many peripheral members.

In addition to the systematic acquisition of arms, military training, and constant perfection of its organizational system and drafting methods, the FPO activities included the successful mining of an army munitions train in July 1942 (the first incident of its kind in Lithuania following the German invasion). The FPO also sent emissaries to other ghettos to warn them of imminent *Aktionen* and across the front line to Russia in order to transmit to the world at large detailed information about the fate of the Jews under the occupation. However, this mission failed in its final stages.

In the course of continuous efforts to communicate with anti-Nazi partisans, the FPO succeeded in establishing direct contact with a group of Soviet paratroopers in the summer of 1942. The paratroopers recognized that the FPO was an integral part of the Soviet partisan movement, and decided to collaborate with it. Together, they established a base for sabotage operations, conducted military training, espionage, and sabotage missions, and acquired arms and explosives. Then, in the midst of these initial efforts, contact with the group was suddenly lost; only later did the FPO ascertain that the paratroopers' group had been almost totally liquidated by the Germans. The search for contacts with the outside world continued, however, and the Communist members of the FPO began discussions with the former mayor of Vilna, Vitas, and induced him to set up a unified command for partisan activity in Lithuanian territory. The command, which included Wittenberg as FPO representative, recognized the FPO as the combat division of the ghetto area. This connection also enabled the FPO to step up anti-Nazi propaganda activity. Distributing posters in Lithuanian and Polish, they called upon the population to join the partisans and warned them against working in Germany. Colonel F. Markov, the commander of the Byelorussian *Voroshilov* partisan brigade, thus became aware of the existence of the FPO. In the spring of 1943, Markov sent a letter to the FPO command in which he exhorted the youth to leave the ghetto and join his unit. However, because the FPO emphasized fighting within the ghetto, and because Markov stipulated that only armed men could join him, the FPO leadership rejected his suggestion at this stage, despite the ferment which this decision caused within the ranks of the organization. Other offers on the part of Jewish emissaries from Stankiewicz, the commander of the *Leninski Komsomol* unit in the Nacza forests were similarly declined, as was an offer to permit Svencian youth organization members to join its ranks, despite confirmation from Sidyakin, the commander of the *Chapayev* partisan group, of their trustworthiness.

At approximately the same time, in Spring 1943, the series of discussions conducted by social and political groups which, for ideological and personal reasons, had remained outside the FPO, came to an end. Until then, the groups had undertaken limited social and cultural activities and had even acquired arms, but now they decided to establish a united framework with the FPO. This cadre, first called the "Fighting Group" *(Kamfsgruppe)*, was later named *Yechiel*, after Yechiel (Ilya) Sheinboim, who had led the Hehalutz group in the ghetto after the departure of Mordechai Tenenbaum and served as Chief of Staff of the Fighting Group. Other members of the command were Revisionists who disagreed with Glazman's tactics, S. Brand, L. Bernstein, Y. Faust, and two ghetto police officers, N. Ring and B. Friedman. The Fighting Group, which included quite a number of soldiers, was oriented toward "partisan activity in the forest, to which all its members, as well as all other ready and willing Jews, were to be transferred."[5] The Fighting Group's policy, as well as the relative ease with which candidates were accepted into its ranks, resulted in the rapid growth of its membership from a few score (including a considerable number of policemen) to a hundred or more, including peripheral members.[6]

On April 21, 1943, some ten members of the Fighting Group, under the leadership of B. Friedman, organized themselves into a vanguard group, and with the help of a guide from outside the ghetto, went out to the forest. They encountered a German patrol in the Rudninkai forests about twenty-five miles south of Vilna and most of them perished. In part, because the group included police officers, the Jewish authorities in the ghetto, headed by Jacob Gens, became less tolerant, and sympathetic towards the Fighting Group. Their relationship with the FPO was strained further when the FPO did not conceal its criticism of the Jewish police's participation in the *Aktionen* against the Jews within the Vilna ghetto and elsewhere. As a result, the resistance organizations were persecuted by arms raids, imprisonment, and the exile of their leaders to labor camps. These tactics caused violent clashes, particularly between the FPO and the police. Against this background, and in view of the fact that an SS officer named B. Kittel had, upon his recent arrival in the Vilna ghetto, liquidated the Jews in the nearby labor camps, the FPO began negotiating with the *Yechiel* organization to form a coalition. The ideological gap between the two organizations as well as what appeared to be organizational problems, but were in fact personal (disagreements, for example, over whether members should join the FPO collectively or individually and whether arms should continue to be purchased separately) complicated the negotiations. By the summer of 1943, however, these problems had been settled.

In the meantime, tension between the FPO and the ghetto authorities reached a new height. Following the arrests of Communists in Vilna who had been in contact with Yitzchak Wittenberg, the Gestapo asked the ghetto authorities to hand Wittenberg over. When the ghetto police failed to find him, their commander, Jacob Gens, invited the members of the FPO staff to a meeting in his house on July 15, ostensibly to inform the staff as to the situation in the ghetto. In the middle of the meeting, Gestapo men appeared and arrested Wittenberg. On his way out of the ghetto, he was rescued by an FPO group and taken to one of their hideouts. In response, the ghetto authorities launched a campaign of inciting the community against the FPO, based on the claim that the refusal to hand over "Wittenberg, the Communist" was liable to bring disaster upon all the Jews. The next day, the FPO command was subjected to heavy moral pressure from both the Jewish masses and the community leaders to take pity on the ghetto. Imbued with fear of a civil war in the ghetto, the heads of the FPO allowed their commander-in-chief to decide for himself whether or not to surrender. "History will probably blame us for this," states the protocol of that FPO staff meeting, headed by Abba Kovner. "It is probable that no one will ever entirely understand the situation in which we were placed and the actions which resulted from our great responsibility to the ghetto and to the masses against whom we could not, indeed might not fight."[7] The day after Wittenberg gave himself up to the Gestapo, he was found dead: apparently he had been poisoned (or had committed suicide) before they could interrogate him.

Prompted by the atmosphere of depression which reigned after the loss of their commander[8] and their disappointment at the behavior of the masses, as well as by differences of opinion with respect to the value of their ties with the ghetto, the FPO leaders decided to send a group of members to the forest. The group was composed of twenty-one activists—most of whom had systematically suffered from persecution by the ghetto authorities. The group was dubbed "Leon" (Wittenberg's underground alias) and led by Joseph Glazman. On July 24, the group left the ghetto for the Narocz (Naroch) forests with a young guide from Svencian, Yashike Gertman. On the Novo-Vilejka (Naujoji Vilnia) bridge, some twenty miles east of Vilna, a German ambush suddenly opened fire on the group and nine of its members, including five scouts, fell. The survivors (including Glazman) succeeded in reaching the Narocz forests together with the guide. When animosity toward the underground movements grew even more intense, five more groups numbering some two hundred persons in all, left for the Narocz forests with the active assistance of the FPO. The majority were young people from the towns in the district and refugees from Grodno who had contacts with underground circles in the Vilna ghetto. In the fact of imminent deportations to Estonia and rumors of the liquidation of the ghetto, an almost complete coalition was effected between the FPO and the *Yehiel* organization. So on September 1, when the ghetto was attacked by soldiers and police to preclude mass resistance to the deportations to Estonia, the FPO was ready. They published a statement: "Jews! Defend yourselves with weapons!" and prepared a plan of attack against the Germans, with the additional objective of confronting the ghetto inhabitants with a *fait accompli* of a revolt.[9] However, most of the members of the FPO's second battalion were captured before they had succeeded in arming themselves when the Germans launched a surprise attack on their mobilization site. They were sent to Estonia. Then there were exchanges of fire between the Germans and an armed unit led by Y. Sheinboim, positioned behind a barricade in Strashun Street. Sheinboim was killed in the fight, as were a number of other underground fighters when their position was blown up by the Germans. The Germans then retreated from the ghetto, and the rest of the deportation was implemented by the Jewish police. Consequently, the FPO staff decided upon a mass evacuation to the forest.

By September 15, some 150 men, most members of the FPO, had joined Markov's units in the Narocz forests; approximately seventy full and peripheral members of *Yechiel* left for the nearby Rudninkai (Rudnicki) forests. On September 23, the eve of the final liquidation of the ghetto, the last 150 members of the FPO, including their commander Abba Kovner, left the ghetto through the sewers. These groups established four partisan units in the Rudninkai forests: *Mestitel* ("Avenger"), *Za Pobedu* ("To Victory"), *Smert Fashizma* ("Death to Fascism") and *Bor'ba* ("Struggle"). (See appendixes.) In the Kailis and HKP labor camps, which continued to function in Vilna until July

1944, the remaining FPO members and their adjuncts concentrated on getting people to the Rudninkai forests. With the help of Jewish partisans in these forests (former members of the FPO), three large groups, numbering some 150 persons in all, were brought out of the camps between September and November.[10] Only a minority of them were members of the FPO; the majority (including a considerable number of women) were not affiliated with any group. Later, when supervision of the camps was tightened and the partisan command in the Rudninkai forests changed their policy, such parties were no longer brought to the forest. But individuals from the camps continued to penetrate into the forests, and after acquiring a number of pistols and grenades, an underground cell established by members of the FPO in the HKP camp dug a tunnel through which to escape. Denunciation by a Jewish policemen, however, led the Germans to the tunnel. They blocked the exit, demanding that the Jews surrender. Refusing to come out, the group opened fire, upon which the Germans threw grenades and gas bombs into the tunnel and liquidated all those inside.

There were underground groups organized for flight to the forests in nearly every camp in Estonia. Most of them arose spontaneously and were unaffiliated, and the majority did not succeed in making contact with Estonian or Russian partisans.[11] On the other hand, in those camps where the leaders were members of the FPO, methodical, wide-ranging and efficient activity was perceptible, stressing social and communal aspects. The FPO members in these camps were affiliates of the second battalion that had been captured in the ghetto while preparing an attack against the Germans. Headed by the battalion commander Grisha Zipelevicz, ten activists in the Soski camp began to organize underground activities, including sending men out of the camp in order to make contact with a group of Soviet prisoners and attempting to carry out sabotage operations. An order of the day concerning role distribution and a short code of regulations was read to the activists at a meeting to mark the anniversary of the October Revolution. In February 1944, the members of the group, (which grew to twenty members) decided to join the partisans, but due to the transfer of the Jews to the Goldfilz camp, the plan was not carried out. On the strength of his former rank in the FPO, and because of his moral influence and energetic character, G. Zipelevicz was recognized as a leader by the majority of the FPO members, including those in other camps. On his urging, an underground framework in the FPO tradition was established in the Ereda camp which, in the course of time, totalled between ninety and one hundred members.[12] Some of its members organized sallies to the forest, and at least one party succeeded in reaching its destination. However, out of the group's 144 members, only thirteen were still alive by the time the Red Army arrived. Pursuant to an order by battalion commander Zipelevicz, a number of FPO activists were smuggled into the Klooga camp in order to organize underground activities there. In Goldfilz, too, the members of the FPO stayed together. A number of them participated in organized escapes involving scores of men, including FPO member Hirsh Glick, composer of the organization's hymn, "*Zog nit, keyn mol, az du geist dem letzten veg* ("Oh do not say, this journey is my last.") Only a few lived to see the liberation.

The underground in the Klooga camp, founded by members of the FPO, numbered fifteen groups of five on its first day.[13] Apart from devising plans of escape, it prepared for mass self-defense against the eventual liquidation of the camp and acquired a number of pistols for this purpose. However, on September 19, 1944, the day before the liberation of the camp by the Red Army, the SS organized a mass slaughter of the camp inmates on the spot; from among the hundreds who attempted to flee, only about a hundred escaped. After the liberation, FPO members among the survivors of this camp, as well as other camps in Estonia, were recognized as partisans by the Soviets.[14]

THE KOVNO GHETTO

The first attempts at organized armed resistance in the Kovno ghetto crystallized during the *Aktionen* of fall 1941. Two Jewish police officers, I. Greenberg and P. Padison, presented a predominantly Zionist group of community leaders who had assembled in the apartment of Officer M. Bramson with a plan for a ghetto uprising in the case of an attempted massacre. To this end, they suggested that units be established immediately to train young people for armed resistance. As a result of this meeting, a pistol was acquired with *Ältestenrat* funds and training units were set up under the leadership of I. Greenberg. The units existed until the beginning of 1942, but achieved no practical results. After this abortive attempt by the Committee for Self-Defense (*Zelbstshutz Komitet*), the initiative was transferred to political organizations, which became the ghetto's new underground framework. They included Communists, who were divided into a number of factions unaware of one another's existence and Zionists, among whom were movements and groups from the *Eretz-Yisrael ha-*

Ovedet bloc, *Mizrachi*, General Zionists, the *Irgun Brit Ziyon* (IBZ) set up during the Soviet regime in 1940, and the bloc of organizations belonging to *Ha-Histadrut ha-Ziyonit ha-Hadashah* (New Zionist Organization): Revisionists, *Betar*, and *Brit Ha-Hayal* (Convent of army veterans).

At first, most of these organizations focused on taking a census of members still alive at the end of 1941; publishing warnings of imminent danger; giving succor to the needy, and seeking employment, particularly in ghetto institutions and the police force. They also sought to reinforce their links with organizations with similar ideological outlooks. It was then that the Communists made their first tentative contacts with key personalities in the Zionist camp like the *Ältestenrat* member Zvi Levin, a renowned Revisionist leader who had been imprisoned under the Soviet regime. Then on December 31, 1941, the majority of the Communist groups merged into the "Activists' Union" *(Aktivistn Farband)*, later known as the "Anti-Fascist Organization." It was headed by a committee first of five, and later of seven, under the *de facto* leadership of Chaim Yellin.[15] In April 1942, they created the Viliampole Kovno Zionist Center, called *Matzok* (Distress). Apart from bringing members of the Zionist parties and movements into the *Ältestenrat* in the hope of influencing its general policy, *Matzok* also worked to strengthen ties with Jewish and non-Jewish elements outside the ghetto. They also helped to install a radio transmitter.

At the same time, other groups were also trying to arouse world public opinion by means of propaganda and reprisals against the Germans. But when they realized that they would not succeed on their own, they joined the umbrella organizations. One was called *Zorg*, short for *Zelbstshutz Organizatsie* ("Organization for Self-Defense") and the other *Bar-Giora*. *Zorg* joined the Communists and *Bar-Giora* became affiliated with IBZ and afterwards *Betar*.

The majority of these organizations, with the possible exception of the Communists (who had already carried out a series of sabotage operations and were making concrete preparations for both fighting in the ghetto and joining the partisans)[16] continued to focus on internal consolidation, cultural and educational activities, and, to a certain extent, on establishing contacts outside the ghetto. These quests, however, were to no avail. When the idea of resistance was raised in any underground Zionist circle, it immediately became the subject of bitter argument, due to apprehension about the fate of the ghetto. The proponents of these ideas were mainly refugees from Poland and elsewhere. The arguments were especially characteristic of the IBZ, but also plagued *Hashomer Hatza'ir,* which from an ideological point of view was close to the Communist party. Nevertheless, the youth movements as a whole were more receptive to the concept of self-defense than were their founding parties, or their representatives in *Matzok,* and they stepped up pressure particularly after a visit from Irena Adamowicz, the emissary of the pioneering underground in the Warsaw and Vilna ghettos, in July 1942. At the end of that year, an attempt was made to establish an organization under the name of AYO—*Algemeyne Yidishe Organizatsie* ("General Jewish Organization") to defend the ghetto. Members of various movements were organized into groups of five and met two or three times, but for reasons which are still unclear, the activity did not continue at this time.

Amidst general chaos in the spring of 1943, ferment within the underground movements increased. A series of events, including the defeat of the Germans at Stalingrad and the subsequent *Aktion;* the Warsaw ghetto uprising; the massacre of the Jews in the small towns of Eastern Lithuania, and also stories from refugees there about the existence of partisan units in the forests forced the organizations to consider future tactics for the underground under the new conditions. The argument was increasingly heard among the Zionist youth movements, most of which had secret groups for military training, that the time had come to map out a clear plan of action either for revolt inside the ghetto or for fighting outside of it. *Hashomer Hatza'ir* members sought practical means for rebellion which, since Irena Adamowicz's visit, had been their primary concern. Among the members of the IBZ, too, there was a lively discussion, and the command of the organization was requested to reexamine its policies. It was contended that one should not concentrate on educational and cultural activities; defense and rescue should become the primary aims. The Communists reacted to the new situation by increasing their efforts to contact the Lithuanian underground, but in the ghetto itself, they realized the necessity of emerging from their isolation and cooperating with the other underground organizations in an active struggle.

At the beginning of the summer of 1943, the Communists, on behalf of the Anti-Fascist Organization, presented an official proposal to *Matzok* concerning collaboration between the two movements. Representatives of *Matzok* accepted the proposal.[17] The agreement, signed by the four participants in the negotiations, stated:

> The two camps, the Zionist camp and the Jewish Freedom Fighters (the Communists) will reorganize the "Fighting Division" and will avoid

separate activity. Each side will recruit its own men and will receive training and supplies. . . . There will be a united program for training and activity until departure to the forests . . . and the members of the movement will avoid any attempt to pressure or influence one another ideologically.

The joint organization was simply called "The Organization" *(Di Organizatsie)* or "The Fighting Organization." Its full name was *Yidishe Algemeyne Kamfs Organizatsie,* the General Jewish Fighting Organization, or the JFO. During its peak period, the organization had a membership of close to six hundred.[18]

On the basis of this agreement, joint supreme commands were set up. The Communal Committee, was the highest authority for general policy and represented the fighting force in the ghetto institutions and the general public (for fund-raising and similar purposes). The Coordinating Commission, also called MTK, the *Militerishe Tekhnishe Komisie* ("Military-Technical Commission"), planned the Communal Committee's policy and executed it. As the JFO briskly took its first steps towards reorganization in fulfilment of the agreement, there was a division of labor. The Zionists devoted themselves mainly to the mobilization of funds, with semi-open appeals for "the Hebrew Rebellion Movement" and "the fight against the Germans," and to gathering money and supplies from the ghetto authorities. The Communists redoubled their efforts to make contact with their comrades outside the ghetto, hoping to contact the partisans who, according to reports, were already active in Lithuania. It was, in fact, through a JFO liaison officer that a Communist underground movement, which was known as the "Union for the War Against Fascism in Lithuania," and had been active for a number of months since March 1943, was discovered in Kovno. The two sides soon came to the realization that their aims were identical and decided to work closely together. During the summer of 1943, they met regularly once a week not far from the ghetto on the banks of the river Nėris (Wilja). The two organizations devised united acts of sabotage, distribution of informative material, and preparations to establish partisan units. The Jewish organization received from the Union illegal local newspapers from Moscow and they, in turn, prepared a rubber stamp for the Union in the ghetto as well as equipment for duplicating posters. The latter included a German duplicating machine that had been "removed" by a member of the JFO.

On the other hand, attempts to establish a joint partisan base in the forests in the Kovno area were doomed to failure. After huts and a small quantity of arms and supplies (boots, fighting equipment, and clothes) brought from the ghetto had been stored there by both sides, the Gestapo surprised the few Soviet partisans and killed them. The rest of the leaders of the Union were captured, interrogated, and brutally tortured, while some of the JFO were forced to go underground, hiding in the subterranean *malines* they had prepared earlier.

Attempts by the Communists in the JFO to discover partisan bases in eastern and southern Lithuania in August and September also failed. Two of the five groups sent out to reconnoiter, armed with light weapons, compasses, and maps, clashed with the police, and eight of their members, who were among the elite of the JFO, perished. The others returned to the ghetto having encountered no partisans.[19]

There was a decisive change in relations between the Lithuanian Communist party and the partisan command, largely as a result of the visit the Jewish paratrooper Gessia Glezer ("Albina") paid to the Kovno ghetto at the end of September 1943.[20] During the few weeks which she spent secretly in the ghetto, the Yiddish-speaking paratrooper met primarily with the Communist activists, but also with *Hashomer Hatza'ir* representatives from the JFO, and the commander of the Jewish police in the ghetto, M. Levin, who represented the Revisionists in *Matzok* and the JFO. The central figure in Communist and JFO circles, Chaim Yellin, was also invited to meet with her at a partisan base in the Rudninkai forests that had been established by the Lithuanian Brigade under the command of the paratrooper "Jurgis," (Yurgis) G. Ziman, (Zimanas) the Jewish teacher and well known Communist leader from Kovno. On the basis of the discussions with Ziman, as well as those with Albina, the JFO developed a plan of action, which almost certainly was founded on instructions from Moscow. It stipulated that attempts to establish partisan bases around Kovno should be continued, and that communication should be made with a partisan unit under the command of the Jewish paratrooper L. Solomin ("Pranas"), (also known as "Petrovich") located in the Jonava (Yaneve) forests, so that at least part of the JFO could be sent there. The plan was, however, principally concerned with sending armed groups from the JFO to the Augustow forest, the meeting point for the borders of Lithuania, Poland, and Eastern Prussia some eighty miles south of Kovno. The groups who were supposed to leave from the ghetto were charged with setting up partisan bases there with the help of fighters from a special Soviet unit, *Spetzgruppa*, which had already been parachuted in.

Despite the Zionists' grave reservations about the Augustow

plan, its execution was hastened mainly because of external factors—namely, the ghetto's transfer of authority to the SS, its division into a number of concentration camps, and the deportation *Aktion* to Estonia, which was planned for October 26. While JFO representatives had been incorporated into the ghetto authorities' Relocation Committee in order to prevent members of the underground from being included in the lists of candidates destined for work camps, nevertheless, the JFO leadership knew that the camps marked the first stage in the final liquidation of the ghetto. They therefore felt that the opportunities offered by the Augustova plan, however slight, should not be overlooked.

The first vanguard group bound for the Augustow forests comprised twenty persons. They left in mid-October, in carts belonging to the ghetto authorities, with each person carrying two pistols, three grenades and a long knife, manufactured in the ghetto. After traveling some twelve miles to the south of Kovno, the carts returned to the ghetto leaving the group to continue its journey on foot. Because of an encounter with the forest patrol and their unfamiliarity with the road, most of the group lost contact with the main party and only with difficulty managed to return to the ghetto. Still more disastrous were the failures of the following groups which left, similarly equipped, at average intervals of one day. Out of nearly one hundred participants, whose trips continued until mid-November, approximately ten men were killed in clashes with the police or peasants; forty-three of the underground's finest young activists fell into the hands of the Gestapo, of whom twelve were taken to Fort Nine and employed in burning the tens of thousands of bodies of those who had been massacred there; about fifteen died in prison, and only a few succeeded in escaping and returning to the ghetto, mainly as a result of intervention by the ghetto authorities. Only two succeeded in reaching the Augustow forests—N. Endlin and S. Mordkovski, who subsequently became two of the best liaison officers.[21] They reported that there were no partisans in the forest after all.

Against a background of sharp criticism for the ill-conceived planning of these journeys, the "existentialist" inclinations of those who had been unenthusiastic about the Augustow plan, intensified. Thus, for example, the IBZ, ZS, and even the *Hashomer Hatza'ir* emphasized the value of escaping and remaining together as a group. The foundations were thus laid for Kibbutzim or communes, in which the members of these movements, some of whom had remained isolated after the Estonia *Aktion*, gathered together. *Hashomer Hatza'ir*, disenchanted with the Communists, established a kibbutz at 7 Mildos

Street, together with *Hehalutz Hatza'ir-Deror* and other youth movements of the *Eretz-Yisrael ha-Ovedet* bloc. Their intention was to build a *maline* there and, at the same time, to send female members who looked Aryan to live with peasants.

Concrete possibilities for escaping to the forest first emerged in mid-November, when it was learned that Ziman had instructed K. Radionov, the commander of the Kovno partisan detachment *Smert Okkupantam* ("Death to the Conquerors") in the Rudninkai forests, to accept ghetto fighters at his bases, and that partisan guides had already been sent to bring the first group of fighters to the forest. On November 24, the first group of ten armed men left for the forest, a journey of ninety-four miles. As a result of bloody clashes with German patrols during the journey, only six of them reached their destination. In order to avoid similar mishaps, they decided from then on to drive the escapees to the forest in trucks, which is how they got the next nine groups, totalling some 180 persons, to the forests.

JFO arms suppliers also found various ways to supply arms and military equipment to those leaving for the forest. The ghetto police not only did not hinder them, but actually protected them; members of the force who had previously served in the army even trained those who were leaving in the use of arms. As a result of the preparations for departure and the JFO's semiofficial campaigns, the organization's existence was once again no secret either to the ghetto inhabitants or to the Gestapo. Although the JFO did not hesitate to expel a number of traitors,[22] the Gestapo succeeded, within the space of twenty days, in dealing four blows directly to the underground: 1) At the end of the *Aktion* against the elderly and children on March 27 and 28, 1944, the commander of the ghetto police, Moshe Levin, and his deputy, Yehuda Zupovitz, were executed at Fort Nine, together with almost all the officers and sergeants and a number of privates in the force, forty men in all, 2) On the charge of collaboration with the partisans, the members of the *Ältestenrat* were also arrested and beaten. Of them all, only Dr. E. Elkes returned to his post and then served as the *Judenälteste;* 3) The central personality in the JFO and its *de facto* commander, Chaim Yellin, died after an exchange of fire with members of the police who organized a manhunt for him in the main streets of Kovno on April 5;[23] 4) A week later, in an ambush near the ghetto the Gestapo opened fire on a truck that was taking a JFO group to the Rudninkai forests. Out of the twelve members of the group, only four survived, including A. Diskant, a guide from the forest. During the shooting, the defenders succeeded in killing several Gestapo men.[24] The 150 JFO activists who remained in the ghetto were henceforth obliged to remain on their guard against the new Jewish police force. The latter not only offered no assistance to the underground, but actively interfered with their activities. They also had to move the store of arms still remaining in the ghetto to the woods. The organization was from then on led mainly by the Communist delegates. When the eighth group left the ghetto, all contact with the Rudninkai forests was broken, and only individuals managed to break through the ghetto fence and reach the base of the Kovno detachment.

During May and June, JFO groups made three or four further attempts to break through the ghetto fence in order to find additional partisan bases in the vicinity of Kovno, but to no avail. All the escapees were shot by the guards, despite the fact that a special group existed which was expert in breaching the fence and transferring men out. Out of three organized JFO groups numbering a few dozen persons that left in the direction of the Kazlu-Ruda forests (approximately twenty miles south of Kovno), only a few safely reached their destination. They later joined an organized partisan unit called *Korchagin*. With the help of the JFO, a number of armed groups succeeded in reaching various forests in Lithuania. The groups included JFO members, peripheral members, and independents who had become acquainted with the forests before the war.

In addition to evacuating its members, the JFO occasionally undertook other activities between the first half of 1944 almost until the liquidation of the ghetto. A few female activists managed to hide sixty children during the "Children's *Aktion*," and other members forged documents and developed a workshop for manufacturing rubber stamps.

The general upheaval which reigned within the ghetto at the beginning of July, when the decree concerning evacuation to Eastern Prussia was annouonced, also affected the members of the JFO; they realized that they had no one to rely upon and that anyone who could, would have to try to save his life on his own. In fact, the structure of the organization had already undergone a change: its activists had joined forces with Dr. Wolsonok and others. They had, at first, formed an iron resolution not to obey the evacuation order for "it definitely means liquidation . . . and we must, therefore, take all possible steps to prevent the decree from being executed."[25] However, apart from distributing slogans in this view among the general ghetto population (the majority of whom were in any case entrenched in *malines* in order to resist deportation to Germany), and an abortive attempt to dig a tunnel in order to escape from the ghetto, there was no organized activity to further the ghetto defense plan. While SS men set fire to the ghetto houses and combed the area for those in hiding, the members of the JFO command and the organization's activitists sat in *malines,* practically unconscious and without arms, air, food, or water, until they were discovered and dragged out to join the transports to concentration camps in Germany. Only a few escaped on the way to the trains or from inside them.

The survivors of the JFO incarcerated in the Kaufering K.Z. (concentration camp) and the *Aussenkommandos* (Branch camps) of Dachau in Bavaria were extremely active until the liberation. Their main concerns were culture and national education. A number of intellectuals, such as the writer M. Burstein and others who had not belonged to underground organizations in the ghetto, joined the JFO activists. Their intention was to create "a select group of exceptionally talented men who would bring comfort and encouragement to every hut."[26] In fact, they organized lectures on political, literary, and historical themes and made sure that the handful of teachers, writers, and academics who still remained in the camp received easier work and an extra soup ration wherever possible. Meanwhile, the IBZ activists continued to organize political activities. They were mainly concerned with what would happen after the anticipated liberation. The first sign of renewed activity in the camps was the appearance of the Hebrew newspaper *Nitzotz* (The Spark) which came out on Hanukah 1944, in the central camp at Kaufering. Its headline was from the "Hatikvah": *Od lo Avdah Tikvatenu* ("We have still not lost hope").[27]

As a result of lengthy negotiations between the IBZ activists in the concentration camps and the members of Eretz-Yisrael Haovedet Block and also of the *Massadah* organization from Shavli, a new body arose called *Hitahdut ha-Noar ha-Leumi* (Federation of the National Youth). Its aims, detailed in *Nitzotz*, volume XXXVIII; which appeared for *Tu bi-Shvat*, were as follows: (1) to create an organized framework among the Zionist youth in the concentration camps, to unite the national forces, and to create a suitable cadre for after our liberation; (2) to strive for a complete change in the social structure of the Jewish homeland; (3) to strive for a revival of Hebrew spirit and culture and the creation of a new Zionist way of life in *Eretz Yisrael*. The main demands from the non-Jewish nations, which are stated further on, include the establishment of a "Jewish homeland" as a solution for the Jewish question, the punishment of war criminals, and the granting of restitution to the survivors by an international judicial decree. Even the cultural activities of the Federation had a primarily national bias. For example, a "Hebrew Circle" was established on February 23, 1945, and debates were held on Jewish issues. The Federation also organized mourning sessions, apparently in cooperation with general underground circles, and a "National Song Evening" on *Adar 11*—the anniversary of the fall of Trumpeldor and his companions.

During the last weeks before the Allies liberated the camps in Germany, underground activist circles concentrated on discovering SS intentions with regard to the surviving internees and making meticulous preparations for the period between the expected retreat of the SS and the arrival of Allied soldiers. The preparations included the manufacture of armbands for members of the internal police who were to keep order during this period. Liaison officers to represent the camp inmates to the liberating armies were likewise appointed in advance, but there were sharp differences of opinion on this point between the Zionist faction and the Communists, who were not prepared to allow a Zionist to represent them. The last edition of *Nitzotz* in the Kaufering camp, which appeared on April 25, 1945, was already devoted to the liberation. Its leading article was entitled *Dor Aharon le-Shiabud ve-Rishon li-Geulah* (The last generation in servitude and the first of the redemption). After the liberation, the underground activists from these circles did, in fact, play an important role among the survivors in Germany until the majority emigrated to Israel at the end of the 1940s.

CHAPTER 14
IN THE SMALL GHETTOS—SHAVLI AND ŠVENČIONYS (SVENCIAN)

IN THE SHAVLI GHETTO

THE QUESTION OF RESISTANCE IN SHAVLI WAS FIRST DIS-
cussed publicly at a meeting of community leaders and representatives of political Jewish organizations on the eve of ghettoization.
Among other things the possibility of setting the ghetto on fire was
debated and rejected on the grounds that it amounted to suicide. No
practical decisions were made at this meeting, but, even so, organized underground activity existed from the time of ghettoization until
mid-1942, mainly within the following factional frameworks: (1) the
Zionist Socialist bloc (ZS), which included a group of Polish *halutzim*
(pioneers), survivors of the local branch of the *No'ar Ziyoni-Halutzi*
(Zionist Pioneering Youth—*Netzah)* and *Hashomer Hatza'ir,* and older
members of the ZS party; (2) the Revisionist bloc, which included
survivors of the local *Betar* group, a group of Polish Betarites, a number of local veteran Betarites, and members of the Revisionist party;
(3) the Communist bloc, composed of veteran members of the party
and the Komsomol and those who had joined during the Soviet regime.

Unlike the Communists, who had become disorganized and
ideologically insecure as a result of the war, the Zionists were active
from the first, while the youth movements, especially the refugees,
had become organized during the period of their clandestine activity
under the Soviet regime. At this stage, all the movements worked
separately, while maintaining contact with other groups of similar
ideological outlook. The Polish refugees continued to live together in

the ghetto, pooling their resources and energetically organizing social activities, particularly among themselves.

The social movements at first undertook cultural and educational activities: they published a newspaper, *Ha-Tehiyah*, and organized parties to mark dates of national importance. Adults were not integrated into these activities on a large scale, although some of them were employed at communal work in the ghetto.

This began to change, however, when in July 1942, Irena Adamowicz arrived in Shavli as an emissary of the pioneering underground movements in the Warsaw and Vilna ghettos. Meeting with representatives of the pioneering group, *Netzah*, and *Hashomer Hatza'ir*, as well as with members of the Jewish council, she gave detailed accounts of what was happening in the Polish ghettos as well as in Vilna and Kovno. She also stressed the need for organized self-defense.

After preparatory inter-movement talks designed to organize the youth under a single leadership, *Massadah* was established in August 1942 by a group of Zionist students. Although the Communists and other leftist groups did not join *Massadah*, because of the Left's traditional aversion to bourgeois organizations and some of the members of *Betar* maintained independent activities concurrent with their membership in *Massadah*, *Massadah* soon had a membership of 120 young people, mostly from nonaffiliated Zionist circles. Ideologically speaking, *Massadah* favored armed resistance, even to the point of identification with the motto, "Let my soul die with the Philistines," and they actually made a few preparatory steps in that direction, including collecting arms and drilling in their use. But they directed most of their attention at first on educational and cultural activities from a Zionist and nationalist point of view. For these activities, often involving a large number of nonmembers, *Massadah* enjoyed the sympathy as well as indirect aid of members of the Jewish Council. There was also mutual understanding, and even cooperation, between *Massadah* and the heads of the Jewish Council with regard to the defense of the ghetto. After the battle of Stalingrad, *Massadah* and the Jewish Council held a special meeting on defense on February 5, 1943. Those present assumed that before the Germans retreated from Lithuania, the Jewish remnant would be destroyed. The questions were whether to prepare for resistance immediately or to wait and what to do in the meantime, whether to leave for the forests and make contact with the Lithuanian underground or not. They also discussed the possibility of joining an armed Jewish band led by the Chaluzin brothers, which was roaming around at the time in western Lithuania. This proposal was turned down on the grounds that it would endanger the ghetto as a whole. A proposal to send out a group of armed youth to eastern Lithuania, where there was already widespread partisan activity, was also rejected. Nor was a plan to arm the ghetto inhabitants and to prepare for resistance within the ghetto itself enthusiastically received by the participants in the meeting.[1]

Within *Massadah* internal opposition also increased rapidly. This opposition stemmed from three causes: the atmosphere prevalent in the ghetto; disinterest on the part of the *Massadah* command in acquiring arms; and desire for revenge for the hanging of a member of the movement on the charge of profiteering.[2] At the same time, however, the general situation in the ghetto, particularly the expected transfer of some two thousand men to labor camps in the vicinity, motivated the creation of a new organization called *Zelbstshutz* (Self-Defense), comprising members of *Hehalutz, Netzah,* and the Communist bloc as well as *Massadah. Zelbstshutz,* which in the summer of 1943 totalled some two hundred members, was headed by a command composed of representatives from its various member organizations.

When some 1,340 men, including many of working age and many members of *Zelbstshutz,* were sent to four or five labor camps in a woody, rural area, the focus of underground activity also relocated. In the dynamic conditions of the labor camps, where many young men organized themselves spontaneously into groups, *Zelbstshutz* activists became the center of local working committees, on which Communists, members of *Betar, Massadah, Netzah,* and other organizations served. The *Zelbstshutz* command in the ghetto coordinated activities, while *Massadah* leadership in the ghetto was forced to accept a *fait accompli.* They gave sanction to collective organization within the camps in retrospect, helped the groups financially, and supported them when arguments arose with the Jewish administration in the camps. While the melancholy atmosphere and widespread mysticism[3] hampered the *Zelbstshutz* command in the ghetto, the atmosphere in the labor camps was more conducive to activity. In some of the camps, plans were made to break through the fence at a suitable moment, close to the anticipated liquidation of the camp, and to cover the escape of a large number of Jews to the surrounding woods. The activity in the camps reached its peak in the summer of 1944. Despite the precise planning and extensive preparations by devoted activists who completely disregarded personal risk, the escape plans failed. Only a few dozen succeeded in leaving the Shavli ghetto or the labor camps in the vicinity like Linkaičiai Daugeliai, HBA etc.

Immediately after this aborted attempt to escape from the camps, the Germans transferred the inmates to Shavli en route to detention camps in Germany. Further attempts to escape and disturbances in the deportation schedule, did not impede the transfer; the Germans, with the help of the member of the Jewish Council named G. Pariser, had their way.

Members of *Zelbstshutz*, the *Massadah* command, and many activists, along with the rest of the Jews of the Shavli ghetto, were taken to the same camps in the Dachau complex to which the Jews of the Kovno ghetto had been brought a few days earlier. In meetings that were held between underground activists of the Kovno and Shavli ghettos, and particularly between members of IBZ and *Massadah*, they learned that the ideologies of the two organizations were very similar. Hence, they formed a coalition that continued after the liberation.

IN THE SVENCIAN GHETTO

The first underground organization in the Svencian ghetto was established immediately after the German occupation. A group of young people, who had met only periodically until then, installed a radio in a hideout and listened to the news from Moscow and Jerusalem.

When the majority of the Svencian Jews were liquidated in the fall of 1941, leaving some two thousand people (mainly from the surrounding hamlets) in the ghetto, the underground group grew and their organization crystallized. It concentrated mainly on collecting arms from various sources and arms training. The underground's existence was no longer a secret, howevever, after May 1942, when one of the members was wounded while handling a pistol and was arrested by the Gestapo, together with a friend. After three days of interrogation and torture, both were executed. But attempts by the Jewish police to break up the group and to destroy its weapons were fruitless; moreover, the Judenrat (Jewish Council) was threatened and forced to contribute money to enlarging the group's arms supply. After arguments among the members of the group, the majority decided to leave for the forest, where it would be possible to fight actively against the Germans, despite the minority's claim that "leaving might endanger the ghetto's existence."[4]

Scouts sent to the forests and villages to search for partisans were unsuccessful in their mission. However, when the group learned of the expected transfer of the ghetto inhabitants to the Vilna and Kovno ghettos, they decided not to postpone departure for the forests any longer, despite the absence of any contact with the partisans. On

March 5, 1943, twenty-two armed men left the ghetto. A month later, thirty more people escaped to the forests. Most of them, like their predecessors, reached the Narocz (Naroch) and Kazian (Koziany) forests, where they were integrated into the *Chapayev* unit and other units of the Byelorussian *(Voroshilov)* Brigade (commanded by F. Markov), as well as units of the Lithuanian *Zhalgiris (Žalgiris)* Brigade.[5]

Several dozen refugees from the Svencian ghetto also reached these units at the end of summer, 1943. They had taken refuge in the Vilna ghetto after the Kovno Action, and had encouraged the youth to escape to the forests. A number of young people from Svencian, who had belonged to the underground group, were also active within the Vilna ghetto. They were sent by their partisan commanders, Markov and Sidyakin, to the FPO to convince the FPO to send its members to the forest. Since the FPO refused at that time to accept this proposal, the emissaries arranged for the departure to the forest of nonaffiliated youth, particularly from their hometown. The emissaries were arrested more than once by the Jewish police during their stay in the ghetto and badly beaten. Nevertheless, they were received by the head of the ghetto, Jacob Gens, who, after long discussion, consented to let them leave the ghetto with their arms and even permitted them to take some twenty-five of their fellow townsmen with them.[6] When the FPO changed its mind about fighting in the forest, some of the emissaries served as guides for FPO groups in the fall of 1943. Among the guides were Y. Gertman, I. Volfson, M. Feigel, S. Yechilczik, and M. Shutan.

CHAPTER 15
THE SOCIAL AND IDEOLOGICAL BASIS

THE FEAR THAT THE EXISTENCE OF AN UNDERGROUND ORganization in the ghetto might prematurely endanger all the inhabitants forced the resistance movement to act with extreme caution and secrecy. This, in turn, determined the standards employed in mustering manpower, its structure, and its activities. The strictness governing the acceptance of members was also partly responsible for the fact that the resistance organizations, even at their peak, did not comprise more than 5 percent of the population in any of the ghettos.

Since the movements did not wish the ghetto inhabitants to know of their existence during the first year of organized underground activity (1942), members were accepted into their ranks only if they were trustworthy from every point of view, including the certainty that they would give no hint of their activities even in their most immediate circles.[1] Thus, the character of a candidate was one of the criteria that guided the organizers in the acceptance of new members.

In the Shavli ghetto, the Jewish authorities were not suspected of infiltrating spies into underground organizations, so the atmosphere was relatively relaxed. Past members of movements, who were more or less well known, were the first to be accepted into the organization. They were obliged to swear that they would at all times and under all conditions fulfil the demands of the people and the orders of the movement. A similar oath was taken by the members of the IBZ in the Kovno ghetto. However, since suspicion was prevalent in the Vilna ghetto, the FPO was not content with the fact that each youth movement was responsible for the character of its members, but established "pre-FPO" frameworks as well, in which candidates were tested. For example, they would give a candidate an empty box which, they said, contained a bomb and tell him to take it from one street to another, while an FPO member disguised as a policeman followed him. If the candidate discarded the box, the FPO would not accept him. If he proved himself, he was received into the movement at an impressive and mysterious ceremony.[2]

Even after the summer of 1943, when the organizations reached the peak of their activities, and their existence was known, they continued to exercise caution. Despite the fact that the reservoir of the movement had been drained, and they had begun to muster peripheral members, a number of young people in the Lithuanian ghettos, including some who owned weapons, had not succeeded in making contact with the underground organizations.[3] The movements' policies regarding the acceptance of new members changed with the organized dispatch of fighters to the forests, however.

The basic components of the resistance movements were cells of three members ("threes"). Each of the three members of the cell knew only one other member and the group leader, who acted as a liaison. At first, all the members of the groups belonged to the same political movement. Later, the cells were enlarged to groups of five which were politically heterogenous, principally for two reasons: first, they decided they could increase the efficiency of the cells by basing their plans for recruitment and defense on regional and geographical considerations; and second, they realized that their experiments in close collaboration and mutual trust in the high command as well as within other units where members of various movements were brought together, had been successful. Moreover, since promotions to positions of command and instructorships were granted according to achievement, there was disparity between the ranks held within the organization and those held in other movements or parties. This organizational development was particularly characteristic of the resistance movements in the Vilna ghetto and, to a lesser extent, those in the Kovno ghetto. In Shavli, groups of five were used from the onset, in accordance with the tradition of underground activity under the Soviet regime.

While there were almost no intermediate ranks between the groups of five ("fives") and the highest echelons in the Shavli ghetto, the FPO in Vilna was built up according to clear principles of military hierarchy; each unit was precisely defined by size, authority, and subordination. In order to avoid uncertainty and confusion, a clear set of regulations was draw up as follows:

The FPO is comprised of two battalions. Each battalion will number between six and eight platoons; each platoon—three squads; each squad will comprise five fighters. A squad is led by the squad commander, a platoon by a platoon commander, to whom the squad commanders are subordinate. The battalion is led by a battalion commander who is a member of the high command, and the platoon commanders are subordinate to him. Each battalion will place a reserve platoon at the command's disposal. The battalion commander has a special liaison officer, who will be employed if the need arises. The highest order is that given by the commander of the FPO.[4]

The last section of the regulations was devoted to the establishment of a shadow command in an emergency, if the existing command was incapable of functioning for any reason. A number of special sections were directly subordinate to the command, for example, liaison, training, and sabotage. The Anti-Fascist (Communist) Organization in the Kovno ghetto had a similar, if less precisely-developed, structure.

In addition to the network of cells ("threes" and "fives"), the organizations had a system of passwords and code-names to insure secrecy, which proved particularly efficient in the Vilna ghetto.[5] The period of relative calm within the ghettos permitted routine work patterns to crystallize, and the activity of the cells was planned according to a fixed schedule. While the form of the various activities undertaken by the organizations was generally dictated by technical and organizational considerations, the character of each was determined by the highest aims of the resistance movements. Therefore, the importance of the principal activities varied in each organization.

THE SOCIAL AND IDEOLOGICAL BASIS

Considering the composition of the ghetto population, and the nature of the activity expected of the underground resistance movements in the ghettos, it is not surprising that the bulk of active members of the organizations were young, unmarried men and women.

Duties were generally distributed among the age groups as follows: leaders of the organizations—26 years and above; responsible positions—21–25 years; rank and file—under 20 years.

The percentages of nonindigenous members of the resistance movements were 20 percent in Vilna, 12 percent in Kovno, and 8 percent in Shavli. The inclusion of these foreign elements greatly

enriched the underground organizations. Nevertheless, because of
their different backgrounds, they did not always identify with the
methods and aims of the organizations, especially as far as the principle of collective responsibility and concern for the ghetto was concerned.[6] On the other hand, their membership in the resistance
movements greatly facilitated their social integration into the ghettos,
prevented them from feeling lonely and bitter, and also diminished
the risk of deportation or forced labor to which many foreigners and
isolated individuals in the ghettos often fell victim.

Although developments in the resistance movement later
wrought a schism within the traditional party frameworks, veteran
political organizations and their recently created counterparts, like
Matzok and IBZ in Kovno, the Coordination in Vilna, and its counter-
part in Shavli, formed the primary basis for underground activity in
the three ghettos, and the framework for meetings and discussions
which initiated the establishment of the fighting underground movement. Even after clearly defined underground resistance movements
such as the FPO in Vilna, JFO in Kovno, and *Massadah* in Shavli had
crystallized by the beginning of 1942, political considerations over-
lapped with military goals for a long time. For instance, the communal living quarters occupied by members of parties and youth
movements, such as the *Hashomer Hatza'ir* commune in the Vilna
ghetto and the *Eretz-Yisrael ha-Ovedet* kibbutz in the Kovno ghetto,
became military training bases for the general underground organizations. Although in theory, acceptance into the resistance organizations took place only after individual examinations, the admission of
new candidates was, in fact, effected in the majority of cases either as
a result of active membership in or on the periphery of one of the
parties or youth movements (such as the JFO in Kovno or Massadah
in Shavli) or upon their recommendation. It should not be inferred,
however, that all members of parties and movements were automatically accepted. In the Vilna ghetto, for example, there were many
Betarites whom the *Betar* command itself was not prepared to recom-
mend, because admission into the FPO was most stringent. Furthermore, the highest echelons of the resistance organizations were made
up of representatives of parties and movements in proportion to
political strength. Thus, for example, the large staff of the FPO consisted of representatives of the *Bund, Hanoar Haziyoni* (Zionist Youth),
Communists, Revisionists, and *Hashomer Hatza'ir*. The *Gezkomitet—
Gezelshaftlikher Komitet* (Communal Committee) and the *Militerishe-
Tekhnishe Komisie* (Military Technical Commission) in the Kovno ghetto

and *Zelbstshutz* in the Shavli ghetto were formed according to a similar principle. At the same time, the general tendency within organizations to strive for a broad political basis and to unite all the organized forces of the ghetto was conspicuous. As we shall see later, the specific importance of the Communists far exceeded their actual comparative quantitative representation. However, while members of parties and youth movements were the principal constituents of the underground movements, the resistance did contain other elements. Not sufficient from the outset, the parties' resources were soon drained. At the same time pressure (particularly from fall 1943 on) on the part of unaffiliated young people to be admitted into the ranks of the organization increased; they wanted to escape to the forests with the movement. In the course of time, unaffiliated groups, which were mostly organized on the basis of personal acquaintance, also joined the underground. Some of the aims of these groups were identical with those of their more systematically organized counterparts.[7]

A comparison of the declared aims of the resistance movements in the Lithuanian ghettos reveals that nearly all include the following: (1) *Self-defense:* that is, organized, violent opposition or revolt, using weapons if necessary, in the face of "danger to the existence of the ghetto as a whole," or during an *Aktion,* which was judged to be the "beginning of the end";[8] (2) *Combat:* that is, fighting against the enemy (both the Germans and their collaborators) by every means and in every place, whether in self-defense or not, be it separately or in conjunction with any form of partisan movement; (3) *Rescue:* that is, saving Jewish lives by mass or individual escape either to the forest within organized partisan frameworks, or to hideouts in the city or forest. However, the emphasis placed on each of these aims varied. Thus, for example, the supreme objectives of the FPO in the Vilna ghetto were characterized by the order of their appearance in the military code of regulations: self-defense, combat and rescue; the stress was on mass armed resistance *within the ghetto.* For the Vilna underground, combat, relegated to a secondary position, signified the following: acts of sabotage and terror in the enemy's rear and joining the partisans and aiding the Red Army in the common war against the Nazi invader, which were not connected to their schedule of defense for the ghetto. Even after the events in Vilna in July 1943, when some FPO members felt, "The ghetto doesn't need us—it's against us," and the movement was compelled to send a group of fighters to the forest, the FPO did not forsake its principal objective— the secret hope that when the time came, the group would serve as a base for the uprising in the ghetto. Moreover, it was determined that the fighting unit of the FPO would remain inside the ghetto where it would continue to work despite ever-increasing difficulties.

The FPO's adherence to self-defense was clearly reflected in a proclamation published on September 1, the eve of the expected liquidation of the ghetto: "Only armed resistance can save our lives and our honor. Brothers! It is better to die fighting in the ghetto than to be led like sheep to Ponary! An organized Jewish force exists within the ghetto walls which will resist with weapons. Support the rebellion!"[9] However, as they attempted to actively resist in the streets, they learned that the Germans were not sending the Jews to Ponary for immediate extermination but, for tactical and administrative reasons, transporting them instead to Estonia. Therefore, when there was no hope that the battle, which was being carried on by a handful of fighters, would become a revolt, they decided (with certain reservations) to transfer the fighting unit from the ghetto to the forest.

The other organization within the Vilna ghetto—The Fighting Group of *Yechiel*—stressed combat outside the ghetto. They believed that combat within the ghetto would neither harm the Germans nor save Jewish lives, whereas partisan warfare in the forest by national Jewish units was a fight for Jewish honor that also afforded the possibility of saving hundreds of thousands of young people, while participating in the universal struggle against the Germans. The obvious conclusion in light of this objective was to send out large numbers of young people to the forest.[10]

In the Kovno ghetto, too, self-defense was stressed from the outset as a basis for partial rescue or at least honorable death in the tradition of Massadah. After a few weeks, however, on December 31, 1941, the Communists summed up the direction that their underground organization was taking in these words: "We are not actually abandoning the ghetto, but our main objective is open combat within the ranks of the partisans."[11] In the IBZ, and to a lesser extent the pioneering movements in the ghetto *(Hehalutz-Hatza'ir—Deror, Gordonia, Netzah)*, social and educational matters for a long time took precedent over self-defense. Even in 1943, at the height of JFO underground activity, combat and rescue were given equal weight by the organization, and emphasis of one over the other was left to the choice of individual members. The wording of the last will and testament of Chaim Tiktin, one of the IBZ leaders in Kovno, is characteristic: "Our last wish is: keep alive vengeance against the enemy; for them—for the remnant of the Hebrew nation—total rescue! Masha!

Menahem! You who have taken the way of rescue and you who have chosen the way of vengeance, keep the banner of the IBZ—the banner of solidarity of the survivors of our people—flying high."[12] At the same time, due to Communist influence and the victories of the Red Army, the inclination to fight the Germans actively outside the ghetto without abandoning the idea of self-defense within the ghetto steadily gained ground within the ranks of the JFO.

In the Shavli ghetto, the principal organization, which eventually claimed to represent the entire underground in the ghetto, was given the symbolic name of *Massadah*—a clear hint of the hopes that its founders had for it. Until the last day, the survival of the ghetto and its branches was favored above rescue, and combat was hardly considered at all.

While the principal objectives of the Jewish underground organizations in Lithuania revolved around Jewish values and honor, the FPO in Vilna set itself an additional aim—an aim which was unknown at least at that time in organizations in Lithuania and elsewhere. Concerned with the fate of all Jews in danger, the FPO stated at its founding meeting: "The organization will inculcate the concept of self-defense in other ghettos, and will contact forces outside the ghetto."

The tempest that overtook the underground organizations in the Lithuanian ghettos in the summer of 1943 forced many to change their priorities. Thus, in both the Vilna and Shavli ghettos self-defense gradually gave way to rescue. Circumstances also forced members of the underground, to switch roles. Thus, for example, a member of the FPO staff, Joseph Glazman, was killed in a clash with Germans while carrying out a partisan mission outside the ghetto, while Yechiel Sheinboim, an architect and leader of the underground movement, died behind a barricade in the ghetto while defending the ghetto against anticipated liquidation. In addition to bitter arguments about the "ghetto or forest" question, controversy arose over more tactical matters such as a propitious moment to begin operations were liquidation of the ghetto to appear imminent. The question was when, and with what criteria, could the "beginning of the end" be determined? And as far as leaving for the forest was concerned—which forest? The nearest one to the ghetto, or one which would be decided upon in view of other considerations?

The change in these aims and in the order of priorities—whether through differences in outlook and perceptions of the situation and the future, or through only superficial differences, at times camouflaging personal ambition—stirred acrimonious debates between various organizations and within them. The result was a split between the established parties and movements, and even the Communist party, which was by nature monolithic, did not always succeed in presenting a united front.

CHAPTER 16
"ROUTINE" UNDERGROUND ACTIVITIES

ARMS ACQUISITION

SINCE THE PRACTICAL REALIZATION OF RESISTANCE DE-manded the acquisition of arms as well as arms training, this became an aim in itself. The movements did not hesitate to endanger the fate of the ghetto to a certain extent in order to carry out this objective. The weapons also had a symbolic value in that they increased the fighting spirit among the members of the organizations. For instance, a Belgian pistol, which had been "removed" from a German arms depot, was not passed around at the founding meeting of the FPO in Vilna in vain; the underground decided there and then to steal weapons from the Germans. Despite a series of daring operations carried out by the underground in the Vilna and Kovno ghettos, in which scores of firearms of various types were removed from German arms depots, it became essential to acquire weapons by other means as well.[1] Due to the difficulty of buying pistols and, to an even greater extent, rifles and machineguns, because of the continuous rise in prices[2] and the dangers, the organizations built up stocks of other weapons including axes, bayonets, iron gloves, knives, bars, and so on. The FPO in Vilna produced hundreds of Molotov cocktails and hand grenades, some from old electric lightbulbs filled with inflammable material. Attempts were made to produce bombs by a similar method in the Kovno and Shavli ghettos. Because of the great risk involved in smuggling weapons into the ghetto, those who intended to join partisan units concentrated their arms in hiding places outside the ghetto, in the cemetery, for instance, or in huts in the suburbs of the city. Furthermore, because the partisan command stipulated to the Kovno and Vilna underground that the majority of those who went to the forests must be equipped with long weapons, some organizations, like the JFO in Kovno and *Yechiel*, the fighting group in Vilna, were forced to accept help from private sources. They also accepted nonmembers in their groups who had the required weapons, or were able to finance their acquisition. However, the principle of sharing arms was upheld almost until the end in the FPO.

The JFO in Kovno probably possessed the largest quantity of long arms in all the three ghettos: at least thirty rifles and ten machineguns were stored in a depot inside the ghetto and in dumps outside it. In the Vilna ghetto, the number of rifles belonging to the FPO and *Yechiel* was smaller. However, it appears that there were more pistols in the Vilna ghetto, where the purchase of weapons in large quantities, to be used for the flight from the ghetto, began in the summer of 1943.[3] An original list of arms[4] (presumably the only remaining one of its kind), detailing the holdings of five secondary FPO units, each named after its commander, supports this impression:

Ruzhka
1 pistol and 1 reserve bullet (Grisha Levin)
1 parabellum and 50 bullets
1 lightbulb (Molotov cocktail)
Vitka
1 SS pistol, caliber 6
3 grenades
Rashka
1 Mauser, caliber 7, and 10 reserve bullets
1 Walter, caliber 6.35
Chaim
4 grenades
1 pistol, caliber 7
1 Belgian pistol, caliber 4, and reserve magazine
1 TT pistol, caliber 7.62, and 50 reserve bullets
Shames
24 bottles
M9 and 3 [bullets] sic
1 P.38, and 57 reserve bullets
1 Parabellum and 49 bullets
1 Mauser, caliber 1.56, and 7 reserve bullets
5 grenades
Demolition group
1 bottle
1 pistol, caliber 7.65, and 9 bullets
3 grenades
4 knapsacks
33 round green boxes—smoke candles

A1:
The three Spanye brothers, all members of the Lithuanian Division.

A:2
[th]e staff of the Anti-Fascist Organization in the Kovno ghetto, with their [lead]er, Chaim Yellin ("Vladas"), center.

A3:
Jewish partisans from the Kovno detachments known as "Death to the Conquerors," "Forwards," and "Vladas Baronas."

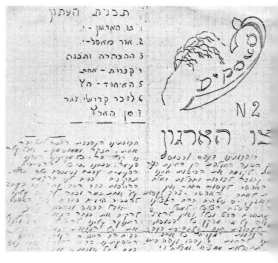

B1:
"Let us not go like sheep to the slaughter!" Partisan proclamation written by Abba Kovner, January 1942, to the inhabitants of the Vilna ghetto.

B2:
The first page of the second edition of the underground paper Mi-Ma'amakim, published in the Shavli ghetto.

B3:
Roster giving particulars on seventy-six fighters from the "Struggle" partisan detachment, July 25, 1944.

C1: Major Wolf Vilenski, Battalion Commander in the 249th Brigade of The Lithuanian Division, Hero of the Soviet Union.

C2: Staff Sergeant Kalman Shur of the 249th Regiment of the Lithuanian Division, Hero of the Soviet Union.

C3: Rosa Deweltov, a medical officer in the Red Army, Heroine of the Soviet Union.

C4: Itzik Meskup ("Adomas"), commander of the first operational group, which parachuted into northern Lithuania in March 1942.

C5: Itzik Wittenberg ("Leon"), the first commander of the FPO in the Vilna ghetto.

C6: Eliezer Hotz, a soldier in the Lithuanian Division, who parachuted into Lithuania for partisan activity and later emigrated to Israel, where he fell in the Jordan valley during the War of Independence.

D1:
Abba Kovner, ("Uri"), the second commander of the FPO in the Vilna ghetto, leading the funeral procession of Yehiel Sheinboim, who fell defending a barricade in the ghetto on September 1, 1943.

D2:
Partisans entering Vilna during the liberation, July 1944.

D3:
Major Levitatz at the head of a procession soldiers from the Lithuanian Division, receiving flowers at the liberation of Vilna.

D4:
Ilya Ehrenburg, the noted author, with Jewish partisans celebrating the liberation of Vilna, July 1944.

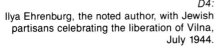

In the Shavli ghetto, where combat was last in the order of priorities, there were about ten pistols (more than half of which belonged to private persons) and a number of grenades. However, the underground group in the Linkaičiai and Daugeliai work camps owned some rifles and a few dozen grenades, which they intended to use in breaking out of the camp.[5]

The first arms that were smuggled into the ghettos were immediately transferred to small groups that undertook systematic training in their use and maintenance. In Kovno and Shavli, the trainers were primarily ex-soldiers. In Vilna, groups of young people who had taken a special course sponsored by the FPO acted as instructors. The scope of the training was subsequently enlarged to include additional kinds of weapons (grenades, rifles, machineguns) and different subjects, like liaison, first aid, fieldcraft, and topography. Theoretical courses in the use of arms or, as they were generally termed in the IBZ in Kovno, "the theory of defense," were also held for groups of young women, concurrent with educational and political activities.

Nearly all activities connected with the acquisition of arms—their maintenance and preservation in secret depots—entailed coordinated operations and experts in a variety of technical fields. These experts were scattered at first in various secondary units of the organizations. In the course of time, special units were formed dealing mainly with arms, which not only raised funds with drives, but also by "removing" articles from German storehouses and selling them.

SABOTAGE

Acts of sabotage apparently arose from the combat clause of the declared aims of the underground organizations. In practical terms, combat meant the obligation to fight by any means in every locale. Sabotage, however, was initiated by members of the organizations (as well as the majority of ghetto inhabitants) to strike at German possessions and equipment. Motivated by hatred for everything connected with the Nazi regime and an ardent desire for revenge, as well as the hope of damaging the Germans' war effort, members of the underground carried out various acts of sabotage in their places of employment more frequently than operations initiated by the command. The underground leaderships in the Kovno and Vilna ghettos not only regarded these activities in a favorable light, but actually encouraged them and even publicized them. At the beginning of 1942, C. D. Rattner was appointed operations coordinator of the Anti-Fascist Organization (later part of the JFO) in the Kovno ghetto. His task was, *inter alia*, to receive reports from those implementing acts of sabotage and to record the operations. From these fragmentary reports, it is possible to infer the dimensions of the sabotage operations and the method of execution. For instance, according to one source:

> In March, sacks of produce were partially filled with snow which caused the contents to rot; in April, two hundred liters of benzine were poured into the sewers; in May, a box of rare medicines was broken in a military hospital; in June, filters were removed from six hundred gas masks; in July, the batteries of ninety-eight army cars were irreparably damaged by the addition of too much water; in August, one thousand pairs of army boots were spoiled.[6]

Members of the organization employed in the railroad station and its workshops acted more systematically: they changed the destination cards and lists of required repairs, removed screws from the locomotives, and shifted the signaling equipment. This led to chaos in the station, quarrels among its higher officials and, on more than one occasion, collisions. During other operations, members of the organization set fire to three large carpentry workshops on the banks of the river Neris (Vilja) opposite the ghetto and blew up Soviet arms depots that had remained in the Fifth Fort near Kovno.

Those who took part in sabotage activities were not unaware of the actual danger that these represented to the peace of the ghetto. Therefore, it was not without good cause that even members of *Hashomer Hatza'ir* refrained from participating in acts of sabotage, despite the fact that they were the closest to the Anti-Fascist Organization (Communists) in general ideology and in their demand for active combat against the Nazis in particular.[7] All the resistance organizations in the Shavli ghetto displayed no interest in sabotage operations. The Communists also took no action, despite the call from Moscow by the general secretary of the Lithuanian Communist Party to "burn the ground of Lithuania under the feet of the German invader."

Of all the underground umbrella organizations of the Lithuanian Jews, only the FPO, as stated above, included among its principal objectives sabotage operations in the enemy's rear. In addition, individual FPO members first carried out various acts of sabotage on their own initiative, albeit with the encouragement of the organization's leadership. Members of the FPO who worked in the arms depots in Borbishok were particularly active in this field. They put hundreds of guns, a hundred machineguns, and scores of vehicles out of action.

The FPO command's approach to the subject of sabotage changed, however, after it made contact with a group of Soviet paratroopers. During talks, they decided that "the FPO will organize espionage missions at all important military and economic points within the Vilna area, and will also continue sabotage operations."[8] This agreement also encouraged the FPO to carry out operations of military value, such as gathering information about German units and their positions and the movement of military and civilian trains in the area, which was transferred to the Soviet group. The FPO command likewise initiated and planned the mining of a military train carrying arms and ammunition. The mine was assembled in a *maline* inside the ghetto according to instructions in Soviet army pamphlets that had been smuggled in by members of the FPO. The operation was successfully carried out on July 8, 1942, by three FPO members, including one young girl; the train was derailed and blown to pieces. A meeting to discuss the incident, which seems to have been the first of its kind in Lithuania, was held that evening between representatives of the various political factions comprising the FPO, who met together for the first time.

LIAISON

The underground organizations made many efforts to break through the tight siege under which the Germans had placed the ghettos and to communicate with the outside world. Most of these contacts were limited to local branches of the Communist and Soviet organizations and to other concentrations of Jews. With the exception of an occasional letter or an isolated piece of information smuggled to Jewish organizations abroad, communications with Jews in other ghettos were limited to Lithuania and Poland.[9] For the sake of caution and convenience, as well as perhaps from force of habit, most of these contacts were made through party and movement channels and originated in the underground communication between branches of the *Bund*, the Zionist movements, and other organizations in Poland and Lithuania in the first stages of World War II (1939–1941).

While the chief motive of the political parties (assisted by the ghetto authorities) in the Kovno and Shavli ghettos was to maintain contact with and receive information about the Jews in general and their comrades in the underground in particular, the various organizations which eventually comprised the FPO, on the other hand, aimed much higher. Once they reached the conclusion that a self-defense organization was essential, they wanted to inculcate other ghettos, especially Warsaw, with the same idea.[10] Once established, the FPO adopted the same stand in a slightly different form somewhat later.

In October 1941, the young Pole, H. Grabowski, was sent to the Vilna ghetto by the Warsaw ghetto *Hehalutz* movement to make contact with the movement in the Bialystok area. An eye-witness to the deportations of the Jews from Trakai (Troki) and elsewhere in Lithuania, he brought back to Warsaw the news that the Germans were "massacring the Jews and that some tens of thousands had already been exterminated."[11] His mission was to no avail, however, and contact was subsequently entirely cut off. At the end of December 1941, a delegation of four, representing three movements— *Hano'ar Haziyoni, Hashomer Hatza'ir,* and *Betar*—were sent to Warsaw by the Zionist Coordinating Committee of Vilna. The delegation's aim was again to warn the Jewish community in Warsaw and convince them that what had happened in Vilna was no chance incident but rather the beginning of a systematic program of extermination that would eventually include Polish Jewry as well, for they knew that Hitler was "planning to destroy all of European Jewry and that the Jews of Lithuania were only the first in line."[12] They knew that the only possible course of action was to organize armed self-defense. The community leaders in Warsaw replied that the German extermination campaign was aimed at taking vengeance on the Jews in the territories previously occupied by the Soviets, while Warsaw was in the heart of Europe. In response, yet another delegation went to Warsaw, as well as to other ghettos, with testimonies of escapees from Ponary about the mass murders there, and a special proclamation by the FPO which appealed to all the Jews under Nazi occupation with the cry, "To arms!" Two young female emissaries from *Hashomer Hatza'ir,* who left Vilna in April 1941, perished near Warsaw. The proclamations, however, reached not only large centers such as Warsaw, Bialystok, and Grodno, but also smaller towns such as Mezricz and Hrubieszow.[13] Then, in the summer of 1942, two more female FPO emissaries made a daring attempt to smuggle coded documents, including material about Nazi crimes in Lithuania and Poland, across the Russo-German front, in the hope that the truth would reach world Jewry by way of Moscow.

Concurrent with these missions, and at times in coordination with them, some ten emissaries from Zionist movements traveled constantly between Vilna, Bialystok, and Warsaw. Along with news about the movements both in Poland and in Palestine, some of the emissaries brought money to finance movement activities. A number of *Hehalutz* and *Hashomer Hatza'ir* activists left Vilna at the end of 1941 and the beginning of 1942 and returned to their posts in Poland in order to organize a resistance movement there. Among them were Mordechai Tenenbaum, Chaika Grossman, and Edek Boraks, who went to Bialystok, and A. Wilner, J. Kaplan, and Tossia Altman, who went to Warsaw. All of them subsequently played key roles in the revolts in these ghettos.

After a comparatively long break in the visits by emissaries, a Christian social worker from Poland arrived in Vilna in June 1942 on behalf of *Hashomer Hatza'ir* and *Hehalutz*. Her name was Irena Adamowicz. A former senior instructor in the Polish scout movement, she imparted detailed information about the destruction of Jews in Poland and the preparations for organizing self-defense in the Warsaw ghetto. After her return to Warsaw, she was sent by the FPO command to the Kovno and Shavli ghettos from which, despite their geographic proximity and inclusion in the same political and administrative framework as the Vilna ghetto *(Generalkomissariat Litauen)*, only hazy reports had thus far been received. Adamowicz held similar meetings in Shavli, where she arrived in July 1942. There, as in Kovno, her visit precipitated the decision to begin organizing groups for self-defense. On her way to Vilna, she again visited the Kovno ghetto and reported to *Matzok* about the situation of the Jews in Shavli.

Another Pole, Jadwiga (Jadzia) Dudziec, travelled to Kovno from Vilna on a similar mission. When the Germans' intentions to liquidate the Oshmyany (Oszmiana) ghetto in September 1943, with the cooperaton of the Jewish police of the Vilna ghetto, became known, the FPO sent Lisa Magun to the ghetto. The aim of her mission was to warn the Jews of the imminent *Aktion,* to organize the youth for flight to the nearby forests, and to call for resistance in case the Germans tried to deport them in order to exterminate them. As a result, a considerable number of the young people in the Oshmyany ghetto did attempt to flee to the forest, and at least thirty of them succeeded in joining the partisans in the nearby forests. Another FPO representative implemented a similar mission in the Svencian ghetto before its liquidation.

PROPAGANDA

Nearly all the underground organizations in the Lithuanian ghettos systematically listened to the military and political news carried on foreign radio stations and distributed a summary of newspapers, which were censored by the occupying authorities. While the FPO in Vilna, however, concentrated particularly on current news from the fronts and in the political arena, which they published in the form of a daily handwritten leaflet in Yiddish,[14] activists in the Shavli ghetto produced at least five underground newspapers and bulletins stressing themes of a national Jewish character from different historical periods, reports of the Holocaust, and news from Eretz Yisrael.

In February 1942, the Anti-Fascist Organization in the Kovno ghetto installed a radio (connected to the electricity network outside the ghetto) in a *maline* to hear the news broadcasts from Moscow. From these broadcasts, they compiled a weekly bulletin in Yiddish, which was duplicated and distributed to all underground cells. *Matzok* circles in the Kovno ghetto also organized shifts for listening to a radio that had been installed under the pharmacy and established a news distribution system. Announcements concerning events at the fronts and in other ghettos, which called to the youth to defend themselves, were published by *Hashomer Hatza'ir (Tohelet)* and IBZ *(Shalhevet)*. At the same time, an IBZ newspaper *(Nitzotz)*, an underground organ created during the Soviet regime, continued to appear at intervals.

These bulletins were all designed to provide members of the underground movements with quick, reliable information, not only for activists but for the general ghetto population. The organizations' information service became so efficient that there was hardly an important political or military event about which the Jewish community did not soon learn. Special typed proclamations in Yiddish were published by the FPO in the wake of serious incidents such as "Wittenberg Day" (July 15, 1943), or at the onset of the mass deportation from the ghetto on September 1, 1943. One proclamation ("No one will enter the railway cars!") was published by the JFO in July 1944 on the eve of the liquidation of the ghetto.

Not all underground publications were addressed to the Jews, however. At least six proclamations in Lithuanian, Polish, and German were composed, edited, typed and distributed by the FPO among the non-Jews in the Vilna area. At least one proclamation in Lithuanian appeared on behalf of the underground in Shavli.[15] It was likewise intended to supply the non-Jewish population with reliable military information, and it was hoped to create enough dissent between the Lithuanians and the Germans to encourage the Lithuanians to fight against the Germans.[16] These proclamations were issued under the names of fake organizations to conceal their true origins. From time to time, the FPO also provided Soviet soldiers interned by the Germans under conditions of severe degradation and isolation, with up-to-date information about the situation at the fronts.

Unlike the FPO in Vilna, activists in the Kovno ghetto put considerable emphasis on culture and education. No clear distinction was made between the JFO umbrella organization and its political components. Thus, for example, the IBZ for a long time gave preference to cultural and educational activities rather than to rescue and self-defense. The cultural activities had two aims: to teach Zionist and pioneering values and to imbue the youth with Jewish knowledge. Lessons were taught in Hebrew; members learned the history of *Eretz-Israel* and Zionism and acquired basic concepts of the Hebrew settlement in Palestine. Some even learned written Hebrew. The IBZ also held lengthy ideological debates (particularly among its adult members), the conclusions fo which were published for the information of all its members.

In the Shavli ghetto, the *Massadah* organization and other unaffiliated pioneering groups also gave preference to cultural activity, continuing the pattern of the days of the Soviet regime. The *Massadah* leadership also felt that there were no other concrete ways to raise morale in the ghetto, and used every national festival as a pretext for some sort of party.[17] A considerable part of *Massadah's* ideological activity, like that of the IBZ, was based on the need for unity in the Zionist camp. In *Hehalutz* circles, however, the stress was rather on ideology. There was, however, no real discrepancy between cultural activity and actual combat, since the former acted as training for the latter. In fact, cultural activity in the underground organizations was in inverse proportion to their work in the field of combat.

CHAPTER 17
MAJOR RESISTANCE PLANS AND THEIR EXECUTION

WHETHER ARMED COMBAT WAS THE PRINCIPAL OBJEC-
tive of the resistance movements, as it was in the Vilna ghetto, or
whether it was relegated to a secondary position, as in the Kovno and
Shavli ghettos, its very nature obliged the underground organizations
to design a practical plan of action.

The resistance organizations realized that timing was crucial.
Furthermore, because the issue was an important part of each movement's ideology, on the one hand, and because it was critical to the
welfare of the ghetto on the other, combat was discussed in detail in
each organization's basic guidelines. The FPO also prepared explana-
tions of the regulations, along with a paragraph of the decisions taken
at the founding meeting, which mentioned "mass armed resistance in
the face of any attempt to liquidate the ghetto." The FPO's commentary also clarified problems of timing: "The FPO will take action during an *Aktion* which is considered to be the beginning of the end,"
while "the time when action is to be taken will be determined by
headquarters through an appraisal of the situation and in accordance
with the information it possesses." In other words, the FPO was
inclined to establish H-hour in accordance with the principle that just
as premature action is akin to irresponsibility, so belated action is
tantamount to criminal negligence. This permitted a reappraisal prior
to a final decision and was logical from a tactical and military point of
view; nevertheless, because it was also liable to different assessments
of the situation, any actual attempt at resistance was doomed to fail.
In the Shavli ghetto, the general inclination was to wait until an
Aktion was actually in progress.[1] In the Kovno ghetto, however,
where the plan was to offer stubborn resistance and to exhort the

151

ghetto inmates not to surrender easily, the question of timing was left open, since one never knew the date when final liquidation was to take place.

One of the principal problems in determining a propitious time for combat was that the German regime kept its intentions secret and disguised its aims with diversionary tactics and dissimulations. In an attempt to overcome this problem, the resistance organizations organized speedy and efficient mobilization systems that could work automatically in a number of possible situations. Plans for sudden mobilization of the JFO in Kovno, for instance, provided for three possibilities: (1) that children, elderly persons, and invalids might be taken away or shot on the spot, while the rest of the population was at work; (2) that all the inhabitants (including those fit for work) might be liquidated or deported at the same time; (3) that the entire ghetto might be totally exterminated. The FPO's code of regulations also included nineteen detailed rules (sections 18–37) for mobilizing the fighting forces and stationing them at their posts. This was to be effected either through instructions from headquarters, with the signal "Liza calling" or by automatic mobilization if the ghetto were suddenly endangered and the inmates fled to their hiding-places.

In the course of time, plans for defending the ghetto were perfected with a combined program which, along with static defense, also included attack from a central position outside the ghetto walls (at 11 Rudnicka Street). According to this program, the Communist force outside the ghetto was expected to implement sabotage both as a diversionary tactic and to create the proper political atmosphere. The last stage of the program was designed to blaze a way out to the forest for the fighters as well as for ghetto civilians, either under the cover of darkness or during an anticipated temporary retreat on the part of the Germans. The JFO's detailed program of defense was further determined by the Kovno ghetto's strategic position.[2] Krikš-čiukaičio Street (a bottleneck area in the ghetto) was fixed as the first target for attack, as its seizure would prevent the Germans from dividing the ghetto in half. The JFO also decided to neutralize the German guards in the ghetto who would be able to serve as a bridgehead to the Germans. This attack would also allow the Jews to disarm the guards and distribute their weapons among the fighters.

The JFO plan also provided for the division of the ghetto into eight defense zones. A commander was to be appointed for each zone and two meeting points would be decided upon, one for the general population, and the other, which would be secret, for the fighting units based in the area. The small quantity of arms in the underground's possession would be divided among the fighters in accordance with their duties, while the rest of the men would be provided with axes, iron bars, knives, and so forth. A clandestine workshop was set up to prepare such equipment. If the Germans brought army or police units into the ghetto with the clear intention of taking away the inhabitants in order to murder them or of massacring them on the spot, the ghetto inmates would immediately be called to their meeting points. Some of the fighting divisions, and especially those based in the areas where the Germans might begin their activities, were scheduled to attack the enemy with all the weapons at their disposal. The aim of the attack would be to kill and disarm as many Germans as possible and to divert the German forces, thus giving the fighting division in the border areas of the ghetto time to break down the fence and enable the ghetto population to flee. The incendiary divisions, equipped with Molotov cocktails and other inflammable material, also had an important task to fulfil: they were to set fire to empty houses within the ghetto and on the Aryan side when the fighting was at its height, in order to increase the confusion among the Germans who would find themselves trapped between the burning houses and the hail of fire from the ghetto defenders.

In the Shavli ghetto, on the other hand, there was apparently no plan for resistance that was acceptable to all sections of the underground, even though programs had been discussed from the first day of the ghetto's existence. As in the Kovno ghetto, a common factor in all these tentative plans was to set the ghetto on fire and ignite the fence.[3] The plan in Kovno relied mainly on a fighting unit that was to break down the fence and set fire to the houses on the Aryan side of Old Slobodka.

In theory, the underground organizations never abandoned plans for defending the ghetto. But when events shook the ghetto and the underground, like the relocations in Kovno and Shavli and the death of the underground commanders in Vilna and Kovno and when leaving for the forests became increasingly popular, they were no longer inclined to devote all their time, energy, and means to developing and perfecting major plans. Such plans were revived at the last moment, however, near the eve of the liquidation of the ghetto, and a new strategy was formulated.

When, for example, the Vilna ghetto was suddenly surrounded at dawn on September 1, 1943, and Estonian units filled the streets to implement the deportations to Estonia, there was a delay in the distribution of weapons, and the defense strategy had to be altered. According to the new plan, the main battle with the Germans would take place throughout the entire expanse of the ghetto, supported by forces concentrated at the central headquarters.

The Germans also frustrated the defense plan in the Kovno ghetto by evacuating the Jews from the first district of Old Slobodka and concentrating them in an area bordred by the river on one side and empty fields on the other. The new plans were at first capricious and impractical, and more demonstrative than effectual, including, for example, the plans to throw sand into the eyes of the Germans during the evacuation in order to enable a few people to flee, and to have the inmates throw themselves on the ground *en masse* in order to demonstrate their opposition and to prevent the Germans from carrying them away. A plan for setting the ghetto on fire was also considered. The plan that finally proved acceptable to the majority of activists, however, was concerned with escape; the plan was to dig a tunnel some thirty yards long, which would emerge beyond the ghetto fence. Unfortunately, despite precise planning by the best engineers in the ghetto and the vast amount of effort which went into its building, the tunnel collapsed during the last stages of its construction.

In the Shavli ghetto, two strategies for defense were drafted. One was drawn up at a meeting of *Massadah* on the day before one of its members, Z. Mazovetzki, was to be hanged for smuggling provisions into the ghetto. It was a proposal to blow up the gallows and kill the Germans who came to watch the spectacle.[4] The other was a plan against an imminent *Aktion* against children. It called for a special unit, some of whom would be dressed in German uniforms, to divert the Germans at the gate by attacking them with bayonets and revolvers, while the Jews in the ghetto resisted with knives and refused to surrender the children.[5] Neither plan was ever effectuated.

In contrast to the FPO's plans, which were made on the eve of the liquidation of the Vilna ghetto in September 1943 when the front was still far from Lithuania, the plans drawn up in July 1944 in the Shavli ghetto, before its liquidation and the liquidation of the labor camps affiliated with it, were aimed at escape and self-preservation and were made when the front was very near. And unlike the tunnel plan in Kovno, which included technical stages (building, assembling people, and so forth), the Shavli plans, especially for the labor camps, were of a military nature, relying on the use of arms, distribution of duties, and coordination with an outside armed force. Thus, for example, the planned mass escape for the 270 persons interned in the Daugeliai camp during the last days before their evacuation to concentration camps in Germany at the beginning of July 1944, was based on the following known facts: a group of armed youths who had left the camp earlier had received concrete promises from partisans in the area that they would support the operation from the outside; a considerable number of families in the camp had already prepared hiding places with peasants in the district; the conspicuous change in the Lithuanians' attitude toward the Jews had given rise to the hope that other Jews who were unable to join the partisans might also be sheltered. The plan included the following stages: (1) A group of scouts would approach the camp by night, and one of them would give a signal from the top of a telephone pole. (2) A return of the agreed signal by the commander of the operation in the camp would indicate to the group outside that they should cut the telephone and electricity cables. (3) A sniper inside the camp would then shoot the sentry on duty at the gate. (4) Armed units would take groups of men, women, and children, who had been previously organized and drilled, out through the gate. (5) Units armed with rifles, and especially grenades, would divert the local SS guards. (6) Some of the escapees, together with the partisans would then gain control of the nearby arms depots, and distribute weapons to everyone capable of using them.[6] But on the appointed night, the agreed signal was not given. And although the signal was given outside the camp on the following night, no answer came from the camp; there had been some complaints among the civilian prisoners. The program then apparently reached the Germans, who quickly evacuated all the prisoners to Shavli and then to Germany. Eye-witness accounts and descriptions make it seem that the plan failed not for technical reasons, but for human ones. Although the program had been designed for the benefit of the Jewish population at large, and was dependent upon it at certain stages, the population was an untried factor. They were also responsible for the failure of the Vilna plan. While the first stage of the FPO's strategy was executed by members of the organization, who incurred several losses, the second stage, in which the ghetto masses were to have played an active role, was never put into practice. The masses did not participate in active resistance on that day or at any time thereafter in the Vilna ghetto.

The battle of September, however, was different. It was the only armed confrontation between the Germans and the Jewish underground in Lithuania that was part of the underground's basic strategy and in accordance with its fundamental ideology. It was not the only battle, however: a series of fights preceded it, both with German security forces, and, on a different plane, with Jewish authorities who obeyed German orders. These fights began when the Germans attempted to interfere with the underground's activities. The first was a violent clash between the German security service agents who arrested the leader of the FPO, Yitzhak Wittenberg, on July 15, 1943, and a group of FPO members who rescued him from their hands. About a week later, there was a second confrontation, involving far greater numbers. That was the shoot-out of July 24, between an FPO group called "Leon" that was leaving for the forests and the Germans who were lying in wait for it by a bridge near Naujoji Vilnia (Novo-Wilejka). Nine partisans, former ghetto inmates, died in the incident, and thirty-two of their close relatives were subsequently shot. The last clash took place on Subocz Street during the liquidation of the Vilna ghetto on September 23, 1943. Several FPO members, including Abraham Chwojnik, a member of the command, opened fire on a German patrol that had stopped them to examine their documents. One German was apparently wounded in the incident, but the FPO members were all caught and hanged.

JFO members in the Kovno ghetto were apparently prepared for similar action. For instance, on the day of the Estonia *Aktion,* the JFO members hiding in *malines* were ordered to open fire on potential assailants. By chance, the German units combing the area missed the *malines.* And in addition to the indirect steps taken by the JFO to resist the German authorities, like the execution of B. F. and other German agents, there were a number of open clashes in the Aryan part of Kovno. Two of these took place in April 1944; one when Chaim Yellin was captured, and the other during the ambush of a truck transferring underground fighters to the forests.

CHAPTER 18
RELATIONS WITH GHETTO AUTHORITIES AND COMMUNISTS

THE UNDERGROUND AND THE *ÄLTESTENRAT*

RELATIONS BETWEEN THE GHETTO AUTHORITIES (THE *Ältestenrat* or the *Judenrat* and its employees, like the ghetto police) and the underground resistance movements were apparently greatly influenced by the basic differences in views: "procrastinating and gritting one's teeth in order to gain time and perhaps survive until the liberation," versus rebelling openly against the torturers with the cry, "Let my soul die with the Philistines!"[1]

In actual fact, these attitudes were not mutually exclusive. Both expressed preference for a certain course of action without necessarily damning the other forever. Moreover, it was not unheard of for one side to adopt the principles of its opposition, even if only temporarily. The chairman of the Jewish Council in the Shavli ghetto, for example, did not hesitate to propose a plan for general revolt by the ghetto inhabitants; similarly, the FPO did not refrain from advising restraint in certain cases and tended to maintain that "the life of every Jew is worth defending." What is more, certain people were active on both levels. In addition, because the ghetto authorities resisted passively from the outset, while the underground organizations did not deny their responsibility for the welfare of the ghetto inhabitants, the two sides, at least at first, recognized one another *de facto* and distributed tasks equitably. Thus, for example, the *Ältestenrat* in the Kovno ghetto was aware from the outset of the establishment of the various underground movements and did nothing to prevent their existence, and afterwards accepted them as a *fait accompli*. The problem that the ghetto authorities faced was rather the possibility of influencing their activities and, at the same time, not injuring the interests of the ghetto, as the *Ältestenrat* saw them.

Not only did the *Ältestenrat* in the Kovno ghetto refrain from blocking the underground, but they even helped the activists in various ways, such as providing financial assistance for the acquisition of arms. And even the Anti-Fascist Organization, along with the Zionist organizations such as IBZ, *Betar,* and the *Eretz-Yisrael ha-Ovedet* bloc (who had special ties with the *Ältestenrat* as the latter included members of *Matzok*) enjoyed this generosity. In addition to regular help, such as employing members of the underground in the ghetto police and in places where they would be able to make contact with Lithuanians, and removing the names of members from lists of candidates for deportation or anticipated *Aktionen,* the ghetto police and official institutions helped Communist activists to hide from the Gestapo and the Lithuanian police. Nevertheless, the official attitude of the Anti-Fascist Organization towards the ghetto leaders took the following form: 1) They refused to accept the principles of the *Ältestenrat,* whom they considered "servant of the invaders and the executor of their commands"; 2) They severely criticized members of the *Ältestenrat* and its institutions who took advantage of their position to protect themselves and their families from deportations and *Aktionen* and those who led luxurious and unruly lives; 3) They singled out members of the *Ältestenrat,* including Dr. E. Elkes, who had proved their integrity and courage in the execution of their duties as leaders of the ghetto.[2] Nevertheless, the Anti-Fascist Organization did not hesitate to infiltrate ghetto institutions (including the police) in order to serve the needs of the organization.

The two sides cooperated most closely when the JFO's activities reached their peak. The *Ältestenrat* placed carts and drivers at the disposal of JFO members leaving for the Augustow forests despite fear of disastrous consequences for the entire ghetto should the plan fail. Later on, when departure to the Rudninkai forests was organized, most of the equipment for the escapees was supplied by the ghetto workshops with the full consent of the *Ältestenrat* chairman, Dr. E. Elkes.

In both the Kovno and the Shavli ghettos, there was continuous cooperation between the underground organizations and the ghetto authorities, as long as the latter acted not only in their official capacity, but also—and principally—as ethical authorities. Even the leadership of the *Massadah* movement in the Shavli ghetto was criticized at this time by extremist elements in its midst for its moderate approach towards the ghetto authorities. In these two ghettos, however, the sympathetic attitude towards the resistance organizations was not adopted by the *Ältestenrat* as a body, but only by some of its members, such as Dr. E. Elkes and M. Leibovitz, chairmen of the supreme governing institution in the ghetto, who were held in high esteem by everyone and enjoyed great personal prestige. Nevertheless, contact with the Jewish authorities at nearly every stage in these two ghettos—and even more in the Vilna ghetto—was kept highly secret. As a rule, no one outside the organization was told more than necessary to carry out a particular operation. And while the underground exhausted all possibilities of help from the ghetto institutions, the organizations were nevertheless careful to entrust the majority of their operations to members of the underground, especially during their crucial stages; for this purpose, members infiltrated the Jewish institutions or recruited workers from them.

The relations between the two sides changed drastically, however, when the internal government was transferred at the beginning of 1944 to foreign representatives such as B. Lipzer in Kovno and G. Pariser in Shavli. The altered conditions in the ghetto also affected their relations. The ghetto leaders previously had been free to choose between supporting, passively recognizing, or totally disregarding, resistance organizations. Then, when the liquidation of the ghetto became imminent, they were forced to decide between active support or active resistance, and relations between the resistance organizations and the Jewish authorities in both ghettos began to deteriorate, although the two sides rarely, if ever, came to open confrontation.

In the Vilna ghetto, on the other hand, the position was different. Changes in the composition of the *Judenrat* (which had promoted Jacob Gens and his deputy S. Dessler to the ghetto leadership) had taken place earlier, and relations with the underground were thus more complex. When Gens first became head of the ghetto, there was still some sort of understanding between him and the FPO. He almost certainly was apprised of FPO activities by spies sent to infiltrate the organization, and FPO leaders participated in various communal activities within the ghetto. However, when the organization was no longer content with routine activities, and began to invade the *Judenrat's* field of jurisdiction in a way that might interfere with the execution of their policy by warning the Jews of Oshmyany (Oszmiana) of an *Aktion* executed by Gens's police force, for example, the relations between the two slid to a crisis. Open war was then waged against the FPO. At first, it was aimed primarily against Joseph Glazman, a member of the command and a popular figure in the ghetto. At the same time, Gens supported and encouraged an opposition group led by Esther Yaffe, a hated opponent of Glazman's whom the FPO had condemned to death for treachery. Thus, the Jewish leaders of the Vilna ghetto provoked the FPO to turn its weapons and its strength against the ghetto authorities rather than against its principal enemy, the Germans. Given the ghetto authorities' general attitude toward the underground, and Gens's policy of "saving what can be saved, and not being led astray by sentiment,"[3] the eventual betrayal of the FPO commander, Wittenberg, was in keeping with the authorities' conduct.

In order to comprehend fully the particular significance of this confrontation, it is necessary to compare it with a similar situation which occurred in the other ghettos. The authorities' attitude toward the sixteen prisoners who had been caught trying to escape from Kovno to the Augustow woods and toward the people who fled to Kovno in December 1943 from Fort Nine (where they were employed at burning the bodies of tens of thousands of Jews murdered there, in order to obliterate the traces of the Nazis' crimes) was quite different. The ghetto police did not succumb to the heavy pressure exerted by the Gestapo to surrender the escapees. Moreover, although the head of the Kovno ghetto police, Moshe Levin, joined forces with the Gestapo in hunting down the fugitives for the sake of appearances, he used to visit the escapees in their hideout, encouraged them, and saw to all their needs. The consequences of this were immediate: the Jewish police were arrested and some forty of them were murdered by the Gestapo. The Jewish Council in the Shavli ghetto adopted a similar stance when it refused to hand over fifty Jews who had smuggled provisions into the ghetto. On the other hand, the Judenrat in the Svencian ghetto did not balk at surrendering to the Gestapo two young members of the underground whose identity had been discovered when one of them was found handling firearms.

Despite these differences in attitude toward the underground, there were similarities in the approaches that the authorities took in the different ghettos. During almost the entire period under discussion, including the time when the underground activity was at its zenith, there was no break in contact between the ghetto authorities and the underground in any of the Lithuanian ghettos. Furthermore, the two sides came to some extremely important practical agreements. According to an agreement made in the Shavli ghetto, most members of the underground were concentrated in labor camps, so that they would be able to continue to live together. Those who remained in the ghetto did so only in order to work in the central headquarters. Another agreement was allegedly made between the

FPO and the ghetto police after the unique clash with the Germans on September 1. It stated that the members of the organization would not be deported to Estonia if they would remain concentrated at 6 Straszuna Street and not interfere with the *Aktion*. Later, the two sides apparently held a second meeting at which the FPO announced that it would evacuate its members to the forest. The police promised "not to interfere with the departure of the fighters on condition that the FPO promise not to evacuate ordinary Jews as well."[4]

Special agreements were also made among the ghetto police in Vilna, refugees from the surrounding hamlets en route to the forests, and representatives of partisan units. When the partisans visited the ghetto in order to take people to the forests, they were usually arrested. But it is also true that the imprisonment of outsiders was usually ended with the personal intervention of Gens and a sort of "gentleman's agreement," according to which they were free to return to the forest with their weapons, taking with them their comrades but not youths from the ghetto.

Gens's statements and actions lend credibility to the supposition that his reservations about departures to the forest stemmed not so much from total opposition to the step as from his conception of the nature and timing of the plan. For example, Gens explained to an emissary from the partisan command who pressed for the removal of ghetto Jews to the forest that this would mean selecting only a few Jews and was, therefore, unthinkable: "How many Jews could you save in this way? A hundred, two hundred, let us say even five hundred. . . . You want to take just these and leave the old, sick, and children, whom the Germans will immediately exterminate, to the mercy of Heaven? I shall not allow it." Gens explained his fundamental opposition to the departure of the local Jewish youth from the ghetto thus: "I need daring young men with arms in the ghetto in order to resist at a given moment. I am aware of the existence of the FPO and all its arms depots. I turn a blind eye to it because I know that there will come a time when I shall need them. I have good connections, and I shall always know when the Germans are planning to destroy the ghetto. At that moment, I shall need all the armed Jewish boys, and then we shall all fight together."[5] Concern that the possession of arms by people who were not affiliated with any organization was liable to lead to irresponsible usage and acts of provocation which would endanger the entire ghetto, perhaps explains why Gens executed a Jew from Svencian who, when preparing to leave for the forest, had wounded several Jewish policemen in a clash with the ghetto police. Furthermore, the FPO and other organizations were equally critical of reckless action, although for different reasons. For example, the FPO once gave the following reply to an emissary of the partisan command: "We, the youth or a minority of it, are still able to save our own lives, but we do not wish to save them; we are living in the midst of this people with our mothers, our sisters, and our brothers, and we are seeking a way to save them and their honor".[6] And eye-witness accounts give the impression that the FPO's attitude toward the acquisition of arms by individuals was, at the very least, ambivalent, if not negative, because they feared both provocation and the staggering rise in prices that accompanied the mass demand for arms. In the Kovno ghetto, the JFO, with the Ältestenrat's knowledge, was forced to execute five arms owners who had not only extorted funds, supposedly for the organization's arms fund, while threatening their victims with firearms, but had actually killed three men in the process.

One of the conclusions that can be drawn from this is that the underground movements and the Jewish authorities in the ghettos had similar, if not identical, attitudes on a number of important issues. One can also surmise that the relations between the ghetto authorities and the underground organizations in the Vilna ghetto, which were particularly tense in comparison to Kovno and Shavli, were a result not only of the gap between their outlooks, but of personal animosities and conflicts, which a combination of circumstances escalated.

THE COMMUNISTS

The importance of the Communists in the ghetto was immeasurably greater than their numerical strength, even at the beginning of the war when they were left unorganized and cut off from their ideological and organizational centers. Their impact on the ghetto was even greater when they became integrated, from an organizational and ideological point of view, and gained recognition and contacts from Moscow. Their prestige was due in no small measure to the fact that they were considered an integral part of the Soviet power upon which the ghetto inhabitants laid their greatest hopes. The Communists were likewise credited with having close connections with both political and military forces outside the ghetto, which could enable them to receive, among other things, information and efficient help when the time came.

The members of *Hashomer Hatza'ir*, who were among the first to advocate the establishment of a fighting underground organization in the Vilna ghetto (the FPO), turned first to the Communists. Their reasons for doing so were as follows: they reasoned that the character of the war necessitated it, and they believed that the Communists had contacts outside the ghetto "and maybe even more." When it became clear that no organized Communist underground was yet in existence, at the very time that the need for allies outside the ghetto became essential for underground activity,[7] the FPO did not hesitate, with the consent of representatives from all its various member groups, to assist the Communists in restoring the party institutions in the city and within the Vilna area. In the Kovno ghetto, the Communists were cut off for a long time even from local Communist circles which, although not systematically organized, were active in various frameworks. However, even when some sort of contact was established with them, they did not exert much practical influence.

The turning-point came when the Communists in the Kovno and Vilna ghettos established direct contact with authorized party representatives from Moscow, and particularly the paratrooper "Albina" (Gessia Glezer). Unlike the paratroopers who had met members of the FPO by chance or the partisan commanders (Markov, Sidyakin, and Stankiewicz) whose connections with the FPO were at best marginal, Albina held meetings with JFO and FPO representatives that were planned beforehand and were part of her official duties as an emissary of the "operative group" of the Lithuanian Communist Party Center in Moscow. For the Communists, who were accustomed to following instructions from higher authorities, the visit was a great boost, both morally and ideologically, for their ambition "to rise up against the invader under the direct leadership of the party" was thus fulfilled.[8] From this point of view, the importance of Albina's visit for the Communists can be compared to that of Irena Adamowicz for the Zionists.

However, being recognized by an authorized representative of the Communist Party Center and aligning themselves with the party in the fight against the Nazis had a recognizable effect on the Communist cells' standing among the resistance organizations in the Kovno and Vilna ghettos and on their plans for action. Thus, for example, the aborted Augustow plan, which Albina introduced and which purported to serve the geo-political and strategic interests of the Soviet-Communists, was accepted by the FPO only after pressure from the Communists, who were also secretly dubious about its practicability. Albina's visit also left the Jewish Communists in the Vilna ghetto with the problem of choosing between adherence to the party line and their responsibility to their brethren in the ghetto. Albina came with clear instructions not to recognize any underground organization within the ghetto except on a municipal, and not exclusively Jewish, basis. She also claimed that there was only one course of action: to leave the ghetto and organize a partisan fight in the forests. The leaders of the FPO, together with some of the Communist leaders in the Vilna ghetto who had a more positive and national approach, convinced Albina that their duty as Jewish fighters lay in remaining with the Jewish community until the end. Even later, when the FPO did decide, for completely different reasons, to leave for the forests, the Communists, like their Zionist comrades, abided by the idea of a special framework for Jewish fighters, so that the Jewish aspect of the fight would not be obliterated.

This attitude was emphasized to an even greater extent in the Kovno ghetto. While the Communists declared that those who went out into the forests were joining the Soviets as partisans in the holy war against German and international Fascism, the Zionists stressed that they were going "as Jews, as escapees from the Jewish ghetto in Kovno, in order to avenge the blood of their relatives who had been slaughtered because they were Jews."[9] In addition to their differences of approach to the national problem, the Communists in the Kovno ghetto were also divided from their comrades in the Vilna ghetto by the nature of their relations with the non-Communists within the resistance organizations. The relations between the Communists in the FPO and other movements were distinguished by sincerity, mutual respect, trust, and deep personal friendship.[10]

After the Communists in the Kovno ghetto had, thanks to Albina, received exclusive control over contacts with the Lithuanian partisan brigade under Jurgis's command, they were in a position to dictate to the JFO command the composition of the groups that would leave. Thus, the JFO demanded, and received, sole authority in the appointment of commanders of the groups. And although this was seemingly an unimportant matter (the appointments were temporary and their validity expired upon the groups' arrival at the partisan base), these commanders did succeed in blurring the distinctly Jewish aspect of the operation and in stressing the "universal" aspect of the ghetto fighters' alliance with the partisans.

In contrast to the Communists in the Vilna and Kovno ghettos, who played an honorable role in the underground organizations, the Communists in the Shavli ghetto remained isolated for a long time. Even when they began to participate in joint activities at the end of 1943, they carried out most of their work in the labor camps, in actions sanctioned *post factum* by the Zionist leadership in the ghetto, after pressure by rank and file members in the camps. Since emissaries from Moscow hardly ever reached the Shavli area at that time, and factional and partisan activity outside the ghetto was very weak, the Shavli Communists' chance connections with their comrades outside the ghetto were of little practical value. The Communists were relatively consistent in comparison to the rest of the movements in *Zelbstshutz* in that they always emphasized that fighting should be regarded as an objective in its own right. In particular, they were among the most active in rescuing Jews from the Daugeliai camp. Despite the fact that the proportion of Communists among escapees from the ghetto and labor camps was remarkably high, their activity in the forest was in general not outstanding, that is, they tended to be concerned with their own survival.

By and large, the underground organizations, with the exception of those in the Svencian and Shavli ghettos, received considerable help from their Communist members and through them, from the Russian military and political authorities operating in the area during the later stages of the war. However, the organizations also suffered many setbacks as a result of their contacts with local Communist circles, despite the help which the underground had given them.[11] Thus, for example, although the FPO provided the Communist underground in Vilna with money for the purpose of acquiring arms, and the latter undertook to prepare hiding places in the city as well as to help with sabotage operations during an uprising in the ghetto, the FPO did not receive from them "the ghost of a revolver, and at the crucial moment, there was no sort of apartment in the city that could have served as a hideout."[12] A rebuttal can be heard in a statement made some twenty-eight years after these events. Speaking at a symposium on Jewish problems, the Jewish commander of the partisans, Ziman ("Jurgis"), said: "When I fought in the land of the Fascist enemy, we did everything in our power in order to rescue the youth from the Kovno and Vilna ghettos. However, our adversaries, the Zionists, persuaded the ghetto internees to give up the fight. The Zionists interfered with the partisan movement and from this point of view, bear some share of responsibility for the deception practised by the Fascists on Lithuanian territory."[13]

CHAPTER 19
DEPARTURE FOR THE FORESTS

AT THE SAME TIME THAT LARGE-SCALE RESISTANCE WAS abandoned in practice if not in theory, escape to the forests to join the partisans gained importance in the underground organizations. There were a number of causes for this. First, the partisans had strengthened and enlarged their organization so that it then stretched to the borders of Lithuania as well as to Lithuania proper. Rumors about the fighting penetrated the ghettos, providing both organized and unorganized activists already interested in joining the partisans with the names and locations of partisan groups to which they could turn. In organizations such as *Yechiel,* and among groups of refugees from the small towns who were living in the Vilna ghetto, internal unrest and pressure in favor of leaving for the forests steadily mounted as partisan leaders, whose forces were concentrated at the eastern border of Lithuania, showed more and more interest in reliable fighters from the ghettos. This unrest also afected many who, at first, had reservations about joining the partisans. The letters of Colonel F. Markov, commander of the *Varoshilov* partisan unit, and Sidyakin, leader of the *Chapayev* unit, sent in the spring and summer of 1943, called upon the youth to leave the ghetto and join partisan units. Among the members of the FPO, these letters raised not only hopes of an immediate and free fight, with prospects of rescue and survival, but also doubts about their current line of action. The organizations in Vilna and Kovno, and especially the Communists among them, were no less influenced by the visit of the paratrooper Albina (Gessia Glezer) a representative of the Lithuanian Communist Party Center, who stressed the need for fighting together with the partisans and objected to passive resistance.

Second, there was growing concern that some members of the organization and periphery would endanger not only their own lives

167

but the lives of everyone in the ghetto. Thus, the FPO command actively helped some two hundred youths escape to the Narocz forests, because they were concerned about the fate of refugees who had reached the ghetto illegally. For similar reasons, the JFO quickly transferred to the Rudninkai forests many of the nineteen young people who had escaped from their jobs as corpse-burners in Fort Nine and had taken temporary refuge in the ghetto. More importantly, after Wittenberg's surrender, the FPO decided that a group of its members (including J. Glazman, a member of the general command), who had already been persecuted by the ghetto authorities and were no longer able to participate effectively in any ghetto activity should flee to the forest and create a partisan base to support future ghetto struggles. In the Vilna ghetto, the pace of departure to the forest was quickened partly as a result of some underground members' deep disappointment with the apathy of the masses during "Wittenberg Day" and the Estonian *Aktion*, and partly because of the FPO command's indecision toward continued resistance within the ghetto.

The third cause was the rise in the number of work camps for the Lithuanian Jews, especially in 1943. Since the majority of the camps (such as Daugeliai in the Shavli area, Baltoji Voke near Vilna, and Kaišiadorys near Kovno) were situated in densely wooded areas, and since conditions there were, in fact, too unfavorable to permit any hope of successful resistance on the spot, local underground activities concentrated on preparing for flight to the forest. As a result, in some cases with and in other cases without the help of underground organizations in the ghettos, some two hundred men from five or six camps succeeded in escaping.

The most enthusiastic support of departure from the ghetto usually came from activists who had already lived in the forest for one reason or another. "Those who lived in the ghetto," remarked one of them, "did not realize what a cage they were living in. When we came from the forests to the ghetto and saw how people were choking there, we knew that they would never be able to fight for the FPO inside the ghetto."

Although the ghetto organizations' decision in favor of departure for the forest finally solved the thorny problem of choosing between ghetto or forest, it raised a range of new problems, some of which, such as weapons, guides, and the distance between the departure-point and the forest, were to have far-reaching consequences. Leaving the ghettos also raised moral and political problems for the underground.

MORAL AND POLITICAL PROBLEMS

Unlike individuals and unorganized groups who were at liberty to leave the ghetto armed or unarmed, without confirming the existence of their destination or its readiness to receive them and, even more important, without any responsibility towards the community they left behind, the resistance organizations were compelled to consider the departure program very carefully. They were forced to make many preliminary reconnaisance trips to the forest, to determine precise absorption possibilities, and to conduct wearisome negotiations with authorized representatives of the partisan movement. Furthermore, they had to employ maximum caution so as not to involve those remaining in the ghetto or camp. For the sake of greater security, the resistance organizations also took care that those leaving did not take with them any documents (including family photographs), and that they did not speak Yiddish among themselves. Such precautions forced them to postpone departure on more than one occasion despite the resulting loss of time and in some cases the loss of unique opportunity. For instance, in the *Heeres Bekleidungsamt* (HBA) labor camp near the Shavli ghetto, a group of Jews, including members of the resistance organization, refused to accept an offer to join the ranks of partisans who had penetrated into the camp and killed the German guard. They argued that their families were in the ghetto and liable to be executed if they fled.[1]

In the intermediate stage, however, before the push to depart for the forests had gained momentum, the FPO and the JFO adopted a plan for setting up bases in the forest which could play a strategic role in defending the ghetto in the event of liquidation. This meant that ties with the ghetto and the organization would not cease after the departure to the forest; bases would even remain attached to the ghetto from the operational and organizational points of view, at least as far as the defense of the ghetto was concerned. The underground was probably naïve regarding the centralized format of the Soviet partisan movement, or possibly wished to pay lip service to supporters of resistance within the ghetto. In any case, there is no doubt that the will to band together in the forest, too, (which was the main condition for the realization of the program) was rooted in clearly national motives.

One can thus understand the hesitation of the FPO command when, on the brink of transferring their remaining forces in the ghetto to the Narocz forests, it suddenly gave orders to send its members to the Rudninkai forests much closer to Vilna, where they could unite with FPO groups who were already in the forests in order to "establish a strong Jewish fighting unit."[2]

The JFO in Kovno faced the opposite problem. Their difficulties stemmed from the conflicting military and political interests within the Lithuanian partisan movement. When JFO members were ordered to go to the remote Augustow forests instead of the far more accessible Rudninkai woods, the argument arose that acceptance of the decision would mean that these men were merely serving as test cases for the Communist party and the partisan movement. The fear that Zionist members of the JFO would come to harm in the forest emerged in lengthy discussions between *Matzok* representatives from the JFO and Communist representatives, in the innocent belief that the Communists were authorized to speak for the partisan movement. It was finally decided that "all those leaving for the forest shall be obliged to obey the district or local commander. During rest hours, social activities will be freely conducted according to the comrades' wishes."[3] Later, the JFO leaders in the Kovno ghetto refused to send men to the Rudninkai forests due to their relative remoteness and the anti-Semitism that had come to light. They preferred the Kazlu-Ruda forests, but those who went there were no more fortunate than the others.

At first, the organizations tried to evade the partisan stipulation that only men with weapons were welcome. They sent many unarmed people, including quite a number of girls, and only a few arms. Subsequently, however, when the partisan command became stricter in their demands, insisting that the activists bring "long" weapons and threatening to send back the girls and unarmed men, the underground could no longer ignore their conditions. Furthermore, when the number and size of the groups were limited (because of the lack of guides, the capacity of the trucks, and the dangers involved in transferring large groups) and the pressure from members of the organization and many other young people to leave for the forest increased, the leaders of the underground were faced with the extremely difficult task of choosing candidates for departure. The resultant overt and covert struggle between the political movements within the JFO, in fact, between the Communist and Zionist elements, led to the establishment of a fixed code for selection, giving women whose husbands were already in the forest a certain priority, for instance. In spite of, or because of the code, unorganized people with arms or the means to acquire them were given preference on more than one occasion over members of the organization in excellent physical condition. In the FPO, too, the number of candidates for departure exceeded the places available, and preferential treatment based on personal contacts was known to be used.

The FPO's difficult decision became a pressingly moral one on September 23, 1943. During the liquidation of the ghetto, scores of unaffiliated young people pressed to join FPO members preparing to leave for the forests through the sewers. The FPO decided it had to stop them with the use of arms.[4] The *Yechiel*, on the other hand, was able to allow a number of unaffiliated and unarmed young people to join their ranks in their flight to the Rudninkai forests.

TECHNICAL PROBLEMS

In addition to the armaments problem, the underground faced the complete isolation of the ghetto or camp, the long and unfamiliar path to the forest, and such obstacles as a hostile population, the army, and police forces.

Most plans for escape were not founded on open breakaways or violent clashes with guards, but rather on evasion and secrecy, with help, at that stage, from both their own forces and their allies in the ghetto. Thus, for example, most of the JFO groups left the Kovno ghetto during the night by way of the main gate disguised as official labor brigades employed outside the city, who, fortunately, had permission to report for work with large bundles of bedclothes and garments. Within these bundles they hid rifles, submachineguns, and other military equipment. Escapees dressed as German policemen acted as an armed escort, a common accompaniment for such groups. For further precaution, the electricity was cut at the ghetto gate, the apparent consequence of a short circuit, but in fact the handiwork of electricians affiliated with the organization. The "Leon" group and others from the Vilna ghetto also employed various camouflage tactics when they left for the forest.

The plan to smuggle out all the Jews interned in the Daugeliai camp also called for the cover of darkness, but the success of the plan actually depended on precise coordination between the inmates of the camp and an outside group. "It was agreed that one of us would cut the telephone lines in the camp," relates a survivor from the outside group, "and would fire a small revolver into the air as a signal for the operation to begin. When we heard the shot, we were to give a signal (a burst of flame from a cigarette lighter) to the camp, whereupon they were to kill the guard (without using firearms). We hid opposite the guardhouse in order to divert the guards by shooting so that the Jews could in the meantime escape."[5] But of course, the signal was never given that night, and the next night, when it was given, conditions in the camp no longer permitted a mass escape. Underground groups from the Kėdainiai (Keydan) labor camp and Fort Nine overcame the physical obstacles by digging a tunnel, drilling through an iron door, and climbing a rope ladder, while the last FPO group in Vilna left for the Rudninkai forests by way of the sewers.

Problems of transport were solved with guides and trucks. They eliminated a great deal of walking, the problem of mastering unfamiliar territory, and many losses of life. However, there were also disadvantages. The guides, hired or sent by the partisan commands, or Jewish volunteers from the small towns in the area, were not under the authority of the organizations whose members they were guiding. As a result, arguments between guides and their groups, especially those regarding times of departure and the inclusion of nonaffiliates whom the guides preferred for personal reasons or by instructions from headquarters were not easily solved.[6] Furthermore, even when the partisans sent former members of the underground organization, these guides now represented the interests of their new leadership, which sometimes opposed the organization's goal to transfer as many people as possible to the forest.

The JFO and, in one case, a *Yechiel* group hired truck drivers to transport groups to a point near the forests, but the success of this method depended upon the reliability of the non-Jewish driver. At least once, on April 14 in the Kovno ghetto, a driver betrayed his charges and caused the liquidation of most of the group.

Naturally, one must leave room for such variables as the different ways in which the underground in the Lithuanian ghettos organized departures for the forest, the ghettos' varying distances from the forest (6 to 125 miles), and climate at the time of departure (Vilna: April to September; Kovno: April to September; Shavli: June to July) but generally, plans for departure took the following course:

1. Choice of candidates for departure from within the various underground divisions, either on a voluntary basis, or by party decision
2. Talks with the candidate to determine physical fitness, motives for leaving, and ability to finance the acquisition of arms
3. Approval of the candidate by the headquarters
4. Intensive military and partisan training within small groups some two to three weeks before departure

5. Training within division frameworks; meeting with the other candidates; memorizing instructions for the journey and partisan tactics; learning useful phrases in Russian

6. Parties or farewell ceremonies

7. The announcement of a state of alert to the members of the group; concentration of all the candidates in a secret hiding-place in the ghetto; inspection of personal equipment, including, in the winter, riding breeches or other army gear, boots, a warm hat with earflaps, a warm jacket, an ammunition belt, a rucksack, three pairs of socks, two sets of warm underwear, sheets or an overall for camouflage, a few sandwiches

8. Final inspection and distribution of the group's short-range firearms and ammunition, including arms which they had acquired privately; distribution of general equipment for the group (medical supplies, etc.)

9. Distribution of tasks among the members of the group; last instructions for the journey, including the prohibition of smoking and severe limitations on speaking, in general, and speaking Yiddish, in particular

10. Assembly of the group next to the ghetto gate

11. Departure through the gate in the form of an ordinary working-party, including the removal of caps before the German guard

12. Sitting in prescribed order in the truck: partisan guide next to the driver; two or three fighters in German police or army uniform near the back wall of the truck, which was covered with a tarpaulin; the group commander inside the truck; and the rest seated in a prearranged order

13. A few miles outside the ghetto, an order to remove the yellow patches which had purposely been only loosely sewn on; collection and destruction of all the patches, with such words as "Now you are partisans!"

14. A short stop at the arms depot (near the ghetto) in order to load the rest of the "long" weapons; distribution of weapons inside the truck; loading rifles with five bullets

15. Leaving the truck some ten to twenty miles from the destination; putting on camouflage overalls; formation in rear line according to a prearranged order; guide, advance guard, commander in the middle column, rearguard; marching in this order, particularly by night; camping by day in the forest in an isolated hut

16. Presentation at the chosen partisan base by a password, letter, or other document from the organization in the ghetto

STATISTICAL ANALYSIS OF UNDERGROUND ACTIVITIES

Some thirty to thirty-five groups, numbering more than 1,150 men and women, left the ghettos and work camps in Lithuania between 1943 and 1944. All left in a more or less organized fashion, according to the procedure outlined above, either in trucks or on foot. Approximately 350 people left the Kovno ghetto and the Kaišiadorys and Kėdainiai labor camps; some 750 people from the Vilna ghetto and Kailis, HKP, and other labor camps; some thirty or forty from the Svencian ghettos; and about twenty from the Shavli ghetto. Further-

TABLE 5

Kinds of Resistance Activity According to Population and Place (or Town)

Location:	Vilna	Kovno	Shavli	Svencian	Total
		(including small towns and labor camps near each)			
Jewish Population	18,000	16,000	4,500	1,500	40,000
Percent of Jewish Population	45	40	11	4	100
Membership of Underground Organizations	700	600	150	50	1,500
Percent of Membership	46	40	10	4	100
Membership Ratio for Every Thousand Jews	39	37	33	33	37
Duration of General Underground Activity (months)	20	30	31	15	—
No. of Clashes between the Underground and the Jewish Ghetto Authorities	5	—	—	1	6
No. of Clashes between the Underground and the Occupying Nazi Forces	5	2	—	—	7
No. of Emissaries Sent to Other Ghettos	5	1	1	1	8
Duration of Major Acts of Resistance (months)	5	8	8	2	—
No. of People Sent to the Forests by the Underground	750	350	20	30	1,150
Percent of Total	65	30	2	3	100
No. of Nonmembers Who Went to the Forests	400	150	40	60	650
Percent	61	23	6	10	100
Total of Those Who Went to the Forests	1,150	800	60	90	1,800
Percent:	64	28	3	5	100

more, approximately 650 people left on their own or in unorganized groups (dubbed "wild groups" in the Vilna ghetto) from the ghettos and towns of eastern Lithuania, including Eišiškes, (Eyshishok), Valkininkai (Olkenik) and Švenčionys (Svencian) and the small towns in western Lithuania, including Kelme and Jurbarkas. In all, therefore, at least 1,800 Jews left the Lithuanian ghettos and labor camps for the forests during World War II. (See Table 5.)

Due to misfortunes which occurred during the journey, ambushes, arrests, and betrayals by local inhabitants, a considerable proportion of the escapees perished before reaching the forest (See Table 5), and many of those who did reach the forests, especially the independents, died either from hunger and cold or at the hands of armed groups of non-Jews before they had time to join the anti-German fighting activities.

The following table illustrates the scope of underground activity in the ghettos, labor camps, and other communities in Lithuania: Table 5 shows that while the numerical dimensions of the underground movements in each of the ghettos was in direct proportion to the population, from the point of view of activities, particularly departure for the forests, the Vilna ghetto was outstanding. This can be explained by the fact that several other nearby towns and labor camps were included within the administrative authority of the Vilna ghetto, which resulted in a disproportionate percentage of escapees from Vilna who were not members of the underground. Out of a total of 1,800 people who left for the forest, only two-thirds were sent by the underground, and even these were not all members.

In light of these facts, it is possible to conclude that the active fight of Lithuanian Jewry in the territories conquered by the Germans in World War II involved, in addition to some 1,800 individuals who escaped to the forest, hundreds of underground members who did not reach the forests. The total number of people who participated in the active fight against the Nazis comes to over 2,000, that is, approximately 5 percent of the forty thousand Jews who remained in Lithuania at the beginning of 1942 after the previous mass liquidation.

The lack of comprehensive and precise data on the losses sustained by Lithuanian Jewry in underground and partisan units compels us to refer to partial information. The findings in Table 6 have been calculated from Jewish sources to provide a representative sample of losses.[7]

TABLE 6

Mortality Rates of Lithuanian Jews in the Underground and in Partisan Units According to Their Places of Origin and Death

Place of Origin	No.	Percent	Place of Death	No.	Percent
Vilna	100	39	In their "home" ghettos	29	11
Kovno	88	34	As emissaries	13	5
Svencian	16	6	In ghettos they were sent to	8	3
Others	52	21	En route to the forests	50	20
Total	256	100	In the forests	156	61
			Total	256	100

PART IV
IN THE FORESTS
—PARTISAN WARFARE

CHAPTER 20
THE PARTISAN UNITS

THE SOVIET-LITHUANIAN PARTISAN MOVEMENT

BETWEEN AUGUST AND OCTOBER 1941, ISOLATED ATtempts were made in the Soviet Union to train suitable candidates among Lithuanian refugees for guerrilla warfare in the rear of the German army. Since the supreme partisan command had not yet been created at the time, training was generally conducted by local military commanders in conjunction with the Communist authorities. Thus, for example, the military commissar of Rostov summoned a group of Lithuanian nationals in August 1941, and informed them that, by dint of a meeting with the Komsomol Committee, they would be sent to learn "the art of war" and afterwards return to Lithuania as partisans. Members of this unit were selected with great care, and after courses in parachuting and sabotage, they were sent, at the beginning of November, across the frontline to attack the enemy from the rear. Similarly, at the beginning of September 1941, sixteen Lithuanian refugees were chosen from Gorki and other towns and sent to a special school in Moscow which trained teams for guerrilla operations. When the Germans approached the besieged capital, however, the school ceased to function, and its pupils helped to defend the city and carried out sabotage and mining operations beyond the frontline.

Through these experiences and others, some refugees from Lithuania became skilled in sabotage work and performed special tasks across the fronts.[1] However, the plan to parachute them into Lithuania was still not put into operation. A practical plan to airlift guerrilla fighters to Lithuania was only formulated in December 1941, at the same time, a Lithuanian fighting unit was established within the framework of the Red Army.

179

The first operative group, was parachuted across the Lithuanian–Latvian border on March 7, 1942. The group was under the aegis of the Lithuanian Communist party and was commanded by the secretary of the Central Communist Party Committee, Adomas (Itzik Meskup). It was armed and well equipped, possessing, among other things, a long-distance radio receiver, and consisted of ten members, including four Jews.[2] The group was expected to organize political activity among the population and to recruit large numbers of people "for a partisan battle against Hitler's invaders." However, the group was uncovered shortly after its arrival, and all its members perished in a clash with the police. A similar fate befell the second group that was parachuted into Southern Lithuania. On November 29, 1942, the headquarters of the Lithuanian partisan movement was set up in Moscow under the leadership of the secretary of the Central Committee of the Lithuanian Communist Party, A. Sniečkus. The command coordinated the activities of the partisan units, integrating them with the Red Army unit activities and supplying the Soviet army command with important information. At the same time, the Lithuanian partisan movement's primary concern was to disseminate propaganda to a Lithuanian population still hostile to the Soviet regime, in order to incite them against the local Hitlerite and nationalist Fascists.

The anti-Soviet attitude of the Lithuanian population and Lithuania's relative distance from the eastern front, which obstructed the infiltration of guerrilla fighters, also contributed to the relative tardiness in the Lithuanian partisan movement's development as well as to its relatively small size in comparison to the partisan movement in neighboring Byelorussia. The Byelorussian partisan movements were, until the fall of 1943, almost the only existing refuge for the Jews from eastern Lithuania who fled from the ghettos and labor camps, and for those who were roaming the forests. Both geographically and strategically, western Byelorussia became the most convenient location for interim partisan bases infiltrated through the front line either by land or by air.

The third group, whose task was to reorganize and strengthen the weak partisan movement in Lithuania, was flown in gliders to a temporary airfield belonging to the Byelorussian partisan movement in the Begomel forests. The group, whose coming heralded a change in the history of the Lithuanian partisan movement, numbered some forty members with sophisticated arms and equipment. It included members of the Central Committee, officers and privates from the Lithuanian Division, and activists with underground experience who had received extensive partisan training in the division's special company and special schools. The group was headed by M. Šumauskas (Kazimieras) and G. Ziman ("Jurgis"), the Jewish teacher from Kovno mentioned above. After a pause for reorganization, the group fought its way west 190 miles until it reached the Kazian forests near the northeastern border of Lithuania in June 1943. That fall, the group went south to the Narocz forests, in order to be nearer to Vilna.

A short while later, the group split into two. The first unit, including G. Ziman and some of the men who had been parachuted in, followed a vanguard group which had previously made its way to the Rudninkai (Rudnicka) forests some twenty-five miles south of Vilna. Their objective was to create a partisan base on Lithuanian territory. The second, with M. Šumauskas and the remaining members of the group, remained at the former base in Narocz, near the *Žalgiris* brigade with its three detachments *(ot ryadi): Kostas Kalinauskas, Vilnius,* and *Vytautas.*

When Ziman arrived at the new base in October 1943, there were already several hundred fighters there, including FPO members and a *Yechiel* group from the Vilna ghetto, organized in four or five units. From these units and others which were already established in the Rudninkai forests, Ziman formed the Vilna, Kovno, and Trakai brigades, which totalled some fifteen partisan detachments. These units, together with the special partisan units *(Spetzgruppa)* and others not belonging to the Lithuanian partisan movement, totaled some two thousand fighters. Ziman became head of the partisan command in southern Lithuania in January 1944, while Šumauskas was appointed head of the partisan command in nothern Lithuania. Their commands, which also served as a coordinating force for party activities in northern and southern Lithuania, were militarily and politically subordinate to the Central Committee of the Lithuanian Communist Party and the Central Command of the Lithuanian partisan movement in Moscow. Radio receivers installed in these two bases had direct contact with Moscow, as well as with the supply and arms bases in Toropetz.

As the front drew nearer to Lithuania, the importance of partisan activities, which were carried out in cooperation with the Red Army pursuant to its instructions, particularly with regard to intelligence and sabotage, increased accordingly. After the Red Army approached the eastern borders of Lithuania, the partisan camps, and especially those units which were only temporarily located there, moved westward. Šumauskas and Ziman were with the groups that moved west, as were the Kovno detachments in the Rudninkai forests. As a result, some of the Jewish partisans who had not yet been absorbed into any movement reached the center of Lithuania, because the bulk of the partisan units that accepted Jewish fighters had been formed mainly in eastern Lithuania at the end of 1943 or the beginning of 1944.[3]

Concurrent with the battle against the German military and civil administration, the partisans conducted a methodical fight against Lithuanian collaborators serving in special German auxiliary units in the peasant militia in the villages, and in police forces on the forests' periphery and at strategic communication points. As the front approached Lithuania, the hostile activity of Polish underground forces, which were connected with the Polish government-in-exile in London and were known as the AK (*Armia Krajowa*), increased sharply. In that area, the AK was nicknamed "White Poles," and one of their aims was to take control of the Vilna area after the Germans' retreat, in order to create a situation that would facilitate *de facto* the Polish annexation of the area after the war. Despite attempts to negotiate with them, the Poles in eastern Lithuania became dangerous and cruel adversaries of Soviet partisans in general, and of the Jews among them in particular.[4]

WITHIN THE BYELORUSSIAN PARTISAN MOVEMENT

Jews from the small towns on the eastern and southern borders of Lithuania who were successfully absorbed into the ranks of the Byelorussian partisan movement were concentrated mainly in the Nacza forests some fifty miles south of Vilna and in the marshy Kazian (Koziany) and Narocz forests some ninety miles east of Vilna. The first Jews reached the Nacza forests at the end of 1941, having wandered there virtually unarmed either in small groups or on their own. After the liquidation of the Radun ghetto on May 19, 1942, many Jews from Radun joined the groups in the forests. Survivors from various small towns in Lithuania and the Vilna ghetto were also accepted by the groups. The groups soon totaled 300 to 350 men, women, and children. In the course of time, some of them organized themselves into fighting and family groups. The few weapons in their possession they acquired from peasants in the area. They also occasionally received arms from groups of Soviet prisoners-of-war in the area, but they had no close or steady cooperation with them. When the parachutist Stankiewicz arrived in the forest in February 1943 as an emissary of the Byelorussian partisan command and organized these Jewish groups into a disciplined framework under the command of the Soviet army, he was wholeheartedly welcomed.[5] A partisan detachment (otryad) was then established under his command and called the *Leninski Komsomol*, which subsequently became a brigade which did most of its fighting on Lithuanian territory.

Nine more Jews, who had arrived armed from the Vilna ghetto, were absorbed into these units at the beginning of April 1943. A few weeks later, a delegation of eleven Jewish fighters was sent, with Stankiewicz's consent, to the Vilna ghetto in order to recruit additional Jews. Despite the opposition of the ghetto police and reservations on the part of the FPO, the delegation brought out some twenty-eight people under the leadership of police officer B. Friedman. However, the group was waylaid by a German ambush on its way to a partisan base in Nacza, and most of its members were killed. After that, there were pracically no more organized attempts to bring Jews from the ghettos to the *Leninski Komsomol.* The Jewish fighters in the unit, and to an even greater extent in the nearby family camps, continued to come primarily from the forests of southeast Lithuania. After ambushes from the Germans and others, a number of Jews from these units escaped to the Rudninkai and Narocz forests. In the main, they joined units which already included Jewish fighters, such as the Vilna detachments and the *Chapayev* unit. After the death of the commander of the unit and his Jewish deputy, however, the attitude towards the Jews in the fighting units and family camps worsened considerably. Many Jews were killed in German ambushes and by "White Poles."

The first Jews to flee from the ghettos to the Kazian–Narocz forests found unorganized groups of non-Jewish partisans there, whose proximity proved more dangerous to unarmed Jewish family groups than faraway German garrisons, and more difficult to withstand emotionally than hunger and cold. It was only at the end of 1942, when the paratrooper Markov consolidated these groups into an organized unit subordinate to the partisan supreme command, that fighters began to be accepted into these units. The unit was called the *Voroshilov* unit and later became a brigade. However, when the youths who had fled from the Svencian ghetto and other small towns in the area reached these units (and particularly the *Chapayev* unit) in the spring of 1943, they were not only accepted as fighters, in spite of the small quantity of weapons in their possession, but, as mentioned above, a number of them were sent as emissaries to bring more Jews out of the ghetto to join the partisans. And yet, even though some commanders behaved kindly toward the Jewish fighters in the units and did not prevent them from helping the many Jews in difficult circumstances in the various family dugouts, the situation of the Jewish fighters was extremely wretched, particularly in comparison to that of the non-Jewish fighters. So when Joseph Glazman, an FPO commander, arrived in the Narocz forests with the remnants of his group at the beginning of August 1943, Markov accepted the suggestion that a Jewish fighting unit be established.

The unit was called *Mes't* ("Revenge"). A Jewish paratrooper from Kovno, Z. Ragovski ("Butenas") was appointed commander of the unit, and Glazman was appointed staff officer. The rest of the staff officers, first commanders, and commanders of the secondary units, were likewise Jewish—in fact, most of them were former FPO members from the Vilna ghetto. Glazman and many of his comrades regarded the unit as a practical solution to the problem of the Jews in the forest, as well as a partial realization of the FPO ideal of Jewish warfare under forest conditions. Within two months, the number of fighters in the detachment increased to approximately 250, most of them from groups that continued to arrive from the Vilna ghetto.

A month after the detachment had been formed, it became apparent that its existence was unacceptable to the partisan supreme command. While the representative of the Byelorussian Communist party, I. Klimov, condemned the detachment's existence from a political point of view, Markov prevented it from receiving any additional arms and even requisitioned from it a number of submachineguns that it had received from Ziman. On September 23, 1943, some seven weeks after the "Revenge" detachment had been established, the entire detachment paraded before Markov, who informed them clearly and forcefully that since a large number of the members were armed but had no military training or fighting experience, and since there were superior partisans without arms in other detachments of his brigade, it was imperative that his first concern be their needs. The fighters among the Jews would therefore be absorbed into a Byelorussian unit while the remainder of the brigade would form a productive supply unit that would serve the entire brigade. The parade ended with a confiscation of weapons from a number of Jewish fighters, particularly from women, despite some vigorous protests. "We haven't come here to hide but to fight! We bought our weapons at a high price, and we should not be robbed of them. We girls proved ourselves before we came to the forest," cried a former female member of the FPO, as the weapons she had brought from the ghetto were taken away from her and given, on the spot, to Byelorussian partisans. A few days later, pistols were also taken away from girls who had exchanged their leather coats for them. Boots, leather coats, and other items of value were likewise confiscated, supposedly in order to exchange them for weapons for the brigade. The dispersal of the "Revenge" detachment and its integration into other units was implemented in an equally coarse and humiliating fashion, partly in anticipation of an enemy siege. A small number of armed fighters, including a number of former FPO members, were accepted by the Byelorussian *Komsomolski* detachment.

The situation of the Jews, and particularly of the nonfighters, deteriorated even more when, after a few days, the partisans began to retreat from the forest in expectation of the siege. The siege did actually occur, implemented by tens of thousands of German soldiers and others aided by airplanes and armored vehicles. Shaulevich, the commander of the *Komsomolski* detachment, permitted only Byelorussian partisans and Jews whose weapons had not yet been confiscated to join him when he retreated. By his order, unarmed Jews who tried to follow him were fired upon. The Jewish members of the professional company formed from the "Revenge" unit were ordered to carry stretchers with the wounded to a certain place and to stay there unarmed; some two hundred Jews were thus forsaken. Despite desperate attempts to hide in the marshes and the depths of the forest, more than half of them, including Glazman and his group, perished during the seven-day siege[6]. Only one girl from Glazman's group survived. Even when the siege ended and the detachments returned to their bases, not all the Jews were accepted by partisan units. Many of them, especially those with families, continued to wander in the forest, seeking food in abandoned partisan bases. The young people among them bought food from peasants, sometimes with the threat of their weapons. Despite the dangers involved, they continued to try to join the partisan units of various brigades.[7]

The lot of the Jews among the partisans did not begin to improve until the beginning of 1944, when the Communist authorities intervened and formed committees to investigate the source of the deterioration in discipline and political stability of the partisans in the area. During the winter following the siege, the remnants of the unarmed Jewish fighters were again accepted, for example, by the *Istrebitel* detachment, and reached a total of forty in the *Kalinin* detachment. Markov's command unit again established a professional company; the former members of the FPO, the writers S. Kaczerginski and A. Sutzkever, were ordered by Markov to research and record the history of the brigade. Four or five Jewish doctors from Vilna and the surrounding area were also employed once again on the brigade staff. And while Ziman refused to accept Jewish fighters into his group, which was about to leave for the Rudninkai forests, Šumauskas agreed, after lengthy negotiations, to include more Jews in his brigade.[8] More Jews were also absorbed into the *Chapayev* detachments and even into a number of special units *(Spetzgruppa)*, which until then had not contained a single Jew. Despite the fact that many of these Jews were legally inhabitants and citizens of Soviet Lithuania, they officially belonged to the Byelorussian partisan movement until the liberation by the Red Army, and when their units were dispersed in July 1944, they received certificates from that movement.

WITHIN THE LITHUANIAN PARTISAN MOVEMENT

While Lithuanians and Russians who infiltrated the front lines or parachuted directly into Lithuania could almost always take refuge in their own houses or in those of their relatives, Jewish paratroopers did not enjoy this advantage. It was totally impossible for the local population to absorb them, and they were, therefore, in much greater danger. Moreover, their Jewish origins gravely impeded contacts with the local inhabitants, because of the population's anti-Semitism and because German propaganda identified Jews with Communists and thus as a foreign element among the Lithuanian people. This was apparently why, after the first partisan group, which was commanded by Itzik Meskup ("Adomas") and which was half Jewish, had been sent to Lithuania, the number of Jews in such groups, was limited to an absolute minimum. This minimum included Jews with wide professional knowledge, talent and organizational experience, and a long history of activity in party affairs. From among these, Jews with Lithuanian or Polish accents and appearances were given preference. It should be added that all of them were given distinctly Lithuanian code names. This is also why the proportion of Jewish paratroopers in the Lithuanian partisan movement and the Communist party did not exceed 10 percent (out of some four hundred members), although the number of Jews who worked in the partisan headquarters in Moscow and its branch offices was relatively greater.[9]

The first Jews to join Lithuanian units were refugees from the Svencian ghetto and its surrounding hamlets who had been roaming around in the nearby forests since the spring of 1943, and had not been accepted into other units, largely because they lacked arms. This changed with the formation of the *Žalgiris* brigade, whose commanders were interested in recruiting personnel. In all, some fifty Jews were taken into the brigade, and those who survived until the area was liberated in July 1944 took part in the brigade's festive march through the ruins of Svencian where not a single Jew had survived.

Jews began to reach the Lithuanian partisan movement in the Rudninkai forests when units were first organized there in fall, 1943. A number of the young Jews sent by Ziman from the Narocz and Kazian forests as a vanguard group were absorbed into the "For the Homeland" detachment that was part of the Trakai brigade in September 1943. In November, a number of Jews who had hidden for many months in villages in southeastern Lithuania were also admitted into the detachment. Some forty Jews from the Kovno area and its surrounding towns, who had fled from the Kaišiadorys and Palemonas labor camps, made their way—with the help of partisan scouts—to the "Free Lithuania" detachment of the Trakai brigade. And a few Jews, including some married couples, were absorbed into the "Liberator" detachment. A total of some one hundred Jews were affiliated with the Trakai brigade.

The first three groups, numbering some seventy persons (mostly former members of *Yechiel*) who came from the Vilna ghetto to the Rudninkai forests at the beginning of September 1943, at first maintained military and organizational contacts with a group of paratroopers operating under the aegis of one of the military branches of the Soviet command. Only a few people from this group responded to the paratroopers' offer to accept some twenty refugees from Vilna as fighters, while the rest remained in a family camp. The majority of the refugees refused mainly because they felt that they could not leave the women and the elderly without arms or sufficient means of defense.[10] When additional organized groups from the Vilna ghetto, some of whom were former FPO activists led by Abba Kovner, reached the Rudninkai forests a few weeks later, the leadership of the ever-growing Jewish camp gradually passed into the hands of the activists. The Jewish camp became integrated into the framework of the Lithuanian partisan movement, the vanguard group of which, as stated above, had just reached the Rudninkai forests. With the permission of the commander of this group, four detachments (listed here in order of their establishment) were formed from the Jewish partisans from Vilna and escapees from the Kailis and HKP camps: "The Avenger," "To Victory," "Death to Fascism" and "Struggle." When the Jews from the nearby villages, who had been wandering through the small towns in the area, joined these detachments— particularly the third and fourth—the four detachments comprised a total of four hundred men. The commander of "The Avenger" detachment, Abba Kovner, was at the outset appointed commander of all four detachments.[11]

Despite personnel changes among the Jewish staff, the situation remained fairly stable until a few months after Ziman's arrival in the forest. As commander of the partisans in southern Lithuania, Ziman opposed the existence of separate Jewish units. An attempt on the part of the supreme command in the forest to transfer for tactical or other reasons some 111 persons, including 36 women, from the third and fourth detachments to the Nacza forest, with the agreement of the Jewish command, was to no avail; they returned to their former base after traveling for approximately six weeks with only eleven rifles and two submachineguns through unknown territory controlled by "White Poles."

At the beginning of 1944, a few dozen non-Jewish fighters joined these two detachments and the Jewish commanders were replaced.[12] In the summer of 1944, shortly before the area was liberated by the Soviet army, the commander of the first detachment, Kovner, was also replaced by a Lithuanian paratrooper.[13] Nevertheless, Jews in these detachments continued to hold such posts as commissars and secondary commanders, in the camp staff, and the Jews also maintained a decisive majority.

From the end of November 1943 onwards, organized groups of JFO members from the Kovno ghetto began to reach the Rudninkai forests; by May 1944, they numbered some two hundred. The majority of them were in the three detachments of the Kovno Brigade— *Smert Okkupantam* ("Death to the Conquerors"), *V'period* ("Forward"), and the *Vladas Baronas* detachment. The brigade was principally composed of Soviet officers who had escaped from German captivity. Some ten Jews from the Kovno ghetto were appointed deputy commanders, most of whom were squad commanders. When the units moved west in the spring of 1944, there were some fifty Jewish fighters among them. In contrast to the large number of Jewish fighters in the Kovno brigade who were killed during operations in the Rudninkai forests (fifty out of two hundred) nearly all those who participated in this movement survived. When the Soviet army reached their camping grounds, the Jews hastened to Kovno, where a few ghetto survivors were still living. The others remained in the base in the Rudninkai forests and participated in the partisans' march in July 1944, which included an attack on Vilna to help the Soviet army to conquer the city.

Two additional concentrations of Jewish fighters within the framework of the Lithuanian partisan movement existed in Central Lithuania (Kazlu-Ruda and Kėdainiai) from May 1944 onward. There were also isolated Jewish fighters in other fighting units of the Lithuanian partisan movement both in the Ponevezh (Panevėžys) area and, from spring 1944 on, also in the *Kęstutis* detachment in western Lithuania, which absorbed some of the Jewish groups mentioned below.

OTHER PARTISAN FRAMEWORKS

Lithuanian Jews also joined other fighting frameworks, some of which were not in Lithuanian territory, including partisan units in Poland, where they were dispersed for sabotage activities.[14] There were also a number of quasi-family groups in Lithuania, most of which were not affiliated with regular partisan units. Nevertheless, they were counted among the fighting frameworks not only because they were armed and willing to use their weapons, but also because they were highly motivated to carry on an armed fight against the Germans and those who collaborated with them. They were especially adept at disturbing military transport and supplying information to the Soviet intelligence service.

One of these groups was founded by a family of farmers called Chaluzin from the small town of Kelme in western Lithuania. The family began to wander from village to village and from one peasant house to another at the end of the summer of 1941, when the Jews of Kelmė and the surrounding area were massacred. The three Chaluzin brothers, Shmuel, Yitzhak, and Zvi, and their cousin Jacob Zak, not only succeeded in placing their wives and families in "safe" peasant houses, but also encouraged their fellow townsmen and other Jews from the Kovno and Shavli ghettos to join them, and aided them to this end. They subsequently acquired arms and clashed more than once with the Lithuanian police, who watched their movements closely. In the course of time, they developed an internal communications and warning system which proved efficacious against the persecution and ambushes of the police force. The group also pressured, even terrorized, the peasants whom they suspected of betraying Jews to the Germans, and as a result, betrayals ceased almost entirely in that area. In the course of their activities, they also succored Russian prisoners-of-war in the district. News of this group soon spread among the peasants as well as the Shavli ghetto, and we know that the Jewish authorities and the local underground sent them a number of pairs of vitally needed shoes. In the third year of its existence, when the group numbered some twelve men and eighteen women and children, the majority of the men began spying, mining, and harassing the Germans, in cooperation with a group of Soviet paratroopers based in the area. On the eve of the liberation, the Chaluzin brothers and several members of their group were officially counted among the fighters in the *Kęstutis* partisan detachment, of which the above-mentioned Soviet paratroopers formed the core. At the same time, the group continued to the very end to systematically ensure the safety of the wives and children in their various hiding-places, and after the liberation, they brought a number of the peasants and police who had persecuted them to justice.[15]

Another group of fourteen men and women, most from the little town of Simnas in southern Lithuania, was formed near the town in 1943. It was led by A. Weinstein-Gefen.[16]

NUMERICAL ANALYSIS OF PARTISAN UNITS

The 1,800 Jews who escaped from the ghettos, labor camps, and other places in Lithuania were absorbed in the forest as follows: approximately 450 people were accepted into the fighting units of the Byelorussian partisan movement; approximately 850 people were taken into the fighting units of the Lithuanian partisan movement; approximately 100 people fought in units outside Lithuania, and approximately 250 were in family groups or other units. So, at least 1,650 Lithuanian Jews were active in fighting units and various other groups in the forests, while approximately 150 of those who left for the forest did not reach their destination. Partial information on losses among those who reached the forest can be culled from the data compiled according to Jewish sources, although their estimates are not reliable.[17]

(See Table 7 for an analysis of Lithuanian Jewish partisans who died during World War II.)

Only about half of those who escaped to the forests belonged to underground organizations. (See Table 5.) Thus, the demographic composition of the various partisan frameworks—especially in the family groups, Byelorussian units, and even in a number of Lithuanian units—was different from that of the ghetto undergrounds. This difference resided particularly in the relatively advanced ages of the men and the great number of women, children, and families among them. Among those who left for the forest on their own initiative were a great many from small towns who did not blend in with other Jewish fighters as a whole, particularly in the frameworks mentioned above.

According to a Soviet Lithuanian source published in 1967, the Jews comprised 7.9 percent of the partisans in Lithuania (731 per-

TABLE 7
Lithuanian Jewish Partisans Who Perished during World War II
According to Units and Circumstances of Death

Units	No.	Percent
Total Byelorussian units	52	33
Voroshilev and Spartak brigades	37	24
Leninski Komsomol brigade	15	9
Total Lithuanian units	85	55
Detachments of the Vilna brigade	28	17
Detachments of the Kovno brigade	38	24
The Trakai (Troki) brigade	10	6
The Žalgiris brigade	9	6
Other	19	12
Total	156	100

Circumstances of death	No.	Percent
Total killed in combat	112	72
By Germans	83	53
By "White Poles"	14	9
By Lithuanians	9	6
By peasant guards	6	4
Total killed by partisans	16	10
Officially punished	10	6
Other reasons	6	4
Suicides	9	6
Disease	5	3
In security assignments after leaving the forest	14	9
Total	156	100

sons), a smaller figure than the 850 mentioned above. The Soviet source similarly provides an incorrect figure—four out of ninety-two—for the number of Jewish detachment commanders, while in fact it is known that at least seven Jews occupied these positions in the units of the Lithuanian partisan movement.[18]

The usual ratio of men to women (79.6 percent: 20.4 percent) is not valid with respect to most of the Jewish fighters in these units. Only in the Kovno detachments was the proportion of women among the Jewish fighters identical to their proportion in the Lithuanian partisan movement in general. This phenomenon can be explained, among other things, by the strict supervision and exact quotas imposed on those who left from the Kovno ghetto, especially when compared with the spontaneity characterizing the hasty departures from Vilna and Svencian. For the same reason, there were at least forty-two families with two or more persons (12 percent) among the 303 Jewish partisans from Vilna and the surrounding area, while among the two hundred Jewish fighters from Kovno, there were eighteen (9 percent).[19] An additional demographic peculiarity among the Kovno Jews was that they were relatively younger—between twenty and twenty-five years of age—and, possibly as a result, all had at least some elementary education. At least thirty-five of them had high school or even higher education. At the same time, due to their youth, only some fifteen of them had done military service. Approximately thirty fighters gained experience on the journey to the Augustow forests before they reached the Rudninkai forests. Nearly all came from urban environments, and thus the forests and villages were strange to them. Since they all came from one locale and even belonged to the same umbrella organization (the JFO), the majority of them had already become acquainted in the ghetto or even earlier, in school.

CHAPTER 21
THE JEWISH PARTISANS IN ACTION

THE EXTENT TO WHICH LITHUANIAN JEWS WHO SUC-
ceeded in reaching the forests participated in fighting operations was
largely determined by factors over which they had no control. The
partisan commanders' policies, for example, were determined by
political considerations and sometimes by their disdain for the
fighting potential of the Jews, as well as by their desire to seize arms
for their own purposes. Their age and physical condition as well as
their expertise in skills essential to partisan warfare (for example,
medicine, arms repair, cartography, and printing) also affected the
extent to which they were accepted. Nevertheless, it is possible to
distinguish between those who, for ideological or emotional reasons,
aspired to military roles, and those who, for personal or family reasons, perferred noncombat activities.

Generally, these differences in outlook can be traced to attitudes
former underground members and other Jews held before coming to
the forests as well as to the demographic composition of the groups
and their general attitudes toward active combat, although some
changed once they reached the forest. For instance, some
nonaffiliated Jews became excellent guides and fighters, famous
among the partisans,[1] while several former underground fighters
chose roles not directly linked to combat, or even chose to hide
among the peasants or return to the ghetto. Hence, due to the unique
form of partisan warfare, Jewish partisans were involved in a large
variety of activities in the forests of Lithuania and Byelorussia.

SERVICES AND SECURITY

Although the procurement of arms and supplies and other services
was often as dangerous as the partisans' military activities, incurring

contact with the enemy and personal risk, they were nevertheless rated lower than such "classic" operations as mining trains, attacking enemy garrisons, and destroying lines of communication.

Routine camp services and special services were the two major areas of for Jewish partisans in noncombat service. Routine camp services consisted of preparing and distributing food, setting up and operating health installations (baths, laundry, etc.); maintaining a constant supply of fuel and water; and guard duty. Old men, women, invalids, and wounded men were employed in these activities. Despite the low opinion which the partisans on the whole held of these tasks—essential though they were—they were extremely important as a means of absorbing Jews from the ghettos and labor camps. From the organizational point of view, most of those employed at these tasks were affiliated with the quartermaster department. Since, in the majority of fighting detachments, the administrative department formed an important source of manpower for acquiring arms and supplies in the villages and small towns in the vicinity, some of the lumberjacks and kitchen helpers also participated in fighting activities. Special services consisted of tasks requiring professional knowledge. This included, for example, doctors, nurses, printers, cartographers, and translators. Due to the scarcity of such professions in the forests and to the importance of their role in fulfiling the military and political objectives of the partisan movement, they were highly esteemed by the general partisan population and were in great demand. Senior commanders like Markov and others tried to find Jewish doctors and even sent special emissaries to bring them from the ghettos. Thus, most of the doctors in Markov's detachments were Jewish. A similar situation prevailed in the medical service in the Rudninkai forest. Gunsmiths were also in great demand. Workshops for repairing arms in a number of detachments in the Rudninkai forests such as "Death to the Conquerors" and the "Avenger" were founded and operated by Jewish locksmiths. All the above artisans, as well as tailors, cobblers, and others, did guard duty in the camps, and, of course, fought beside their comrades in the fighting units during ambushes, route marches, and so forth.

COMBAT ACTIVITIES

One indication of the combat success of the Jewish partisans from Vilna comes from a speech by the president of the Lithuanian Supreme Soviet on the day of Vilna's liberation by the Soviet army. It

TABLE 8
Targets of Successful Partisan Attacks

	No. of derailed trains	No. of locomotives	No. of railroad cars	No. of plants	No. of storehouses	No. of bridges	No. of vehicles	Railroad tracks (in miles)	Lines of communication (in miles)	No. of tanks	No. of enemy soldiers
The Vilna detachments	242	113	1,065	12	12	35	257	1,409	4.2	11	4,809
The Kovno detachments	31	40	157	10	5	18	64	370	27.3	1	774
The Svenčionys (svencian) detachments*	143	135	766	21	—	15	48	946	140.4	26	650
The Trakai (troki) brigade	45	—	171	1	5	15	13	374	215.0	—	400
Total	461	288	2,159	44	22	83	382	3,099	355	3	6,633

Source. Staras, *Partizaninis judėjimas Lietuvoje, Vilna, 1966 p. 229.*

195

TABLE 9
Damage Caused to the Enemy by Partisans

	No. of trains derailed	No. of locomotives destroyed	No. of railroad cars destroyed	No. of soldiers injured
By the entire Lithuanian partisan movement	577	400	3,000	14,000
By the 22 detachments (listed in Table 8) in which the majority of the Jews served (viz Tab. 8)	461 (79%)	288 (72%)	2,159 (71%)	6,663 (48%)

praises the way they "broke away to the forests on the day the ghetto was liquidated and continued to fight together with their Lithuanian brothers."[2]

The fighting activities of the four Jewish detachments from Vilna and the surrounding area are listed in more detail in table 8, taken from a Soviet-Lithuanian source that includes data on the damage all partisan units in the Lithuanian partisan movement did to the enemy.[3] Table 8 deals with twenty-two partisan units encompassing 90 percent of all the Jews in the Lithuanian Partisan Movement. A summary of their activities and a comparison with the total number of operations, which, according to another Soviet source,[4] were carried out by the partisan units in Lithuania as a whole, appears in table 9. As the table shows, twenty-two detachments out of the ninety-two in the Lithuanian partisan movement (approximately 25 percent) achieved—in at least four kinds of clearly military operations— between 48 and 79 percent of the total damage. In sum, the majority of the Jewish fighters in the Lithuanian partisan movement belonged to units with distinguished fighting records. Moreover, the four Jewish detachments—which, with respect to the number of their fighters, formed a majority among the eight Vilna detachments (420 out of 760)—had the most outstanding record.

Another, and perhaps more reliable way of determining the military achievements of the Jewish detachments from Vilna is an analysis of the diary of its commander, which describes some of the "Avenger's" activities, under the command of Abba Kovner.[5] The diary tells of a total of 623 male and female fighters under eighteen commanders (only three of whom were not Jewish) taking part in thirty-nine operations in a span of nine months (October 7, 1943–July

8, 1944). Nine of these operations were carried out in cooperation with the "To Victory" and "Death to Fascism" units (the second and third detachments) illustrating the links between the Jewish units. Data on the detachment's first operation—only a few weeks after the fighters had arrived from the liquidated Vilna ghetto—and the date of the last operation—only one day before it left the forest for liberated

TABLE 10
Operations Carried Out by the "Avenger" Detachment

Kind of Operation	No. of Operations	Results
Sabotage of crucial military targets	8	5 bridges, 11 plants, and various installations wrecked; in two cases, products and manufacturing tools destroyed
Dynamiting of locomotives and trains	6	At least 7 locomotives and 33 railroad cars destroyed*
Destruction of lines of communication	3	315 telephone and telegraph poles destroyed
Ambushes	5	At least 212 enemy soldiers killed**
Reprisals and punishment	4	2 enemy agents and a number of peasants who collaborated with the enemy killed; a farm house which served as an enemy headquarters burned down
Destruction of railroad tracks	3	188 miles of railroad tracks dismantled and blown up
Confiscation of weapons from peasants	3	28 rifles, 2 machine guns, 2 pistols and ammunition taken**
Rescue missions	3	71 Jews brought to the forest and absorbed into partisan units
Reconnaissance operations	2	6 enemy soldiers** taken captive; 4 escapees from a German prison camp absorbed into partisan units**

*In a number of places, enemy losses and damage are mentioned without exact numbers.
**Results of other types of operations are also included.

TABLE 11
The Vilna Detachments' Membership in Communist Organizations

	Total No. of Fighters	Communists	Komsomol Members
the "Avenger"	108	7	4
"To Victory"	125	3	15
"Death to Fascism"	107	3	8
"Struggle"	80	6	4
Total	420	19	31

Source: P. Štaras, *Partizaninis judejimas Lietuvoje* [Partisan Movement in Lithuania], (Vilna "Mintis," 1966), p. 248

Vilna are both measures of the detachment's spirit. Detailed descriptions of the operations testify to the Jewish detachment's efficiency.

Similar information on the "Avenger's" achievements is provided in the Lithuanian-Soviet encyclopedia of 1971: they derailed five enemy trains, dynamited two miles of railway embankment, blew up railway tracks on 350 occasions, destroyed five bridges, two factories, one water tower, and three electricity transformers, and cut more than two miles of telephone and telegraph lines. See table 10.

The extent of the military activities of the Jews from the Kovno ghetto, who formed the majority of the "Death to the Conquerors" detachment, can be determined from a summary of the detachment's achievements in a Soviet source: "The Kovno detachment, 'Death to the Conquerors,' destroyed two enemy garrisons (534 soldiers and officers) and derailed sixteen military trains. These fighters were among the main members of the Kovno *Komsomol* and the Anti-Fascist Organization, who had fled from the Kovno ghetto. . . . forty-six partisans from this detachment were killed."[6] It should also be noted here that Soviet sources claim only a few fighters as members of Communist organizations. See table 11.

The intensity of the fighting activities undertaken by the Jewish fighters can be seen from the data on killed Jewish fighters and the data on circumstances of the soldiers' deaths detailed in table 7.

The individual prowess of soldiers and staff often came to the fore during partisan fights which, by their very nature, depended on the concentrated activities of small combat and sabotage groups operating far from their bases. Those fighters who achieved results as saboteurs, especially in mining trains, were particularly esteemed. Among the Jewish fighters in the non-Jewish detachments of the *Voroshilov* brigade who earned renown in this field were B. Yochai, who derailed seventeen trains; A. Leva, who derailed thirteen; L. Warszawczyk, twelve; M. Bushkanitz, ten; S. Bushkanitz, ten; M. Burstein, ten; and Z. Lifshitz, five. A few saboteurs also managed to distinguish themselves in other fields. For example, in addition to blowing up thirteen trains, the fighter Y. Rudnicki ("Tolka") from the *Vilnius* detachment, destroyed a power station in Svencian and a peat-processing plant, helped in the rescue of a wounded partisan from captivity, the destruction of two bridges and three cars, with German soldiers in them, and the capture of four policemen.[7] The painter A. Bogen was also a distinguished fighter and guide. The fame of the veteran fighter, L. Zayontz, (Zaytsev) a squad commander in the "Forward" detachment, spread beyond his own unit for his raids on Lithuanian villages. Scouts were also respected among the partisans, because their jobs required not only excellent fighting abilities but also familiarity with various kinds of intelligence work. Y. Yoels from the *Vladar Baronas* detachment was among the few Jews in a reconnaissance group from the Kovno detachments.

These lines from a document signed by the leader of the Vilna brigade exemplify the activity of Jewish women in the various units. They are about the partisan Sima Kaganovitz, a former FPO member; "She participated in military and administrative duties in the detachment. She was commended twice before parades of the detachment. She was self-disciplined, fulfilled orders correctly, and was a fearless partisan."

It is also noteworthy that a few years after the war, the national Polish government decorated several Jewish fighters. Among them were N. Endlin and P. Klatchko, who received the "Partisan Cross." G. Ziman ("Jurgis"), and A. Chwojnik, (posthumously) received the "Virtuti Milatari" decoration.

SPECIAL PROBLEMS

Many circumstances, not the least of which was anti-Semitism, demanded that the Jewish partisans be more than good fighters. Since the Jewish partisans' role in the acquisition of arms and supply, for instance, was liable to give credence to German propaganda claiming that partisans were synonymous with Jews and robbers, Jewish fighters in this field were ordered to camouflage their origins. Moreover, while the peasants generally behaved civilly to non-Jewish partisans and accepted the expropriation of food from their farms as a necessary evil that was pointless to resist, their reaction to Jewish partisans, at least during the first part of the war, was one of contemptuous opposition, which at times erupted in violent resistance and bloody ambushes. Jews were expected to be more prepared, more belligerent, and more capable of dealing with delicate situations than non-Jews. The relatively large number of Jews who fell at the hands of Lithuanian, Polish, and Byelorussian peasants suggests that a long time elapsed before the peasants learned that "a bullet shot by a Jew strikes home in the same way as a Russian bullet."[8]

In general, fighting operations were dictated by military, political, and economic needs, but occasionally partisans were able to satisfy their own personal and political motives. More than once, Jewish fighters took advantage of situations to take revenge on the murderers of their families: A number of German and Lithuanian prisoners identified as perpetrators of the Jewish massacres in 1941 were shot by Jewish partisans from the *Korchagin* detachment. The desire for revenge was also clearly behind Jewish fighters' enthusiastic participation in punishing Nazi collaborators and in executing Nazi agents who fell into their hands. And in a number of cases, Jewish partisans initiated special revenge operations against identified murderers. A squad of Jewish fighters from the "Avenger" detachment under the command of E. Magid, for example, was sent to catch one Pole who, according to the testimonies of survivors, had taken part in the murder of Jews in the town of Eišiškės (Eyshishok) and had also handed over escapees to the German authorities. There was, however, also a case where the partisan command prevented Jewish fighters from harming a peasant "whose house was decorated with parchment from Torah scrolls and who was reputed to have killed Jews."[9] The reason for the prohibition was that he was a partisan liaison officer.

The dread of being captured which afflicted most of the partisans was particularly strong in the case of Jewish partisans, for certain death, as well as torture and humiliation, usually awaited them. No wonder, therefore, that Jewish partisans preferred to commit suicide rather than fall into enemy hands. The fighter Tania Vinisheski from the "Death to the Conquerors" detachment, the sole survivor of a group of sixteen (including thirteen Jews) who fell in a fight against a garrison in Večioriškiai, killed four Germans and herself with a hand grenade. Apparently, there were at least eight similar cases. It was not always possible, however, for fighters to commit suicide. Such was the case of the paratroopers D. Guterman ("Drutas") and A. Joselevitz (Žiugžda). In a desperate fight against superior enemy forces, they found themselves alone without a hand grenade or bullet with which to kill themselves. The Germans captured them, put out their eyes, and paraded them through the town until they died in terrible agony. There were also cases in which fighters were forced to kill a wounded comrade so that he would not be captured alive. The belief that Jewish fighters would never surrender and that if they were captured, they would never survive was so pervasive that even on those isolated and exceptional occasions when Jewish fighters succeeded in escaping from captivity, it was difficult for them to convince the partisan command that they had not been released by the enemy in order to spy. Such escapees were subjected to long interrogations and regarded with great suspicion even when they returned to their own bases.

CHAPTER 22
THE JEWISH MOTIF

THE FIGHT TO ESTABLISH JEWISH UNITS

THE DELIBERATIONS OF THE LITHUANIAN JEWISH UNDERground organizations with respect to sending their members and other Jews to the forests were based on the supposition that once the escapees had succeeded in reaching the forest, they would organize and fight within the national Jewish units. They would thus stress the national Jewish aspect of the war and be able to implement special military operations on behalf of the Jews interned in the ghetto. On the basis of this supposition, as well as the expectation that the fighters would be able to join the large force that was already concentrated in the Narocz forests, the FPO command delayed the departure to the Rudninkai forests of the majority of its members still remaining in the ghetto. Moreover, quite a number of FPO members considered their move to the forest only a matter of "transferring the front from the ghetto to the forest,"[1] where they would not be obliged to disband. Therefore, immediately after the two FPO leaders arrived in the Narocz and Rudninkai forests with their men, they systematically began to take the necessary steps for establishing exclusively Jewish units.

At first, they were successful, largely because of the timing, for the Soviet partisan movement in the Narocz and Rudninkai forests was then being founded. Furthermore, Jewish and non-Jewish units already existed at that time in Byelorussia, the Ukraine, and Poland, so there were precedents, apparently because certain aspects of Soviet policy encouraged partisans of various nationalities to join the movement. What is more, against this background, F. Markov, one of the commanders of the Byelorussian partisan movement, and G. Ziman, a representative of the Lithuanian partisan movement, agreed to the establishment of a Jewish detachment. In a passionate speech at the detachment's swearing-in ceremony, Markov emphasized the terrible tragedy which had befallen the Jewish people and suggested that the Jewish detachment be given the symbolic name "Revenge."

This detachment was disbanded, however, only seven weeks after its establishment, in accordance with instructions from Moscow, following a new political policy aimed at serving Russia's interests more efficiently. At approximately the same time, Jewish units in other places were also disbanded, as was the Polish *Kosciuszko* unit.[2] I. Klimov, the representative of the Byelorussian Communist party, explained the reasons for his actions quite openly: he believed that the partisan movement was basically composed of national units according to the country in which they were active. Therefore, because the majority of the Jews in the Narocz district were Lithuanian and Byelorussian citizens, they should belong to the territorial units of their own countries. Klimov also hinted that the existence of a Jewish unit was liable to indirectly corroborate German anti-Semitic propaganda, which claimed, as stated above, that partisans were synonymous with Jews and robbers. When Ziman, the representative of the Lithuanian partisan movement, arrived in the Rudninkai forests and found that Jewish fighting frameworks, established by escapees from the Vilna ghetto, were already in existence, he repeated Klimov's claims at his first meeting with the Jewish commander, Abba Kovner. He also underscored the connection between Jewish units and the increase in anti-Semitism: "The partisan movement on Lithuanian soil will one day be the liberator of Lithuania. All Lithuanian partisans, regardless of their religion or origin, are therefore expected to fight against the conquerors within the framework of this movement, unless they have separate objectives!" Kovner's answer was: "We wish to continue in the forest what we began in the ghetto, and to prove that the surviving remnants of those defenseless masses who were slaughtered will continue to fight unresistingly against the murderers of the Jews and their people."[3]

In contrast to the Byelorussian partisan command's ruthless dissolution of the Jewish "Revenge" detachment in Narocz, the Lithuanian partisan command in the Rudninkai forests acted somewhat differently. They did not disband the Jewish Vilna detachments in one fell swoop, but instead gradually replaced the senior Jewish commanders by non-Jews, while they accepted a continuous influx of non-Jewish fighters. The fact that the Jewish Communists who had influence in the Jewish detachments were not united in favoring a continued separate nationalist existence also made it easier for the command to carry out its policy almost until the end of partisan activity in the area.[4] However, because this policy was adopted relatively late—after the four detachments had already succeeded to a large extent in becoming crystallized from an organizational and social point of view—and because it was slow to take effect, the results were only negligible. The detachments continued to remain Jewish both in their composition and in their nationalist and cultural character. The presence of a few dozen non-Jews among 420 Jewish partisans in the Vilna detachments made very little difference.

RELATIONS BETWEEN JEWISH AND NON-JEWISH FIGHTERS

In the absence of a clear military constitution or code of regulations concerning the partisans' duties and relations to each other and to the command, the fate of the Jews in the forest was largely determined by the attitude of their companions-in-arms, on the one hand, and their commanders, on the other. Therefore, in addition to the challenge of adapting to the physical conditions in the forest, Jewish fighters also suffered greatly as a result of their relations with the non-Jewish fighters.

Although cases of Jewish fighters being murdered by non-Jewish partisans were an extreme expression of the attitude of the non-Jews towards the Jews, they were undoubtedly a reflection of the hostile atmosphere in the forest in general and in some of the mixed units in particular. The fact that some of these murders took place during the execution of military duties supported the fears of Jewish fighters who declined to work with non-Jews. For example, S. Shapira, the first casualty among the Jewish partisans in the Rudninkai forest, fell while on a supply mission at the hands of Russian partisans, although he had given the agreed password. From then on, the Jews in the Rudninkai forests tried as much as possible not to include non-Jews in their operations.

In addition to assaults from their comrades the Jewish partisans were the victims of various accusations from the day of their arrival in the forest. For instance, they were frequently ridiculed with the question: "Why did you stay all this time in the ghetto and give the Germans money, and then come here to save your skins?" In military matters, it was widely held that the Jews were cowards and avoided danger. On the other hand, they were criticized as being overly severe in punishing policeman and peasants who had murdered Jews, actions which were said to arouse the population against the partisans. At the end of the siege of the Narocz forest, Jews were even accused of betraying military secrets to the Germans. All in all, Jewish partisans were constantly forced to defend and justify themselves, and refuting these accusations convincingly became one of their chief aims. Thus, for example, the Jewish partisans in the Lithuanian *Kostas Kalinauskas* detachment in the Kazian forests decided that it was essential for them to prove their military prowess. With the agreement of the commander of the detachment, Karvelis, five Jews led by S. Valonas were tested by being required to blow up a train on the Vilna–Leningrad line. And although a special non-Jewish observer reported that the operation was successful, there was no conspicuous change in tthe detachment's attitude toward the Jews. There were, of course, cases of mutual respect, cooperation, and personal friendship between Jewish and non-Jewish partisans, and even an occasional mixed couple, but these were exceptions to the rule. Relationships of this kind were generally described along these lines: "You really are a courageous fighter and excellent partisan, and you don't resemble a Jew at all!"[5] Even in the mixed units, where the soldiers had to come to terms with co-existence and where there were relatively few racial incidents, jibes and jokes at the expense of the Jews abounded, and the distinction between "ours" and "yours" remained until the very last day.

Until the very last day, too, some of the non-Jewish partisans in the forest remained suspicious of the Jews in other detachments, particularly the members of the Vilna detachments whose self-confidence and stalwart nationalism intensely irritated the non-Jews. An incident that took place a few days before the partisans left the forest exemplifies this. The "Avenger" detachment had seized the small town of Rudninkai (Rudniki) unaware that negotiations were then taking place between the Lithuanians and "White Poles," who were also on the point of seizing the town. When the "White Poles" had made the exclusion of any Jewish partisans from Rudninkai town a chief condition of the agreement, the Lithuanians complained that because of the Jews, they had been forced to fight against the Poles.

In sum, a state of near anarchy reigned in the forest until mid-1943, with every armed group acting on its own initiative. With the supreme command's gradual and increasing domination of these groups, however, the position of the partisans, and particularly that of the Jews in the forest, came to depend on the attitude of individual partisan commanders. Moreover, the manner in which the local commanders—and even more the senior commanders—dealt with anti-Jewish incidents, from a case of murder down to sharp verbal attacks, was important not only because it could prevent the repetition of such incidents, but also because it affected the Jewish fighters' morale. In fact, it subsequently emerged that some of the commanders, particularly escapes from prisoner-of-war camps and paratroopers from the Soviet Union were prejudiced against the Jews. Thus, a division commmander from the "Death to the Conquerors" detachment, who through negligence led an obstruction unit to its destruction during a battle against a German garrison in Večioriškiai, claimed in self-defense that he had abandoned his unit because the cowardly Jews did not obey his orders. No less characteristic was the commissar's reply to the Jewish fighters who demanded that the division commander get the maximum penalty; he answered that perhaps the division commander's claim had some basis, since it was known that Jews are not soldiers. However, since the number of casualties was exceptionally high, even in comparison to what was usual in the forest (of the sixteen who died, thirteen were Jews), and since Jewish fighters from various detachments exerted heavy pressure on the supreme command, the commander was brought before a military tribunal, condemned, and sentenced to death.

Usually, sentences for murdering Jewish partisans, as in two cases in the sabotage units of the "Death to the Conquerors" detachment, were minimized, even though the incidents were brought to the attention of the supreme command in the Rudninkai forests. The supreme command generally refrained from intervening in incidents between Jewish and non-Jewish partisans, unless they were likely to lead to the general undermining of discipline and cooperation that were vital to partisan warfare. For example, F. Markov, commander of the *Voroshilov* brigade, declared that the battle against the enemy should not be delayed because of the Jews. And the acting commander of the Vilna brigade in the Rudninkai forests, Gabrys, (M. Miceika) when informed of a complaint made by Jewish partisans about a Russian partisan's boast that he had murdered several Jews, only remarked: "A hooligan, and that's all!" Nevertheless, during negotiations with the "White Poles," Gabrys strongly opposed their demand that Jews be dismissed from the partisan movement. So clearly, the partisan command influenced not only relationships between Jewish and non-Jewish fighters, but every aspect of the Jews' situation in the forest, including their daily lives.

The wide-ranging powers granted senior and junior commanders in dealing with disciplinary offenses were often exercised in all their force against Jewish fighters, whose punishments were often harsh and even exaggerated. At least ten Jews, for instance, were shot in the forest. Even when there were extenuating circumstances for their offenses, the inclination to deal strictly prevailed. Thus, while sleeping on guard duty, a Jewish partisan from the Ukrainian detachment in the Rudninkai forests was shot by his commander without being tried. This strictness with Jews was particularly striking in comparison to the tolerance shown to non-Jews in similar circumstances. Thus, for example, an outstanding Jewish partisan in the K. *Kalinauskas* detachment, Y. Czekinski, was arrested and sentenced to death for procrastinating in carrying out an order when he had not finished cleaning his rifle. However, the Byelorussian partisan from the same detachment who was accused at the same time of breaking his rifle, insulting the commander, and creating a scandal was cleared.

Not every apparent attack on the Jews by the partisan command was an expression of an anti-Jewish attitude. For example, it is clear that purely political and military concerns dictated the number of Jews accepted into the partisan movement in the Rudninkai forests, under a Jewish commander, Ziman. These numbers were in proportion to the national composition of the units, although ghetto fighters, sensitive to the fate of their comrades and their families in the ghettos, could not but feel that such selectivity amounted to brazen discrimination, portending the most drastic results. Confiscations were almost exclusively from Jews, but it must be remembered that escaped Russian prisoners of war had already been stripped of their possessions. However, the degrading manner in which the confiscations were carried out and the doubts about the aim of the expropriations often gave an anti-Semitic impression, especially since they reminded the Jews of the searches carried out by the Germans, memories of which were not easily forgotten. More than once, the Jews voiced their deep disappointment with the situation in the forest by comparing it with the state of affairs in the ghetto, and more than one Jewish partisan must have asked himself, "In what way are these partisans better than the Germans?"[6] This comparison was, of course, exaggerated. Nevertheless, it reflected the mood among many of the Jewish partisans, particularly when they first arrived in the forest.

The situation was especially distressing for fighters who had hopes of engaging in a common fight with other nations against Nazism. And yet in units where the Jews formed a majority, the feeling of discrimination was not as widespread as it was in the mixed units, even though it was never totally absent. The Jews' main complaints against the supreme command in the forest focused on the marked discrimination in the distribution of arms that had been parachuted into the forest. Against this background, friction and tension reached grave proportions, culminating in the dismissal of several Jewish commanders. At the same time, in addition to leveling complaints of discrimination against the *non-Jewish* command, some Jewish fighters voiced somewhat similar complaints against the *Jewish* command.

THE INTERRELATIONSHIP OF JEWISH FIGHTERS

Their common fate in the ghetto and in the forest brought the Jewish partisans very close to one another, and this attachment, as well as their mutual ties, helped them forge a compact and tightly unified community.

This unity expressed itself in various ways, including the warm receptions given to new fighters arriving from the ghetto; material help during shortages of food and clothing; moral support and identification against a background of persecutions and discrimination. Expressions of solidarity sometimes exceeded the bounds of the formal relationships that theoretically existed in the forest, although at the same time, it was the partisan movement's flexible structure that enabled Jews to intervene on behalf of each other. At other times, Jews extended help to other Jews in defiance of clear-cut commands, when for example, Jewish fighters from Kovno gave some of their ammunition to Jewish fighters in the Vilna detachments. In the Narocz forests, Jewish partisans secretly supplied food to Jewish children who had been gathered together and were being supported by a former member of the FPO staff, N. Reznik.[7] The Jewish command of the Vilna detachments deliberately distorted an order from the supreme command not to bring Jews to the forest and instructed the secondary commanders to direct any group of Jews found at the entrance to the forest to bypaths so that peasants and partisans from other units would not notice them. In addition, small "primary" groups with a tradition of joint endeavor dating back to their stay in the ghetto and even earlier continued to exist among the fighters in the forest. These groups included the *Eretz-Yisrael ha-ovedet* group from the Kovno ghetto in the "Death to the Conquerors" detachment, part of the *Yechiel* group from the Vilna ghetto in the Vilna detachments, and, of course, family groups, groups of relatives, and fellow townsmen.

In contrast to these groups, whose existence was officially ignored by the command, some Komsomol and Communist party members continued to operate in the forest in recognizably communist frameworks. The part played by Jewish members within these frameworks was generally limited, because the policy was to conceal the Jewish element and because so many Jews were disappointed with the situation in the forest; they felt their intervention and protests went unheard.

However, Jews in the forest, although markedly united, were not free from conflicts, which could at times be very severe. Occasionally, there were grave social crises among the Jewish fighters as a whole, some of which dated back to the internal argument in the underground organizations in the ghettos. For example, Moshe Gerber, a Jewish partisan from Kovno in the "Death to the Conquerors" detachment, was shot after being accused by some of his comrades of treachery after they were arrested during the journey to the Augustow forests.[8] At least five former ghetto policemen from the Vilna detachments were executed for "serious crimes against their Jewish brethren there."[9] The five reached the forest as members of a *Yechiel* group which, as an organization, voiced grave complaints about the FPO's control of the Jewish detachments, even though the FPO had arrived in the forest after *Yechiel,* and this, coupled with the fact that the confiscation of gold and silver among the Jewish detachments also affected past members of *Yechiel,* caused a commotion among the Jewish partisans as a whole.[10] The argument as to whether the Jewish detachments should continue to exist as a separate entity, which, as stated above, split the Communists in the Vilna detachments, was also based on interfactional conflicts dating from underground activity in the ghettos. An additional subject of complaint on the part of the members of the Jewish detachments against their Jewish commanders was the refusal to accept a number of Jews from small towns, including some women, into the partisan units.[11]

Despite the supreme partisan command's attempt to conceal the importance of Jews in the Lithuanian partisan movement for the sake of their nationalist policy, the Jewish partisans organized a uniquely Jewish way of life in nearly every aspect of life, but especially in communications, entertainment and, to a lesser extent, religion and tradition. Since the majority of the Lithuanian Jewish fighters who came to the forest from thriving Jewish settlements spoke Yiddish so naturally and spontaneously, the use of any other language among them usually seemed unnatural.[12] Under certain circumstances, however, it was essential for them to refrain from speaking Yiddish, when carrying out instructions, for instance, or in the presence of non-Jews. Even so, the Jews in the Vilna detachments continued to use Yiddish for giving orders and instructions, as had been their custom during military underground activities in the FPO. And the evening bonfire became one of the most widespread forms of entertainment in the forest. The atmosphere of hope and intimacy which reigned at such times encouraged those present to express their feelings spontaneously in speech and song. Both Hebrew and Yiddish songs were heard on such evenings, often with the voices of non-Jews joining in.[13] This phenomenon also occurred after the Jewish fighters had become firmly rooted in forest customs and had even adopted some of the Russians' customs, like drinking parties spiked with songs and ribald Russian stories. Additional opportunities for such fêtes were provided by the official Soviet holidays, like May Day, that were celebrated in the forest. Furthermore, despite the fact that the great majority of Jewish partisans in Lithuania were not particularly religious, Jewish festivals and holidays were celebrated at least symbolically in a number of partisan bases. Festivities, including the lighting of Hanukah lamps, were held in various places in the Narocz forests, particularly in family camps.[14]

Since the secondary units and fighting groups were widely scattered and very mobile in a large operative range, the forest served as a communications center, not only for the partisans themselves, but also for the partisans and people and institutions outside the forest and outside the country. Relatives and friends who had been separated by the war and had then been absorbed into the ghettos, now met in the Narocz, Nacza, and Rudninkai forests, and elsewhere, either by chance or after mutual searches. Similarly, remnants of the *Hashomer Hatza'ir* movement from Vilna and Kovno met in the Rudninkai forests after earlier efforts to establish contact while interned in the ghettos. At first their meetings took place by chance, but in the course of time, they held them regularly and even appointed liaison officers for the two camps. A special letter from *Hashomer Hatza'ir* written in Hebrew relating what had happened to the movement in the Polish ghettos, the story of the struggle in the Vilna ghetto, and the lessons to be learned from it, as well as veiled instructions for organizing illegal immigration to Palestine after the liberation, was passed secretly from hand to hand.[15] Then, when they had to depart from the forests, they drew up a general plan for maintaining contact under the new conditions.[16]

In fact, contact was maintained between the forest and the ghettos and labor camps almost until the ghettos were liquidated. Groups who arrived in the forest and emissaries and guides were the chief means of contact, and verbal and written greetings, as well as such essentials as shoes, medicines, tobacco, and saccharine were sent to the fighters on various occasions by families and friends. The Jewish partisans also acted as intermediaries between the Jewish remnants in the ghettos who lived in daily terror of liquidation and with Jews in the Soviet Union. Thus, greetings from Lithuanian Jews whom no one in Lithuania imagined to be alive were received by air or radio from the command of the partisan movement in Moscow and from paratroopers, some of whom served in the Lithuanian Division, and transmitted to the ghettos by emissaries and guides.

Valuable documentary material on the Lithuanian ghettos and Nazi crimes, including a copy of a memorandum composed by the eleven partisans who had escaped from Fort Nine. (See p. 168.) was also collected by Jewish partisans in the forests and transported by air to Moscow. Similarly, A. Sutzkever, a poet from Vilna, carried original material about the Vilna ghetto and the mass execution site at Ponary, when he was flown to Moscow from the Narocz forests on March 12, 1944. During his stay in Moscow and elsewhere in the Soviet Union, Sutzkever gave various people and institutions verbal and written descriptions of the fate of the Jews of Lithuania and the surrounding area and delivered a speech at the fourth convention of the Jewish Anti-Fascist Committee in April 1944. When some of this material was published by the local Jewish committee, Jewish refugees in the Soviet Union found their children in a photograph from the Kovno ghetto.[17] While he was in Moscow, Sutzkever also continued to exchange letters with the Jewish partisans in the Narocz and Rudninkai forests. In one of the letters, he was requested by the commander of "The Avenger" detachment, Abba Kovner, to negotiate in Moscow for increased arms deliveries to the Jewish detachments.[18]

With special instructions from Ziman, the head of the Lithuanian partisan movement in southern Lithuania, Abba Kovner wrote a proclamation to world Jewry. The package with the manuscript, which was supposed to be sent to Moscow by "partisan post," also included a Hebrew poem entitled *Ve-hayah Levavkha Kinor* (Let your Heart be a Harp), by Abba Kovner, which he signed with his underground name, "Uri." Unlike the proclamation, which was apparently put into "cold storage" in Moscow, the poem finally arrived in Palestine and was published in the newspaper *Ha'aretz* before the end of the war.[19]

CHAPTER 23
PORTRAIT OF THE "STRUGGLE" UNIT

BACKGROUND

This chapter describes a number of leading traits of the fourth Jewish partisan detachment from Vilna, "Struggle" *(Bor'ba)*. Because it began as a purely Jewish unit and became mixed in the course of time, it represents the general partisan framework in Lithuania from both the inter-Jewish and the Jewish and non-Jewish perspective.

Perhaps an even more compelling reason to study the "Struggle" detachment is the existence of a document, dated July 25, 1944, that describes in detail seventy-six of the fighters in the detachment. This unique document gives rare, first-hand information on the make-up and history of the Jewish partisans and their comrades. (See fig. B3.)

The nucleus of the "Struggle" detachment comprised Jews who arrived in the Rudninkai forests from the Kailis labor camp, a camp for Jewish professionals, located next to the Vilna ghetto that remained in existence even after the ghetto was liquidated in September 1943. Given the haste with which they fled from the camp before the ghetto was liquidated, the group consisted of a considerable number of Jews who had not been members of underground organizations in the ghetto.

When they arrived in the forest, A. Aharanovicz, the former commander of the FPO in the Kailis camp, was appointed commander of the detachment by the Jewish partisan command. Because some of the squad commanders selected were also former FPO activists, it seems that the Jewish partisan command was apparently trying to keep the social and military framework of the "Struggle" detachment aligned with the national and communal tradition of the FPO.

Because the same political commissar was attached for a time to both units, the "Struggle" detachment also shared some of the same military, organizational, and geographical traits as the "Death to Fascism" detachment (the third detachment). And yet, apparently there was little similarity from either the social or the compositional point of view between the first and second detachments—which were primarily composed of veteran underground fighters, activists, and commanders from the ghetto—and the third and fourth detachments, in which Jews from the ghetto predominated. This distinction seemed to bring the leaders of the first and second detachments, and those of the third and fourth detachments closer together, while relations between the political commissars of these units remained tense.[1] All these factors came to the fore particularly when part of the Jewish force in the Rudninkai forests was sent (for tactical and military reasons) to the Nacza forests. There are grounds for assuming that it was no chance decision that the third and fourth detachments were ordered to leave. In any case, the Jewish partisan command decided to reinforce the ranks of those who were leaving and added to their number some commanders from the first and second detachments who were veterans of the underground in the Vilna ghetto.

One hundred and eleven people, including thirty-six women, took part in the expedition to the Nacza forests that began on November 4, 1943. They possessed eleven rifles and two submachineguns. Their path led through dangerous territory, riddled with units of "White Poles," and it was only by the use of careful stratagems that they succeeded in avoiding enemy ambushes.[2] After a few days, to their bitter disappointment, it became clear that at least at that stage, the plan to create a base in the Nacza forests was impractical. The feeling of despair and disappointment heightened when the commanders of the expedition decided to send ninety insufficiently-armed fighters back to the Rudninkai forests, accompanied by two or three squad commanders, while the other commanders continued to search for a more suitable site.[3]

Weakened physically, their morale at a low ebb, and their entire stock of weapons consisting of no more than two rifles, the ninety fighters nevertheless succeeded in returning to the Rudninkai forests (in mid-December 1943), and in accordance with instructions from the command of the brigade, the third and fourth detachments were reestablished. Squad commander İ. Lubotzki, who had led the return journey, was appointed commander of the "Struggle" detachment. The position of deputy-commander was filled by squad leader N. Kaganovicz, formerly attached to the expedition from the first detachment.[4] Later, when the original commander of the detachment, A. Aharanovicz, returned with the team of commanders who had left the expedition at various times, he was reduced to the rank of private. The revived "Struggle" detachment, which then totaled between sixty and seventy Jewish fighters, was aided to a certain extent by arms lent by the third detachment. However, despite the efforts of the new commander, Í. Lubotzki, to raise the social and military level of the detachment, the lack of arms left its mark on the fighting proficiency of the unit. The detachment was also below par from the social and disciplinary points of view; apparently, the detachment's composition and the Nacza expedition, created a profound social rift.

The problem of the lack of arms was partially solved in a dramatic, if not unexpected manner. Some time earlier, it had been rumored that the brigade's command had decided to abolish the Jewish units, to give at least official support to the claim that the partisan movement in the conquered Lithuanian Soviet Republic was the product of Lithuanian mass initiative. What remains surprising is the manner and speed with which this policy was carried out. At the beginning of 1944, the Lithuanian commander V. Šilas (Shilas) arrived in the detachment accompanied by ten well-armed Russian fighters. Soon after, at a parade arranged for the occasion, he announced to the astonished Jews, in the name of the brigade's command that, because of its lack of fighting experience and the inefficiency with which the detachment's partisan activities were implemented, the command would be replaced and reorganized.[5] Šilas himself took over command of the detachment; some of the Russian fighters with him (former prisoners of war) were appointed staff officers and deputy commanders. Captain Ivan Vasilenko was appointed chief-of-staff, and a number of changes were made in the duties of the Jewish commanders.[6] A similar "operation" was carried out on the same day in the third detachment, "Death to Fascism."

The personnel changes, which were startling in their suddenness, were accompanied in the course of time by qualitative changes in the military proficiency of the unit and its social life. These changes apparently evolved because the unit then possessed abundant arms (the only occurrence that was readily and even enthusiastically received by the startled Jews). At the same time, there was a marked increase in combat activities. Military discipline was henceforth far more strict, and with a severity the fighters were not used to. The increased strictness was felt particularly with the appointment of chief-of-staff Vasilenko as commander of the unit. The surviving Jewish fighters who served under Vasilenko hold differing opinions of his personality and attitude toward the Jewish partisans.[7] In any case, they concur that during the period of his command, intensified military activity was coupled with an enormous rise in the number of Jewish losses. The circumstances of the deaths of Tamara Rashel (due to the treachery of a non-Jewish fighter who was afterwards caught and executed in the base) and I. Lubotzki (who was killed with four subordinates when forced to saw through telegraph poles immediately after returning from another operation without sufficient respite being granted them) particularly aggravated the feelings of bitterness and depression. Among the Jews, the incident was also linked to the presence of non-Jews in the command and in the ranks, one of whom, Major Kolosov, the new Russian commissar, who believed in separating couples[8] among the Jewish fighters, was later found to be a traitor who had surrendered to the Germans and was serving them.[9]

It is also apparent that not all the Jews were satisfied with the tremendous increase in military activity and associated it, perhaps correctly, with the presence of Russians in the unit.[10] This certainly did not pass unnoticed by the Russians (some of whom were not free of prejudices against the Jews, which dated back to their captivity in German camps or even previously). In any event, snide remarks and hints to the effect that Jews from the ghettos lacked partisan experience and military skill were heard frequently in the detachment, as was criticism of the presence of women in the camp. The Jewish fighters, for their part, were experts in discovering which of the former Russian prisoners of war had served the Germans as ghetto guards or elsewhere and did not allow matters to rest. In one case, a Russian commander, who had behaved arrogantly during training and pusillanimously in action, was attacked in a caricature that was published in the detachment's wall newspaper. At other times, the two sides came to blows.

Jewish fighters (including women) were nevertheless occasionally recommended by the command and their non-Jewish comrades for efficiency in carrying out military operations and various other duties. And in addition to the official celebrations, which closed the gaps in rank and origin and brought Jews and non-Jews together, their common concerns, like fighting and arms acquisition operations, in which nearly all the partisans participated, and the distribution of weapons that had been parachuted in and were allocated to all the fighters without exception, helped at times to ease the tension.

Each squad now possessed seven submachineguns and eight rifles—a tremendous improvement since the first stage of the detachment's existence.[11] The detachment's strength also increased with the influx of fighters from the surrounding hamlets who had been wandering until then in the forests and from one farm to another. The latter had no military experience but knew the paths in the area well. In addition, they participated in internal camp duties and proved themselves capable of enduring hardship. They particularly distinguished themselves in operations to procure arms and supplies from nearby villages. The ranks swelled again in the summer of 1944, when an enemy train was captured and a number of Russian prisoners were brought to the detachment. As there were doubts as to their reliability, the prisoners were placed under the constant surveillance of the special division. The Jews feared to work with the prisoners and even the veteran Russians "did not like them and perhaps did not believe them, because in the final analysis, each knows his own kind."[12] Nevertheless, since the Russians had arrived at a time when arms were abundant, they received automatic weapons and were integrated rapidly. Whether for practical and justified reasons, or from force of habit, the special division also spied on the Jewish fighters with help from, among others, the members of the Communist Party cell.

While the Soviet-German front drew closer daily and the echo of machinegun fire could already be heard, the harassment of the retreating German army continued at full strength. The fighters in the "Struggle" detachment worked with the aid of arms and explosives which had been parachuted in to them, particularly on the Vilna–Salčininkai highway. On July 8, 1944, the entire brigade with all its fighters and weapons moved in the direction of Vilna in order to aid the Soviet army in mopping up the city, which had just been liberated.

The "Struggle" detachment suffered from a series of crises and hardships. At first, the structure of the detachment was rather weak, particularly as a result of an internal security crisis, which expressed itself, by, among other things, frequent changes in command. And although the command later achieved greater stability and the standard of fighting rose and the unit was closely knit from the military point of view, the period was nevertheless marked by social disturbances and tension between the detachment's two separate groups and a new command which was received unenthusiastically by the "founding fathers," that is, the Jews. With this background, certain events (such as the discovery of traitors among the non-Jews, contempt for discipline on the part of the Jews, or unwillingness to participate in military operations) acquired special significance and served as grounds for complaint against each of the groups. At the end of this period, there were signs of a reconciliation and a *modus vivendi* was established. This ceased, however, with their departure from the forest and the renewed distance between the groups.

"People like you are needed here to start up life again," declared Ziman, who had returned to a high-ranking civil position three days after the liberation, to the commander of the Jewish camp, Abba Kovner, when Kovner proposed that volunteers from among the Jewish partisans be parachuted into Germany. In fact, only a few of the survivors participated for any length of time in the rebuilding of the Soviet Lithuanian Republic.

Most of the partisan detachments in the area reached Vilna from the forests in coordination with the Soviet army and were charged with such duties as purging the city of Germans and guarding installations or storehouses. At the same time, the process of disbanding the units was begun by removing their weapons and placing individual partisans in military and civil jobs. Upon his demobilization from the detachment, each fighter received a written certificate stating the length of time he had served in the unit, his rank and his position. It may be surmised that the list we have used as the basis of this profile was designed to serve as the background for these certificates, as well as for the purpose of distributing civilian clothing sent from the United States to the fighters. It is also probable that the purpose of the document was to authenticate information pertaining to the composition of the Lithuanian partisan movement, which was divided into tens of units all over Lithuania and Byelorussia. And yet, given the date on the document, there can be no doubt that it was revised in Vilna, three weeks after the city had been liberated by the Soviet army. For this reason, and because it was apparently compiled primarily for administrative purposes, the list does not include names of fighters who were killed, wounded, transferred to other units, or flown to Moscow. Still, it is a unique document, which provides a momentary glimpse into a military framework that was chiefly composed of Jewish fighters.

FINDINGS AND CONCLUSIONS

The findings from this document can be summarized as follows:

1. In the "Struggle" detachment of the Vilna brigade, which numbered seventy-six fighters during the last stages of its

existence, the Jews were greatly in the majority (four-fifths of the detachment). Most of the non-Jews were Russian.

2. There were eight times the number of women among the Jewish fighters (usually between the ages of twenty and thirty-nine) than among the non-Jewish fighters.

3. Nearly half the Jewish fighters were related to one another; none of the non-Jews were related.

4. There was a greater range of age among the Jewish fighters than among non-Jews, that is, more of the Jewish fighters were under nineteen and over forty, and fewer of the accepted military age (20–39).

5. Only twenty Jewish men were between the ages of twenty and thirty-nine, which was sixty percent of this age group in the detachment.

6. The majority of fighters, both Jews and non-Jews, were educated for more than seven years. The Jews formed a slight majority of those who had seven to ten years of education; among those with eleven years of education or more, Jews and non-Jews were more or less equally balanced.

7. Approximately three-quarters of the fighters in the detachment had been white- and blue-collar workers before the war. The rest had been students.

8. The majority of these former students were Jewish.

9. There was no great difference between Jews and non-Jews in the general professional make-up of the detachment.

10. Approximately one-eighth of the fighters in the detachment belonged to the Communist party. Most of them were the non-Jewish fighters.

11. Most of the Jewish Communists belonged to the *Komsomol* (Communist Youth Organization), which they had joined after becoming members of the detachment.

12. Nearly all the Jewish fighters were originally from the Vilna area; about half of them were among the group from the Vilna ghetto that had first formed the detachment.

13. Approximately one-third of the Jewish fighters were from small towns near Vilna (including a considerable number from the town of Voronovo), and most of them had not been interned in the ghetto; they had sought refuge in farms and forests in the vicinity. From there, they reached the detachment and found the Jews who had already arrived from the Vilna ghetto.

14. Most of the Jews in the detachment were veterans, as opposed to the Russians, who had arrived relatively late, after having escaped from German captivity.

15. There were eight Russians but only three Jews in command

positions and other important posts in the detachment, that is, in inverse proportion to their ratio in the detachment. Only a negligible minority of Jewish fighters had military backgrounds or experience, and the same is true, relatively speaking, of the non-Jewish fighters.

From these data, it is possible to form a picture of the demographic, cultural, and military character of the "Struggle" detachment, and by analogy, of other mixed units, at least those operating in that area. In addition to the characteristics enumerated above, such factors as their desire for revenge, their ideology (which saw fighting as a means of realizing an ideal), and self-preservation influenced their fighting spirit and motivated them to superior combat. Still, despite the lack of additional data, we can conclude that non-Jews were probably more proficient in combat than the Jews; we know, at least, that the majority of the commanders and those in key positions were non-Jews. A fairly clear picture of the "Struggle" detachment's military hierarchy, and the national composition of each group within that hierarchy emerges as follows:

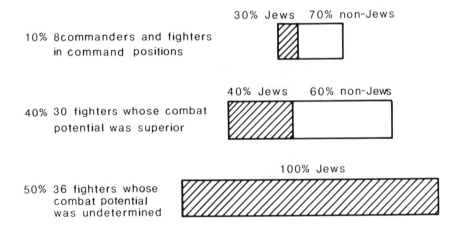

The above is a standard pyramid which applies to almost every independent military fighting framework led by a small command. The middle section represents the active fighting force while the lowest designates those who provide supplies and services. Although the men who acquired arms and supplies were undoubtedly very important, superior fighters, whose main task was to cause as much damage as possible to the enemy, were more highly esteemed. Thus, the military hierarchy more or less corresponds to social status within the detachment. The Jews did not occupy equal positions in each stratum of this social structure. Most of them belonged to the lowest stratum ("hewers of wood and drawers of water"); a minority in the middle stratum (rank and file fighters) and a negligible percentage in the highest stratum. This raises two questions: How much did the social structure influence the quality of the relations between the Jewish and non-Jewish fighters? and, to what extent did it influence the nature of inter-Jewish relations?

A social structure of this kind inevitably causes deterioration in the relations between the various groups. For example, it is very reasonable to suppose that the non-Jewish partisans identified their place within the hierarchy with their national origin; consequently, the non-Jewish fighters were likely to regard themselves as an elite and to cultivate status symbols. In any event, they were liable to regard the Jews as an inferior class (with the exception of those who had succeeded in penetrating the intermediate or highest level). In addition, the facts that the Russian fighters had a common background (Russian culture and their experiences as German prisoners of war) and that the military and political bases of the partisan unit were distinctly Russian (the Supreme Partisan Command was in Moscow and Russian was the language of command) probably augmented the Russians' feeling of superiority. On the other hand, the Jews' internal solidarity, a result of their joint fate and their suffering during the Nazi occupation, was intensified by the injustice of their position; after all, they had been the first to join the ranks of the partisans and to form the detachment.

Another problem in the social structure was the presence of a large number of Jewish women, which not only affected the Jews' fighting potential, but also incited jealousy among the non-Jewish fighters, for two reasons: the number of women among the non-Jews was negligible, and the Russians had spent a great deal of time in the all-male society of captivity, which may well have aggravated their envy. Hence, tensions between the groups may have risen to crisis proportions and, at times, thrown the unit's continued existence into doubt, while hindering their achievement of its principal aim— establishing a strong position against the enemy they wished to defeat.

However, just how divided the groups were and how much the party united the fighters and dissipated the inter-group tension cannot be precisely determined.

It is possible, for instance, that the Communist party cell, the

Komsomol, and others, which penetrated all ranks of the military hierarchy, were able to unite all the fighters under the banner of the higher aims of the detachment. At the same time they may also have been able to organize all its members into special, and necessarily binational framworks and to stabilize relations. The document does show that the Communist party was at least significant enough to be considered in terms of its dimensions and national composition, and it also suggests that the Jews were affiliated with the party (either through identification with its higher aims or with the hope of gaining higher status in the unit).

One must also remember that the command was, in reality, charged with balancing the forces within the detachment. The command was composed of the detachment commander, the political commissar, the head of the special division and the intermediate commanding ranks. In order to fulfill this role, the command (in addition to the official authority it derived both from the confirmation of its powers by the Supreme Partisan Command in the area and from the members of the local command staff) would have had to enjoy a certain degree of recognition from the majority of the fighters from both national groups. And yet, it seems that neither the command nor the party were able to abate continual crises in the unit.

CHAPTER 24
SUMMING UP

THE JEWISH MINORITY IN LITHUANIA ACTIVELY PAR-
ticipated in the country's struggle for independence at the end of
World War I, whereupon they enjoyed full equality of rights and even
cultural and social autonomy within sovereign frameworks. At the
same time, nearly all Lithuanian Jews were involved to some extent in
an educational and cultural network based on Hebrew, Yiddish, and
nationalist principles, which increased their characteristic national
consciousness. This state of affairs continued until World War II.
However, the economic and political position of the Jews, as well as
their relations with the Lithuanians, deteriorated from year to year
and reached a crisis when Lithuania became a Soviet republic in 1940.

The fact that the Jews regarded the Soviets, in comparison with
the Nazis, as the lesser of two evils was interpreted by the Lithuanians as treachery and encouraged them to collaborate with the Nazis
in the murder of Jews, particularly in the wake of the German invasion of Lithuania. The Nazis conquered Lithuania on June 22, 1941,
within days of the invasion of the Soviet Union. Out of approximately
a quarter of a million Jewish inhabitants (including the Jews from
Vilna, which was annexed to Lithuania in October 1939), some fifteen
thousand Jews succeeded in escaping in various ways to the Soviet
Union. The majority of those remaining in Lithuania were massacred
by the Lithuanians and the Germans, particularly in a series of pogroms, mass murders, and *Aktionen* led most effectively by the *Einsatzgruppen*. By the beginning of 1942, only forty thousand Jews
remained in all of Lithuania, and most of them had been incarcerated
in the ghettos of Vilna, Kovno, Shavli, and Svencian. In spite of
further *Aktionen* and deportations, these ghettos survived until 1943–
1944, not long before the Soviet army's defeat of the Germans.

Characteristic of both the Jews who remained in the ghettos and of the refugees in the Soviet Union was their increasing inclination to fight actively against the Nazis, in forms ranging from self-help organizations to active resistance to their liquidation. For most, the realization of this desire depended upon their contacts with the Soviet military and political network, or with the partisan groups under Soviet authority. In view of the fact that during the Soviet regime (1940–1941), the Soviets had tried to demolish Jewish national culture and had forced the Zionist movements underground, their situation was, to say the least, highly problematic.

The acceptance of Jews into regular military frameworks in the Red Army was limited at first, partly because government and army officials regarded the population in the western border area, which had only recently been annexed to the Soviet Union, with suspicion. Two factors were crucial in changing this. First, the Lithuanian's traditional hatred of the Russians, which dated back to the Czarist oppression and the Bolshevists' abortive attempt to renew their dominion over Lithuania in the form of a Soviet republic in 1918, had led to close collaboration between the Lithuanians and the Germans in driving out the Red Army from Lithuania and to mass Lithuanian enlistment in auxiliary units of the German Army. Second, the Soviets were engaged in an ardent diplomatic struggle with their allies in the West over future borders and spheres of influence in Europe, and especially over the Baltic countries (including Lithuania). So, to strengthen her position, the Soviet Union endeavored to prove to the world, in general, and to the Lithuanians, in particular, that not only did the Lithuanian people identify with the war against the Germans, but that they were actively engaged in armed combat for the survival of the Soviet Lithuanian Republic. Among other methods of proving this, the Soviet Union established Lithuanian fighting units, both on the front, with the Sixteenth Lithuanian Infantry Division, and in the rear, with a partisan movement whose leadership was especially parachuted into Lithuania.

Due to the hostile attitude of the majority of the Lithuanian people, it was clear to the Soviets that the principal source of manpower for these fighting units was likely to come from among the Jews. Therefore, when the frameworks were first established, the Soviets strongly encouraged Jews to join them. Subsequently, however, when the front came closer to Lithuania and the Soviets had to win the sympathy of the Lithuanian population and to persuade them to join the ranks first of the partisans and, later, of the Lithuanian Division, they no longer required Jewish fighters, and especially Jewish partisans. The number of Jews in partisan units was strictly limited and in the division, a policy of national control was initiated in order to balance the ratio between Jews and non-Jews in party institutions, from the level of intermediate command upwards, and in the distribution of decorations of the highest order, such as the "Order of the Hero of the Soviet Union."

Let us review the characteristics of this fighting unit, with regard to the Jews' unique position in it:

1. The Jews constituted a majority, at least temporarily, in a considerable number of rifle and other units in the Lithuanian Division.
2. The facts that there was a large concentration of Jews in these units with remarkably strong national cultural traditions (almost all spoke Yiddish, some 70 percent knew Hebrew), and that the staff was composed exclusively of Jews, at least in the intermediate and lower ranks, all contributed to the creation of a thriving Jewish community. The Yiddish language was used predominantly in the Jews' everyday lives, and also served at times as the official military communications language.
3. The common cultural and national background which broke down all social barriers and the large concentration of relatives, fellow townsmen, classmates, and colleagues manifested themselves in widespread mutual help and solidarity.
4. Common concern for the fate of their families and deep sorrow for the slaughter of relatives not only increased the Jews' feelings of solidarity with one another, but also moved a considerable portion of the Jewish fighters to stress the need to fight for personal and national revenge. Military and political commanders also exploited these desires for revenge, particularly on the eve of a battle.
5. The location and special position of the division helped to render it a communications center for Jews throughout the Soviet Union and all over the world, including Eretz Yisrael and Lithuania, during the Holocaust and, even more so, during its final stages. The same was true of some eight to ten partisan units, which belonged to the strongest combat brigades in the Lithuanian partisan movement, after members of Jewish underground organizations and isolated invididuals from the ghettos and labor camps had joined them.

These features, unknown in any other fighting unit during World War II (except for units from within the British Army) were also dependent to a great extent on the political situation into which the units had been born. For example, in the Lithuanian Division there was a campaign to correspond with relatives abroad, including those in Palestine, even though this created an unavoidable conflict in interests when policy demanded that the ethnic-Jewish factor be submerged. In certain cases, this conflict in interests caused friction between the Soviet commanders and the Jewish fighters, which occasionally led to the employment of anti-Jewish propaganda and extreme disciplinary action (as when the Jewish members of the Lithuanian Division suffered a crisis in confidence upon entering Lithuania). At times, organizational action was taken, such as the disbanding of the Jewish units and replacement of commanders (as in the cases of the "Revenge," "Avenger," and "To Victory" detachments).

In the four major ghettos, armed resistance organizations operated clandestinely from the beginning of 1942, with a membership of at least 1,500 men and women—the majority of whom were former members of Zionist youth movements and other organizations. The principal aims of these organizations differed, mainly in the degree of emphasis placed on armed resistance in times of danger; fighting against the Germans and those who collaborated with them; and saving Jewish lives in various ways.

Unlike the resistance organizations in the Kovno, Svencian, and Shavli ghettos, which decided without wracking internal crises to flee to the forests and fight in the ranks of the partisans, the two underground organizations in the Vilna ghetto fought bitterly over whether to fight in the ghetto or in the forest. Due to a number of factors, such as strong ties and contacts with Polish Jewry, geographical location, the ethnic composition of the population in the area, and a tradition of self-defense, underground activity in the Vilna ghetto developed with greater intensity than in the Svencian and Kovno ghettos, and even more so, the Shavli ghetto. Shavli was located in the heart of a hostile Lithuanian population far from a wooded area necessary for clandestine partisan activity. In the Vilna ghetto, the underground also organized a campaign to warn various Jewish communities of the Germans' plans to exterminate them, and on the eve of the ghetto's liquidation, carried out an attack on Nazi security forces that was unique in the history of Lithuania during the Holocaust. Unlike the situation in the Kovno and Shavli ghettos, where the Jewish police actually cooperated with the organizations by furnishing military instruction and aiding them in the acquisition of arms and supplies, in Vilna the tension between the Jewish ghetto authorities and the resistance organizations sometimes had grave consequences.

Some of the members of the underground who were caught by

the Germans and deported to concentration camps in Germany, Estonia, and Latvia continued to develop clandestine cultural activities, as well as plans for escape and resistance. Small organizations also operated in a number of labor camps in Lithuania, either as branches of the organizations in the larger ghettos, or as independent movements, and some of their members succeeded in escaping from the camps and joining partisan units.

Some 1,800 persons fled to the forests from ghettos and labor camps in Lithuania, either on the initiative and with the help of the underground organizations, or individually and in family groups. The majority of them were absorbed by units of the Lithuanian partisan movement and Byelorussian units, and a few by family camps. So, in all, the Jewish resistance and fighting movement in Lithuania numbered at least ten thousand men and women, distributed as follows: some six thousand men served in the Lithuanian Division during the entire span of its existence; some two thousand in other units of the Soviet army as well as in the Polish armies; and more than two thousand were affiliated with resistance organizations in the ghettos and labor camps or served in the ranks of the partisans. This figure clearly demonstrates that Lithuanian Jewry took full advantage of the possibilities for armed struggle against the enemy.

A further statistical breakdown reveals the following: 1) Those ten thousand Jews constitute 4 percent of the 250,000 Jews living in Lithuania on the eve of the Nazi invasion; and 2) They also constitute approximately 16 percent of the total number of Lithuanian Jews who survived in Lithuania and the Soviet Union at the beginning of 1942, that is, after the mass murders which caught the Jews unaware, prior to the formation of the Lithuanian Division and the Lithuanian partisan movement. (This percentage approaches the accepted estimate of the typical civilian draft in wartime: 20 percent.) The particular conditions prevalent in Lithuania, the difficulties in finding acceptance within a partisan framework, the bitter arguments and sometimes sacrifices which accompanied such ventures, lend a further meaning to these figures. In any event, there is no doubt that Lithuanian Jewry played a greater part (at least proportionately) in the anti-Nazi struggle than did the Lithuanian people, to whom Soviet historiography attributes—to the detriment of the Jews—a high place of honor in the "Great Patriotic War."

In this context, and in the light of the bitter internal conflicts among the ghetto Jews, one must wonder whether the Jewish struggle to save Jews was an aim in itself. The question is especially relevant in the light of the following fact: out of a quarter of a million

Lithuanian Jews, no more than 10 percent—25,000—survived the war. The number of survivors among the fighters alone, who are also included in this 10 percent, was between five and six thousand. Against the possible claim that at least five thousand persons were saved through the fighting frameworks, we can correctly assert that, on the contrary, thousands of Jews perished as a direct result of their membership in these frameworks. For example, a relatively greater percentage of Jews (some 15 percent) survived in the Shavli ghetto where the resistance movement was the least developed. In the Val-kininkai Olkeniki community, on the other hand, where the prewar population numbered only some thousand Jews, only forty-one survived: four camp and ghetto inmates; twenty-five escapees to the forest who joined the partisans; nine Red Army soldiers (including members of the Lithuanian Division), and three people who were deported from their hometown to Siberia by the Soviet authorities. This demonstrates that pure statistics do not entirely answer the questions we have posed.

There is no doubt that struggle and self-defense were the natural human reactions to an attempt at the annihilation of the Jews. At the same time, a number of incidents, including the example of the Vilna ghetto, where the battle of the barricades on September 1, 1943, even with its meager results, shows that the urge to fight and resist was more emotional than logical; the preferred course of action was the honorable one, even when it was not necessarily the most practical or productive for the rescue of large numbers of Jews. Hence, the historical importance of Dr. Elkes's words, spoken in defense of extending help to the Jewish underground in Kovno, will always outlive all other considerations: "This is the honorable road which we should choose. I shall bear all the responsibility—it is for the good of the remnant of Lithuanian Jewry, and the Jewish people as a whole. Every opportunity for resistance should be exploited, especially when it is a question of honorable combat."[1]

APPENDIX A
PROFILES OF THE "HERO OF THE SOVIET UNION" RECIPIENTS

THE FOLLOWING IS A DESCRIPTION OF SOME ACTS OF heroism of the Jews from the Lithuanian Division who were named "Hero of the Soviet Union."

Major Wulf Vilenski,
Commander of a Rifle Battalion in the 249th Rifle Regiment

On October 12, 1944, Vilenski commanded a battalion in the Tilset sector against a German infantry brigade reinforced by twenty tanks and a self-propelling cannon. Leaving his main forces to face the enemy, Vilenski penetrated the enemy's rear at the head of a rifle company and a machinegun platoon and hit more than one hundred German soldiers and officers. (Several dozen were bounded by bullets from his own machinegun.) Although he was wounded, Vilenski continued to fire his machinegun while his unit repulsed eight counterattacks for two consecutive days, enabling the division's main force to advance as planned. For this operation, Vilenski was awarded the order of "Hero of the Soviet Union" according to instructions from the Supreme Soviet. He had previously been awarded the following medals: the "Red Banner" (twice), "Alexander Nevski", "The Patriotic War" Class I, and the "Red Star." At the end of the war, he was appointed commander of the 249th Regiment, with the rank of lieutenant-colonel. After the war, he served as commander of the city of Kovno with the rank of colonel. In 1983, he arrived in Israel.

Staff Sergeant Kalman Shur,
Artillery Commander in the 249th Rifle Regiment

In October 1944, when the division was fighting its way across the Nieman river, Kalman Shur ordered the team of gunners he was commanding to shoot at the enemy which was attacking in waves. He was the only one to remain in possession of a cannon, and continued to shoot for hours until he was rescued from the flank. This was the deed for which he was awarded the "Hero of the Soviet Union" on March 24, 1945, upon the recommendation of the commander of the 249th Rifle Regiment, Lieutenant-Colonel Lisenko. In 1979, he arrived in Israel.

Lance Corporal Hirsch (Giršas) Užpalis, Gunner in the 249th Rifle Regiment

Uzpalis was the only gunner to survive the fighting near the Klaipeda-Tilsit railroad. Although wounded while fending off counterattacks from the enemy, he succeeded in damaging two tanks and armored trucks, which had been well camouflaged. When the Germans approached him, he defended himself with shells, and when these ran out, with hand grenades. He fought thus for two days until he was rescued and was named "Hero of the Soviet Union" at the beginning of 1945 when he was already in an officers' training school. After the war, he studied in a school for party activists and embarked upon a political career.

Private Boris Zindel (Cindelis) Gunner in the 224th Artillery Regiment

On October 13, 1944, while the Germans were launching a counterattack near the Nemunas river, Zindel and his Lithuanian commander were cut off from their unit, each with a cannon. With their joint fire, they damaged a number of tanks as they approached in an unbroken line. Zindel continued to shoot even after he was wounded. When the attack was repulsed, the two men were found dead from loss of blood. Zindel was awarded the order of "Hero of the Soviet Union" on December 16, 1948, according to a command issued by a meeting of the Supreme Soviet on March 24, 1945.

APPENDIX B
EXCERPTS FROM SELECTED TESTIMONIES

AN ACCOUNT OF THE JEWISH FIGHTERS' MEETING ON THE EVE OF THE LITHUANIAN DIVISION'S DEPARTURE FOR THE FRONT (FROM *EYNIKAYT,* FEBRUARY 27, 1943)

ON THE EVE OF THEIR DEPARTURE FOR THE FRONT, SOME five hundred Jewish commanders and soldiers, some of whom had already fought in many battles in the patriotic war against the German conquerors, met to discuss the upcoming battle. A senior lieutenant named Wolfson opened the meeting, by describing the cruelty and barbarity of the German Fascists, the suffering of the Jewish population, and the heroism of the Red Army, whose Jewish members were fighting courageously in the sacred war for Russia's independence. Private J. Draznin followed with these comments: "The history of the Jewish people is one of a struggle for progress and freedom against all kinds of barbarians and criminals. Every settlement which the Red Army—all praise to it—liberates from the hands of the German conquerors, saves hundreds and thousands of Jews together with the non-Jewish population."

Red Army soldier Shapira noted the brilliantly lit path of the Jews in the Soviet Union, who enjoyed full equality of rights and who were defending their Socialist homeland together with the two hundred million members of the Soviet nation. Comrades Tilevicz, Kagan, Gozik, the female Red Army soldier Solomin, Spiegel, and Senior Lieutenant Levitan also addressed the gathering. All of them emphasized the determination and willingness of the Jewish soldiers in the Red Army to fight to the last drop of blood against the German robbers. They called upon Jews all over the world to follow in the

231

footsteps of Soviet jewry and actively participate in the sacred struggle against the enemy of all cultured mankind. This sentiment was capped by M. Gluch, a former journalist who was then a soldier in the Red Army: "Cursed be the Jew who stands aloof during this holy war; cursed be the one who fears for his life in the heat of battle." The meeting closed with the speakers' heartfelt thanks to the brilliant organizer, Comrade Stalin, for the Red Army's great victories over the Fascist cannibals. Signed: M. Gluch, H. Ingel, Robinson, S. Yochelis [soldiers from the Lithuanian Division].

AN ACCOUNT OF HOW A JEW FROM THE SMALL TOWN OF
PANDELYS, LEFT THE DIVISION'S CAMP IN THE TULA AREA ON
ROSH HA-SHANAH, 1942 TO PRAY IN A SYNAGOGUE (FROM THE
TESTIMONY OF ZECHARIAH KATZ, 12/54)

"I went into the synagogue and stood in a corner. I felt very depressed and thus, I repeated the morning prayer. The Russian Jews' cantor did not feel well and could not lead them in prayer, so they began to look for someone to take his place. They gave me an ancient prayer book, which was about two hundred years old. I stood before the Ark and they handed me a prayer shawl. I felt so wretched that as I said the first few words of the prayer, "Lo, I am poor in deeds," I began to weep bitterly. I wept for maybe ten minutes, and they all joined in. . . .

"I did not go there the next day. I prayed somehow or other in the camp. In the evening, a jeep arrived with two civilians who were searching for a soldier from Lithuania. 'We don't know his name but he is short and a Cohen.' When they mentioned the word 'Cohen,' the Jewish soldiers realized (for they knew that I was a 'Cohen') whom they were searching for. . . . 'Your prayer of yesterday will always remain engraved on our memories,' one of them said to me, 'not because you were such a good cantor, but because of the sincerity of the prayer which came so spontaneously from your heart. I would like to invite you to dinner tonight. If they make difficulties, then you'll receive a special order from the garrison commander.'

"It emerged that he was from the Central Committee of the Lithuanian Communist Party in Tula and a Communist himself; his father had told him how enthusiastic he and his mother had been about my prayers. He took out a large bar of chocolate and gave it to me in parting. 'Good luck and may we all be saved and our enemies perish.' It was then 6 P.M. At midnight, the order came for the division to leave for the front."

THE STORY OF A YOUNG MAN FROM VILNA WHOSE TRAVELS TOOK HIM TO THE FAR EAST AND WHO FOUGHT ON THE JAPANESE FRONT. HE LONGED TO HEAR A WORD OF YIDDISH, BUT WAS ONLY OCCASIONALLY ABLE TO "HOP OVER" TO BIROBIDZHAN OSTENSIBLY TO PLAY IN THE LOCAL ORCHESTRA, BUT IN FACT TO SEE A JEWISH PLAY AND READ A JEWISH NEWSPAPER. (FROM THE TESTIMONY OF SHEMAIA RUDNICKI, 12/119)

"In December 1941, they loaded me and three thousand other men onto carts and for a month we traveled toward the Far East, finally arriving near Khabarovsk. We entrenched ourselves in the desert and drilled in the terrible cold and snow in order to travel to the front.

"When my course was finished and I was supposed to go with my company to the front, eighteen men were taken out and the rest went to the front. The eighteen men remained after a secret order had been given not to send soldiers to the front whose relatives were in the occupied area. We five Jews were among those who stayed behind.

"I was in the Far East during the entire war. They used us to close the gap which had been created when the army was removed from there to Moscow. We remained there to face the Japanese.

"Years went by during which I did not speak a single word of Yiddish, for even the Jews among us were assimilated. They were mostly youths from Leningrad who did not know Yiddish, except for expressions such as 'A Klog, A Brokh' (Woe is me!).

"When I travelled from Khabarovsk to Birobidzhan and we approached our destination, the non-Jews began to chant *Khitrograd* (city of swindlers) *Zhidograd* (Jewish city). All the time I was with them I suffered from an inferiority complex. Some of the Russians were actually excellent comrades, but the inferiority complex remained and we only got rid of it at the end.

"For five months, I was in the Japanese sector. I gave the Japanese my war rations and I ate with them, all of us sitting in the customary Japanese manner.

"In 1945, we brought down a bridgehead on South Sachaline and a battle broke out, but it was not very fierce for the entire population had fled to the mountains. . . .

"I was demobilized in 1946 when I returned to Vilna after the war had ended. The Yiddish language was so strange to me that for about a week I could only speak it haltingly."

ABRAHAM YASHPAN'S ATTEMPT TO JOIN THE RED ARMY IN THE SUMMER OF 1941 (12/29)

"We reached the Dvina river: across it was the Soviet Union. We had to cross by a makeshift raft. Sebasidze (a Red Army soldier who took Yashpan under his wing) said to me, 'Listen, old chap. I've heard the visitors are forbidden to cross on military rafts, but we'll get you over all right.' 'How?' I was tall, that's to say one might have thought that I was nineteen or twenty, although I was only sixteen. Then he said, 'We'll dress you in army uniform and no one will ask any questions, and you won't be stopped.' 'What about papers?' I asked him. 'Just supposing, Heaven forbid, they ask me about my papers.' He said, 'Never mind. Say you buried them because you were afraid they'd surround us. Some of us did actually manage to bury or tear up our identity cards, and since you're with us, we'll testify for one another that we're from the same company. You come with us. Don't be afraid. Come with us and let's finish the whole business.' Well, I had no other choice. What could I do? Since there were dead and dying soldiers all around, they stripped one of them, and dressed me in his clothes. So there I was, in the uniform of a private in the Red Army, without papers, without any belongings, without a name or an identity, but together with a company, and that was something! That was really something! We went to the river, and got into the raft—the officers, the wounded, the soldiers—and me among them. They didn't ask me for my papers at that moment. There were about a hundred of us. It was a big raft. We crossed the Dvina and then we were on original Soviet territory, that is, land which had belonged to Russia before 1940. We started to march in the direction of Velikiye-Luki . . .

"Then I came to a checkpoint, and I didn't have any documents on me. I stood in front of a table. Opposite me sat some officers. Some of them, especially the party members, had no papers, as they had hidden them, torn them up or burned them, fearing that they would have trouble if they were caught by the Germans.

"We drew close to the table, one by one. Sebasidze said, 'Listen, we'll testify that you're one of us. So if you don't trip up anywhere, everything's sure to go well.' I didn't understand how serious the situation was for if, for example, they had realized that I was not a genuine soldier, they would have finished me off on the spot. But I was a young boy and I didn't realize what was going on. So I put on a brave face and said, 'Everything will be alright. I'll know what to tell them.' I went up to the table. 'Where are your papers and where do you come from, soldier boy?' they asked me in Russian. I answered in such fluent Russian that it was impossible to tell that I wasn't from the Soviet Union. 'I'm from that company.' 'He's one of us,' said the others who were standing round me. They said, 'Where are your papers?' 'I threw them away,' I replied. 'Why on earth did you do that?' 'I was afraid because there were times when I was on my own and I thought I might be taken prisoner—so why should I be captured with my papers? Better that they shouldn't know who I am and where I'm from. . . .' 'Well, if you haven't got any papers, we'll have to make you up some new ones.' 'What's your name?' they asked me, and without my realizing it, I let slip my real name, Yashpan. The man didn't catch the name exactly. He asked me again, 'What? What's your name?' At that moment I remembered I would have problems if I gave them my real name; if the war didn't end and I was taken prisoner, my parents would also be in trouble. It would be better if I had another name, but I couldn't give them a completely different name then, so I changed it a bit and said 'Yashpanov' and he wrote down 'Yashpanov.' 'When were you born?' they asked, and I said I was born in 1920, that is, in one moment, I had become five years older, but judging by my face (which was very dirty and tired), I could have been that old. I was forced to give that year as there was then a group born during that year in the army. If I had said that I was born in 1925, then they would have asked me how I'd gotten into that group, who had all been born between 1919 and 1920. They wrote down 1920 and asked me where I came from. That was really a very difficult question. If I'd said I was from Lithuania, then I would have had difficulties later on if I'd been taken captive, so I said I was from Moscow. It was the most simple answer, for if I'd said I was from somewhere else, then it would have been easier to discover that I was lying. I didn't know the layout of other towns, and if there had been someone just from where I pretended to come from, then he would have been able to prove that I was lying. So I said, 'From Moscow.' Then they asked me, 'From which street?' I thought, what streets are there in Moscow? A Lenin Street, certainly, Stalin Street, certainly. But those streets would be central and that was no good at all. I was sure that there was a Dzerdzhinskaya Street and I thought that it certainly wouldn't be central, so I answered, 'Dzerdzhinskaya.' He asked me what number I lived at, and I gave him some number or other.

"And suddenly some boy asked, 'Is there someone here from Moscow? Which of you is from Moscow?' One of them said he was from there. 'From which street?' He gave me the name of another street which I don't remember exactly and said that it wasn't far away. 'Say,' he said, 'tell me who you are. What's your name?' I said, 'Yashpanov Artiom Semiovich.' He looked at me. I didn't know him. 'So, who do you know there?' Well, who do I know there? I thought. I've fallen into a trap. This is a bad business. I worked out how to get out of the difficulty, and I said, 'Listen, old fellow, do you know Vanya?' He asked which Vanya. There were lots of Vanyas there. 'Vanya Rizhivoy' (Vanya the Redhead). Where isn't there a red-haired Vanya? 'Oh, that Vanya? The one who studied at so-and-so school? Who did such-and-such?' I answered, 'Of course I know him. He broke the windowpanes of this and that neighbor. I remember the day very well.' And so we became friends: 'Listen, come to me. I've got some food left over.' Marvelous. He already liked me. He said, 'Listen, all of you. Get him fixed up at once because I'm taking him with me.' So just by chance, I had found a protector."

THE STORY OF E. TELERANT'S ATTEMPT TO ACQUIRE ARMS FOR THE FPO THROUGH THE KAILIS CAMP (FROM *PIRSUMEI MUZEYON HA-LOHAMIN VE-HA-PARTIZANIM*, NO. 10 [JANUARY 1971], P. 11)

"The Kailis camp was a very important landmark on the FPO map. Most of the arms acquired by the FPO passed through the camp, primarily because the sentries at the gate were members of the underground and obviously had prior knowledge of what was to take place: arms-smuggling, the arrival of liaison officers, the accommodation of people for whom it was too dangerous to remain in the ghetto, etc.

"Since I was fluent in Lithuanian, I made contact with Lithuanian policemen from the nearest station and when I realized that some of them were trustworthy, I began to buy arms and ammunition from them. In the interim period, the price of a revolver was about seventeen thousand Reichsmarks. When the ghetto was about to be liquidated, prices soared to fantastic heights because of the increasing demand by "ordinary" Jews who did not belong to the underground, as well as underground members.

"In our block, there was a carpenter who worked in the YIVO

research institute, which was also an important FPO landmark. He used to bring arms that had been acquired or temporarily housed in Kailis, hidden in a tool box that had a false bottom and sides.

"We hid the arms which we received or bought underneath the floorboards in a barracks occupied by the sentries who guarded the gate until we could transfer them to the ghetto. Sometimes, the weapons were also hidden in our living-quarters. I myself brought most of the arms into the ghetto. Among the sentries at the ghetto gate, there were also members of the underground, and whenever I went to the ghetto, I used to wear a black leather coat to signal that I had arms hidden on my person and that they should make every effort to get me through the gate without being searched.

"Once I arrived at the gate when I had part of a Diakhterov machinegun on me (I smuggled in the machinegun in parts over a period of time). When I reached the gate, I found that great excitement reigned: Franz Murer, who was in charge of the Jews and one of the most notorious Nazi criminals, was standing by the gate and supervising the searches of those returning from work. At such times, the ghetto was always seized by panic and trembling, for things went badly for anyone in whose bag a potato or slice of bread was found while Murer was there. How much worse would it be if they found weapons! I was in a very bad position, but help suddenly came from an unexpected quarter. One of the officers in the Jewish police who had seen me and my black coat fell upon me yelling at the top of his voice, and took me through a small wicket-gate next to the main gate, thus saving me from certain death as well as preventing the grave consequences which the discovery of weapons would have probably incurred for all the inhabitants of the ghetto . . ."

THE STORY OF A. L. SAPIRSTEIN, WHO GUIDED THE LAST MEMBERS OF THE FPO TO THE FORESTS WHEN THE VILNA GHETTO WAS LIQUIDATED IN SEPTEMBER 1943 (FROM *PIRSUMEI MUZEYON HA-LOHAMIM VE-HA-PARTIZANIM*, NO. 12 [SEPTEMBER 1971], PP. 12–14)

"After a short while, the FPO members arrived at the entrance to the sewers. They were led by Abba Kovner and Shmuel Kaplinski. The place was swarming with young men and women, but only FPO members were allowed to go down into the sewers. Kaplinski pointed me out to Kovner and said that I would take them through the canals. I went down first and the FPO members followed me. We began to walk in single file. I felt at home although it had been only two weeks since I had become thoroughly acquainted with the sewers. Despite the darkness, I went in the right direction. Because of the large numbers of people, the water rose to our hips. Progress was extremely slow. Many people fainted from the unpleasant odors. Others felt weak and could not lift their feet from the stinking morass. From time to time, we stopped to rest and waited for those who had dropped behind. Time dragged and the journey seemed endless.

"When we arrived at the exit, it was already dusk. We came out in Ignazio Street opposite the Lithuanian army barracks. The Lithuanians certainly had no idea that there were so many Jews right under their noses. A Lithuanian policeman in uniform, who was secretly a member of the underground, waited for us at the sewer exit. Abba Kovner and Shmuel'ke conferred with him. We were taken to a cellar to rest for a short while and to clean our clothes. After a while, we were told to go out in pairs. We were to speak Polish and laugh and make a noise as though we were coming from a party. In order to reach our meeting-place, we had to pass by German and Lithuanian patrols. It was dark outside, but the places where the patrols were on duty were lit up, and when we passed by, the policemen eyed us sharply, but did not dream that such a large group of Jews would dare to march down the main street. My companion was Musia Krasin.

"I held her arm with one hand, and with the other, I gripped my revolver. If I was arrested, then I would fight my captors. . . ."

FROM THE TESTIMONY OF HAIM GORDON, A VILNA-BORN JEWISH SOLDIER WHO WAS CONSCRIPTED INTO A SOVIET UNIT, TAKEN PRISONER BY THE GERMANS DURING THE FIGHTING NEAR KHARKOV-POLTAVA, AND INTERNED IN TWENTY CAMPS (12/19)

"We were taken prisoner at the end of 1941, and I saw hell for the first time. First of all, any Jews in the camp were taken out and instantly shot. Secondly, there were Ukrainians who betrayed Jews on the spot and that was an immediate death sentence. There were many cases when they told the Germans that Uzbeks and Kazakhs were Jewish, and they were shot because they looked more Jewish than the Jews themselves.

"I immediately joined a group of Siberians who didn't realize that I was Jewish. From the first moment, I pretended to be a Russian by the name of Nikolai Zaytsev, who had been born in Serpukhov. I had never been there but I knew from hearsay more or less how the place looked.

"Sometimes there were searches: they looked for arms, money, and items that prisoners were forbidden to possess; above all, they searched for Jews. One group would go to be searched while the second returned from being searched. While we were walking, I leapt across from the first group to the second. The Germans began to shoot and throw hand grenades, but I succeeded in getting across. . . . All the Jews who were discovered were shot the same day.

"Later they transported us from Germany to an aluminium factory which had been built by the Austrians not far from the Italian border. I was constantly afraid because I was living under a false name. I decided that I had to escape, whatever might happen. I squeezed into a cart that was carrying potatoes and in three or four days, I reached Italy. I said to the *Carabinieri* who arrested me, 'Instead of sending me back to Germany, kill me on the spot.' I was interned in an Allied prisoner-of-war camp until Italy capitulated.

"On September 9, 1943, we were released from the camp and began to march toward the Swiss border. I learned from an Italian Communist that if I crossed the border, I would be interned until the end of the war, but that in Italy, I would be able to joint the partisan fight. I immediately took to the idea. I regarded fighting the Germans as a sacred duty. From stories which I had heard from prisoners about how the Germans had behaved toward the Jews, I was certain that not one of my close relatives had survived. When I was offered the opportunity to fight against the Germans, tears sprang to my eyes and I answered, 'I shall definitely stay with you.'

"I joined a group which was mainly composed of former Italian officers and we performed special duties. One of our tasks, for example, was to terrorize collaborators with the Germans. When it became known in 1944 that a Soviet military delegation headed by Major General Ratta had arrived in southern Italy, I was given the opportunity to join it."

In accordance with instructions issued by the delegation, the soldier was taken back to the Soviet Union via England and was interned in a camp. When he showed papers stating that he had formerly been a prisoner of war and an Italian partisan against the Nazis, he was told that he had better throw them away. "For a hundred francs, you can buy a declaration that you were President of France. . . . If you were a partisan, you had to be active in the Briansk woods." He stayed in the camp with former partisans and prisoners of war from all over Europe for about half a year and was then sent to a forced labor camp until his release in 1952. He later returned to Vilna.

THE TESTIMONY OF YITZHAK ARAD RUDNICKI ("TOLKA") ON HIS SERVICE IN THE PARTISAN RANKS (03/3242; SEE ALSO "PARASHAT HAYIM AHAT," *YALKUT MORESHET* 14 [APRIL 1972], PP. 7–66)

"While I was in the *Vilnius* partisan detachment, I took part in sabotage operations. We worked mainly on the railroad track between Vilna and Dvinsk. All the trains to the northern front went by that track towards Leningrad. In the course of one and a quarter years, I took part in the dynamiting of thirteen trains. Our working method was simple: we would go out in a group of five. Each of us carried two loads of explosives—approximately twenty-six pounds. For a few nights, we would walk in the direction of the railroad track. We would hide one load of explosives in the forest or with a peasant and take the other with us to the railroad line. We placed the load between two railway sleepers and on top of it we placed a mine. The moment the train wheel touched the railway tracks, the mine went off and the dynamite exploded. We generally chose a place where the train was passing across a high embankment and travelling fast. Then the locomotive and about twelve cars would go over the embankment.

"After a while, the Germans perfected their methods and instead of putting the locomotive at the front of the train, they put a few cars with sand in front. They also drove more slowly, and the explosions then would result in the derailment of only two or three cars. In addition to these precautions, they also dug bunkers every 200 to 300 yards, especially in the dangerous zones, and patrolled between them.

"I remember an incident when we approached the railroad tracks to lay a mine. At the very moment when we were about to go up the incline, (there were two of us), a three-man patrol passed us. I am sure that they saw us. We had two machineguns with us and as soon as we realized that they had identified us, we opened fire. That time, naturally, we did not mine the train but returned to our base.

"Towards 1944, it became increasingly difficult for us to carry out these sabotage operations, and our successes diminished as well. The Germans had developed a speedy repair system, since this was their main line to the northern front and a train went by on it every fifteen to twenty minutes. Sometimes we lay down, saw a train coming, ran and laid a mine, and by the time we had run away, a second train would approach and we would hear the explosion before we had got away. In the course of time, the Germans cleared an area of about a hundred yards on both sides of the track. They cut down the trees, and left only dry leaves which made a noise when we stepped on them. Despite these difficulties, we succeeded in derailing thirteen long trains and three short ones . . .

"I happened to be one of the group who rescued the partisan Semyonov, who had been captured by the Germans and lay wounded in the hospital in Svencian (Švenčionys). It happened this way: the Germans had created a Lithuanian army which was supposed to fight together with the German army. As it was already the beginning of 1944, after the German defeat at Stalingrad, the Lithuanians were looking for a way to go over to the winning side. We negotiated with them in order to bring all the units over to the partisans. I personally took part in some of the meetings. In one case, one of our partisans, a man named Semyonov, fell into the hands of the Germans while on a mission to mine a train and was wounded. They brought him to the hospital in Svencian for treatment, intending to have him interrogated by the Gestapo afterwards. Since he knew about our negotiations with the Lithuanian units—which was a very serious matter—our partisan unit was ordered to rescue him from hospital. This was at the beginning of the summer of 1944, shortly before the Red Army's arrival. The nights were very short and it was only dark for three or four hours. Švenčionys was strongly fortified. The Germans had dug bunkers all around and the city was strictly guarded. Our unit numbered approximately a hundred persons, and it would have been very dangerous for us to break into the city in force. I was not the only Jew in the unit.

"We left at night. By the time we had reached the city, it was already light, and it was clear that the entire unit would not be able to break through to the city. During the day, the commander assembled the unit in the forest and said that he needed a few volunteers. I and three others volunteered, including a Russian nicknamed 'Papka.' The commander said that we four were to steal into the city that night and kill the sentry on duty outside Semyonov's room. We knew that he was in a room on the second floor, but we did not know exactly where. We also knew that another Soviet officer who had escaped from captivity and been recaptured by the Germans and wounded, was in the same room. We were told that we had to bring Semyonov out whatever happened, and the officer too, if he could walk under his own steam. If we had to drag him, then we did not have to rescue him.

"We began to make our way to Svencian while it was still light. We wanted to use the hours of darkness for the operation inside the city. When dusk fell, we entered the city by crawling between houses whose inhabitants I knew. I felt strange crawling secretly by night through the town where I had been born and lived. We reached the hospital. The building was slightly lit up from within and we saw the guard walking up and down outside. We kept close to the wall. The moment he appeared at the corner nearest to us, we aimed at his head with a rifle. He lay down. We ran to the door which was closed from the inside. "Papka" pulled it a few times, and the door broke. One man remained below while "Papka" and I ran upstairs to the second floor. Suddenly, a nurse came towards me. I pointed my submachinegun at her and said, 'Where's the wounded partisan?' She was terribly frightened, cried out 'Oh!' and collapsed. I ran to another room in which patients were sleeping and asked where the partisan was. They told me that he was on the other side. I went out and at that moment, I saw "Papka" and another of our boys dragging Semyonov along. I quickly ran downstairs. As I was going down, I suddenly saw a Lithuanian policeman next to the door which had been locked. A Lithuanian policeman apparently sat downstairs in an office on the ground floor, next to the telephone, and we had not known anything about it. When he heard the noise, he telephoned the police and came to investigate what had happened. When he saw that the door had been broken in, he shut it from inside. I did not lose my presence of mind and hit him over the head with the magazine of my submachine gun. He fell down and I rushed outside. When we came out, we heard a number of shots which gave the alarm, and we began to walk towards the Lentupis fields. I ran first, behind me came someone carrying the captured policeman (who had guarded the wounded partisan's room) and after him two more of our group who were dragging along the wounded Semyonov. I was winded. From afar, I saw a horse grazing. I was delighted for I thought we could lay Semyonov on the horse and thus progress faster. I reached the horse and discovered that its forelegs were fettered by a chain. We had thought that they would begin to chase us immediately, but for some reason we were not pursued. We found another horse, seated Semyonov on it, and reached the forest safely near morning. There we met up with our group. The commander told us afterwards that he had not believed that we would succeed but had decided to attempt the rescue, even if it meant sacrificing all four of us. He recommended that we be decorated for the operation.

"Later, we realized why the Germans and Lithuanians did not

pursue us. That night, Soviet planes had passed over Svencian on their way to bomb Königsberg. At the moment when the policeman telephoned from the hospital, the airplanes were flying over the city. They probably thought that the attack on the hospital was connected with a bombing raid or parachuting, and consequently did not pursue us. They also did not immediately grasp what had happened, as the two policemen whom we left there were unconscious. Thus 'Operation Semyonov' came to a close."

THE STORY OF FPO MEMBER A. KEREN-PAZ'S ARRIVAL IN THE NAROCZ FOREST IN SEPTEMBER, 1943 (ABRAHAM KEREN-PAZ, "DEREKH HA-YISURIM SHEL PARTIZAN YEHUDI" [THE SUFFERING OF A JEWISH PARTISAN] *PIRSUMEI MUZEYON HA-LOHAMIN VE-HA-PARTIZANIM,* VOL. 2, NO. 5 [20] [SEPTEMBER 1973, 11–13])

"And thus it came to pass on the morning of the third day, they told us to report with our weapons to brigade headquarters. We did not know why. The great proverb, 'Desire is the father of thought,' influenced us at first. Perhaps we would finally meet Joseph Glazman and the rest of our comrades there, and be officially accepted into the "Revenge" detachment. Or perhaps we were being summoned in order to finally participate in an operation against the Germans. The desire to fight was like a smoldering fire in our bones and we had no more patience for sitting by quietly without doing anything. There was no time for long consideration, however: they urged us to hurry.

"When we arrived, they made us parade with our weapons in our hands. We did not meet Joseph there, nor any other comrade, friend, or acquaintance, not even another Jewish partisan. Instead, they made us listen to a speech which went approximately as follows: 'From now on, you are organized partisans belonging to the great *Markov* brigade, and all rules with respect to organization, order, and discipline, which every partisan has to obey, now also apply to you. We shall ensure that there will no longer be any difference between you and other partisans. This necessitates a number of organizational changes. Firstly, exchanging weapons. Your short weapons—revolvers—are not suitable for partisan activity, which requires rifles and automatic weapons. You will therefore immediately surrender your weapons, and you will shortly receive rifles instead of your revolvers, with which you will be able to carry out partisan activities.'

"That was the first blow. We did not see any ready weapons which would be given to us in exchange. Nevertheless, we understood that we were required in the meantime to hand over our weapons. The latter were dear and precious to us, for we had risked our lives in order to acquire them and to smuggle them into the ghetto under the noses of the Gestapo and their auxiliary police. To acquire weapons and smuggle them into the ghetto was among the most difficult and dangerous operations under conditions where to smuggle in so much as a potato was mortally dangerous. We had trained with those arms in the ghetto and had dreamed of fighting the Germans. We had heard, even before arriving in the forest, that an unarmed person could not be a partisan, and that it had happened more than once that a young man—particularly a Jew—who wished to join the partisans had been told to secure some weapons and then become a partisan. And now, strangely enough, they were intending to strip us of our weapons, without giving us immediate replacements.

"While we were still dazed and hesitating whether to obey the order or not, they urged us to hurry: 'Why are you waiting? Do you intend to disobey an order? Is that why you've come to us? Don't you know that you can't become partisans if you don't accept our authority? Hurry up and give us your short weapons and soon you'll receive better and more efficient weapons instead.'

"This time they did not wait for us to answer but came with outstretched hands to receive our arms. What were we to do? How should we act? Could we disobey an order? Would we begin our careers as partisans by disobeying? In any case, there was logic in what they said, since a fighting unit should be equipped with one type of weapon which would be suitable for use under the prevalent conditions. So there was no choice. We could not forcibly resist an order which came from above. Was it for that that we had come to the forest? Our aim was to fight the Germans, and our only hope of doing so was to prove that we accepted discipline. Sadly, each of us surrendered his pistol and ammunition. That was not the end of the episode, however. Once they had received our weapons, they said, 'Our battle is hard—and expensive. We are obliged to supply all our requirements, particularly arms, on our own. We consequently need supplies of money or valuables, or else we cannot meet our requirements. Now many of you have watches, rings, etc. We need them to exchange for more arms, both for yourselves and for other partisans, in order to continue our common struggle against the Germans. So give us your watches, money, and other valuables.' We gave up our watches and everything else with mixed feelings. On the one hand, we were shocked. On the other, I remembered the famous command given by Samson in Ze'ev Jabotinsky's book, on which we had been reared from earliest childhood: 'The main thing is weapons. Gather weapons. Give everything you have for weapons. Everything must be exchanged for weapons. Nothing is more precious than weapons!' And now these non-Jews, who had certainly never read *Samson* and were not acquainted with Jabotinsky's ideology, were going to fulfil this order: 'Everything must be exchanged for weapons!' Who would have thought that these were all lies, and that they were deceiving us. Worse, it was sheer daytime robbery—as we realized a short while later when we saw that the watches and rings which were taken away from us and our female comrades were adorning the hands of the girlfriends of the non-Jewish commissars and commanders.

"The blows which fell on our heads followed one another thick and fast, each worse than its predecessor. After the 'operation,' during which our arms, watches, and valuables were taken away from us, the parade came to an end and we were free to go. They directed us to leave through another entrance, and there another blow awaited us, possibly even more devastating than the last. As we left, we met many Jewish partisans. Partisans? No. Former partisans. For all of them had drunk from the same bitter cup as we had just drained. All the Jews were unarmed and despoiled like us. We asked them—the most veteran fighters in the forest—how this had come to pass, where Joseph was, and what had happened to the Jewish "Revenge" detachment. It was then we heard the worst: the Jewish detachment had been disbanded. The Jewish partisan unit was no more. Markov had given instructions—according to a command from Moscow which he claimed had ordered the disbandment of all national units—to liquidate the Jewish unit first of all. The "Revenge" detachment had been abolished and disbanded. The *Komsomolets* detachment had been established in its stead. The command had been changed, and Joseph Glazman was no longer its chief-of-staff. A non-Jew had been appointed in his stead."

NOTES

INTRODUCTION
Lithuanian Jewry before World War II

1. In the second Lithuanian constitution of June 15, 1928, the numbers of these sections were changed to 74 and 75. The quotations herein were translations from the Yiddish published in *Yedies,* (News) the official bulletin of the Jewish National Council in Lithuania, November–December, 1922.

2. J. Goldberg, "Finf Yor Yidishe Frontkemfer Farband in Lite" (Five Years of the Jewish Fighting Union in Lithuania) *Di Yidishe Shtime* (The Jewish Voice), October 21, 1983.

3. According to Internal Bulletin No. 242 of the Lithuanian Ministry of State Security (October 12, 1936), Jewish membership in the Lithuanian Communist Party was as follows: 379 in 1932 (53.8 percent of the total); 514 in 1933 (50.1 percent); 754 in 1934 (48.8 percent); 1,109 in 1935 (44.8 percent). J. Žiugžda, ed., *Lietuvos TSR Šaltiniai* (Lithuanian SSR Sources), vol. 4 (Vilna, 1961), p. 631.

4. The figures, based on a report by the Supervisor of Associations in the Lithuanian Ministry of the Interior, were published in *Di Yidishe Shtime* (The Jewish Voice), July 3, 1938.

5. *Alon Statisti* (Statistical Bulletin), Jewish Agency for Palestine (Jerusalem, 1942).

6. M. Schalit, ed., *Oyf di Khurves fun di Milkhomes un Mehumes—Pinkes fun Gegnt Komitet Jekopo* (Book of the Committee of the Yekopo Region) (Vilna, 1931), p. 504.

7. See J. Leshtshinsky, "Dos Sovietishe Yidntum—Zayn Fargangenheyt un zayn Kegnvart" (The Soviet Jews—Their Past and Present), *Yidisher Kemfer* (Jewish Fighters) (New York, 1941); A. Ben Ephraim, "Di Yidishe Studentshaft in Lite" (Jewish Student Life in Lithuania), *Lite II* (Lithuania II) (Tel Aviv, 1965), p. 379; J. Gar, *Azoy iz es Geshen in Lite* (What Came to Pass in Lithuania) (Tel Aviv, 1965), p. 49. These three sources concur that there were 250,000 Jews in Lithuania at the end of 1939. Ben Ephraim, the official closest to Lithuanian government circles in Vilna at that time, estimates that the number of Jews in the Vilna region was 100,000, including 75,000 in the city proper. See also *Di Yidishe Shtime,* October 12, 1939.

8. According to those who went in organized groups to the Soviet Union, mainly to Minsk, Molodechno, Vileyka, Bialystok, and other places in Byelorussia, this spontaneous exodus comprised from 2,000 to 4,000 people, most of whom were youths. Because of the difficulties of absorption and various disappointments, some returned, others were arrested on various charges over the course of time, and some were absorbed into the economy or conscripted into the Red Army. Testimonies, S. Rindzunsky, p. 5; R. Yatziv, pp. 2–15.

9. Within one year, some five thousand Jewish refugees succeeded in leaving Lithuania, many by the following routes: Riga–Stockholm–Holland; Odessa–Istanbul; Vladivostok–Japan.

10. See L. Ran, *Ash fun Yerushalayim de Lite* (Ashes from Jerusalem of Lithuania) (New York, 1959), p. 299, concerning posters and leaflets of that time calling upon Vilna's Jews to "go out into the streets in defense of the lives, property, and honor of Vilna's Jewish population," and towards that end, "immediately to organize an integrated self-defense of all the Jewish housing estates." Ran also cites a leaflet dated November 10, 1939, and signed by the *Yidisher Arbeter Zelbstshutz in Vilne,* (The Jewish Workers' Self-Defense in Vilna) from the Franz Kurski-Bund Archives in New York. See also Testimonies: M. Dworzecki, I, p. 10, referring to a similar leaflet, and to the establishment of a Jewish self-defense committee by the tenants of 64 Nowogrodska Street. According to Zvi N-R's testimony, p. 2, groups of refugee *halutzim* from the Zionist *hachsharah* training camps joined the self-defense formations "at the request of the Zionist movement and of the Labor Zionist Party headquarters." The enlistment of the *halutzim* in the self-defense ranks was especially supported by Mordechai Anielewicz (later to be the leader of the Warsaw ghetto revolt), who also urged the defenders not to accept the arms offered by the Lithuanian authorities, and to face the pogromists "even with our bare hands, or with whatever we can pick up" (see *Sefer Hashomer Hatzair* I (The Book of the Young Guard), p. 442). The New York Yiddish-language Daily Forward of November 3 and 5, 1939, hints that the Lithuanian government had permitted the establishment of a special Jewish militia in Vilna, but this report is not confirmed elsewhere, and it can be assumed that it was leaked by the Lithuanian government in an attempt to placate the American Jews. See also Testimonies: Dr. B. Bludz, I, p. 20, for an account of a Jew from Kovno who fought against the pogromists.

CHAPTER 1
The Soviet Take-Over

1. See the text of the February 10, 1918 declaration of the Russian delegation headed by L. Trotsky in *Soviet Documents on Foreign Policy I, 1919–1941* (London, 1953), pp. 43–45.

2. *Lietuvos TSR Istorija* (The History of the Lithuanian SSR) ed. J. Žiugžda (Vilna, 1958), p. 285.

3. Following the official unification of Lithuania and Soviet Byelorussia (*Lithbyel*) on February 20, 1919, and in view of the difficult security situation, the two republics set up a joint "Defense Council" comprising the Soviet Lithuanian People's Commissar for Defense, Kronik, and also Kalmanovitz and Kapsukas. See *Komunistas*, no. VII (Vilna, 1963), pp. 70–73.

4. The Red Army units sent to Vilna included the 5th Vilna Battalion, which was organized in Russia and composed of Lithuanian refugees. A handbill issued by the Jewish Commissariat in Russia concerning the establishment of the Western (Lithuanian-Byelorussian) Division called on Jews of Lithuanian origin to join the division's Vilna Battalion, which included a Jewish company. See S. Agursky, *Yidishe Komisariatn un di Yidishe Komunistishe Sektsies* (Jewish Commissariats and the Jewish Communist Sections) (Minsk, 1928), p. 111. Some twenty years later, Jews of Lithuanian origin were again to enlist in the Lithuanian Division in Russia.

5. *Soviet Documents,* III, p. 381.

6. According to Soviet sources, 95.1 percent of the eligible voters participated in these elections, of whom 99.19 percent voted for the Communist-sponsored *Bloc.*

CHAPTER 2
The Lithuanian Jews and the Soviet Regime

1. Genrikas (Henry or Genia) Zimanas (Ziman) was the son of a Jewish landowner in the Mariampole area. He was a well-known teacher of Lithuanian and stylistic editor of the Lithuanian-language Jewish periodical, *Apžvalga*. As a former member of the Communist underground after the Soviet take-over in 1940, Zimanas rose rapidly in the party hierarchy. As head of the party's minorities bureau, he went zealously and harshly about the task of persecuting Zionist leaders and suppressing Hebrew culture, but the bureau was soon abolished. During its tenure, he was also editor-in-chief of the periodical *Tiesa* (Truth). See D. Levin, "Zimanas—Derekh Hayim shel Manhig Komunisti Yehudi be-Lita (Zimanas—The Liferoad of a Jewish Communist Leader in Lithuania)," *Shevut* I, 1973.

2. J. Gar, *Azoy iz es Geshen in Lite* (What Came to Pass in Lithuania) (Tel Aviv, 1965), p. 135. Other sources estimate 5,000 Jewish expellees; T. G. Chase, *The Story of Lithuania* (New York, 1951), p. 157. This estimate apparently does not include the Jews of Vilna, who were arrested and expelled during the Soviet occupation between September and October 1939 and later, in June 1941, from Soviet Lithuania, of which Vilna was an integral part. There are grounds for estimating that as many as 7,000 Jews were expelled to Russia. For details of the directives for the expulsion of the "unreliables" from Lithuania, Latvia, and Estonia on June 14, 1941, contained in the telephone dispatch from the heads of the Commissariat of Security in Moscow, Serov and Abamukov, to the security agencies in those countries, see W. B. Walsh, *Readings in Russian History* (Syracuse, 1959), pp. 634–48.

3. L. Garfunkel *Kovna ha-Yehudit be-Hurbanah* (The Destruction of Kovno's Jewry) (Jerusalem, 1958–59), p. 25.

4. "Ha-Rikuz ha-Shomeri be-Vilna" (The "Guard" Branch in Vilna), *Sefer Hashomer Hatzair* (The Book of The Young Guard), pp. 448–49; J. Vidokle, "Yehudei Lita biyemei ha-Sho'ah" (The Jews of Lithuania during the Holocaust), *Kefar Masaryk: Kaf-Heh Shanim* (The Twenty-fifth Anniversary of the Kefar Masaryk) (Kfar Masaryk, 1958), p. 223.

5. Testimonies: Milstein, pp. 3–4; Telerant, pp. 1–2; Shimon Shapiro, pp. 3–4, 18; Shalom Shapiro, p. 2.

6. The underground newspaper *Nitzotz* (Spark) began appearing upon the initiative of the *Irgun Brit Zion*. See also note 27, chapter 13.

7. I. Ivri, "Hamesh Shanim le-Nitzotz—Hamesh Shanim le-Ihud ba-Mahteret be-Lita" (Five Years of the Spark—Five Years of the Unity of the Underground in Lithuania), *Nitzotz*, November 2, 1945.

CHAPTER 3
Lithuanian Jews in Russia

1. The tank columns reached the Dubysa River, about 22 miles west of Kovno, and crossed the Nemunas (Nieman) River 40 miles south of Kovno.

2. P. Štaras, *Partizaninis judėjimas Lietuvoje*, (The Partisan Movement in Lithuania), (Vilna, 1966), p. 45.

3. J. Dobrovolskas, *Lietuviai kariai Didžiojo Tevynės Karo frontuose* (Lithuanian Soldiers on the Frontlines in the Great Patriotic War) (Vilna, 1969), pp. 39–40.

4. R. Korczak, *Lehavot ba-Efer* (Flames in Ashes) (Merhavia, 1965), p. 9.

5. In spite of the theory that the Praesidium of the Supreme Soviet issued an order for the evacuation of the Jewish population (Kahanovich, *Milhemet ha-Partizanim ha-Yehudim be-Mizrah Eiropa* (The Fighting of the Jewish Partisans in Eastern Europe) (Tel Aviv, 1954), p. 202), testimonies indicate that while at some borders the Jews were allowed to pass freely, at other points they were forcibly turned back.

6. In Soviet sources, the number of the evacuees ranges from 20,000 to 42,000. (U. A. Polyakov, *Eshelomy idut na Vostok, 1941–42* (Trains are Going East 1941–1942) (Moscow, 1960), pp. 19, 35.) Even though this source is based on material in the *Komsomol* (Communist Youth Organization) archives, the upper figure seems exaggerated. On the other hand, K. Varašinskas, in his book *Karo Sukuriuose* (The Events of War) (Vilna, Mintis 1970), p. 19, estimates that of 20,000 evacuees, only 8,500 were Jews, based on an official Soviet census of Lithuanian evacuees conducted on May 25, 1943. Varašinskas notes, however, that the data for that census were incomplete, and he cites another researcher who states that "There may have beeı. as many as 30,000." Our estimate of 15,000 Jewish evacuees takes into account the thousands who, because of distance, death, arrest or illness, or because of

their service in units other than the Lithuanian Division, or because they had declared themselves Polish refugees, were not included in the census.

7. See the testimonies of: S. Yaari, pp. 7–8; Oranski, pp. 7–8; Dayan, p. 9; Ronder I, p. 15; Garbarovitz, p. 3; Nurock III, p. 1; and compare E. Bilevicius, *Nemunas grizta savo vaga,* (The Nemunas River Returns to Its Course) (Vilna, 1961), p. 56 and E. Rudnicki, *Shana be-Russia* (A Year in Russia) (Tel Aviv, 1945), p. 128.

8. Dov Levin, "La-Aretz be-Derekh Aruka" (The Long Way to Eretz Yisrael), *Et-Mol* (Yesterday), no. (45)1, vol. 8 (September 1982) pp. 22–23.

9. Dov Levin, "Attempts of Jewish Refugees in the USSR to Emigrate via Its Southern Borders during World War II (1941), *Crossroads,* no. 6 (Winter–Spring 1983), pp. 213–34.

10. P. Štaras, *Partizaninis judejimas,* pp. 39 and 42. Moshe Rotman, from the Rokiskis region, shot a Lithuanian nationalist named Petrys Rotholz, an account of which is in "Meyn Gviyas Eydes" (My Evidence), in *Yizkor Bukh fun Rakishok un Umgegnd* (Memory Book of Rokiškis and Environs) (Johannesburg, 1951), p. 384. See also J. Koriski's article in E. Yerushalmi, *Pinkas Shavli* (Book of Shavli) (Jerusalem, 1959), p. 370; and G. Ritvas, *A Yid in a Nazi Uniform* (Paris, 1971), p. 20.

11. This was said throughout the Soviet Union of anyone suspected of shirking service at the front during World War II. Tashkent had a heavy concentration of refugees, mainly Jews.

CHAPTER 4
The Lithuanian Division

1. J. Žiugžda, ed., *Lietuvos TSR istorija* (The history of the Lithuanian SSR) (Vilna, 1958), p. 427.

2. J. Macijauskas, *Už liaudies laimę* (For the happiness of the people) (Vilna, 1957), p. 53.

3. R. Levitan, "Diviziyah Adumah im Havai Kahol-Lavan" (The Red Division with a Blue and White Tinge), *Be-Mahaneh Nahal,* 7 (1966), p. 12. See also R. Levitan, "Shir ha-Kineret be-Arvot Oriol" (The Song of the Kinneret in the Steppe of the Oriol), *Al ha-Mishmar* (On Guard), September 14, 1958.

4. P. N. Pospelov, ed., *Istoriya velikoj otechestvennoj Voiny Sovietskogo Soyuza 1941–1945* (The History of the Great Patriotic War of the Soviet Union) (Moscow, 1965), vol. IV, p. 228.

5. Because the Red Army suffered great losses during the Great Patriotic War, it changed the organization of divisions at least six times during the course of the war, five times between 1941 and 1942 alone. Thus, for example, the divisional size was set at 9,435 men in December 1942 and raised to 11,706 in December 1944. In 1942–44, about one quarter of the Red Army's divisions comprised 8,000 men each; the rest had between 5,000 and 7,000.

6. The table is from: J. Dobrovolskas, *Lietuviai kariai Didžiojo Tevynės*

Karo frontuose (Lithuanian Soldiers on the Frontlines of the Great Patriotic War), p. 48, and is based on reports of the Lithuanian Division's political section in the Soviet Defense Ministry's archives bearing the signature F.16, 289877, b. 1, 13. Dobrovolskas (p. 49). explains the drop from 12,398 in May 1942 to 10,251 in January 1943 by the fact that the division was reorganized according to a new table of organization because of suspicions of disloyalty, during which it may be assumed that some soldiers were eliminated from the division.

7. These data are based on, among other sources, the testimonies of former officers and soldiers from the division's various units (Testimonies: Ben Zvi, I, pp. 34–36, 55; Niv, IV, pp. 1–2; Bin, p. 22), which were then compared with data given in the Danish newspaper *Militair Tidskrift* (Military News) March 1948 and quoted in *Ma'arahot* (Campaigns), 59 (1948). These data are partially substantiated by incomplete data in *Bor'ba za Sovetskuyu Pribaltiku v Velikoi Otechestvennoi Voine, 1941–1945* (Struggle for the Soviet Baltics during the Great Patriotic War 1941–1945), vol. 1 (Riga, 1966), p. 195; Dobrovolskas, *Lietuviai kariai*, pp. 45–55.

8. In units of usual company strength, the official table of organization provided for a commissar. *Partorgs* (Party organizers) and *Komsorgs* (*Komsomol* organizers) were generally assigned only to smaller units and had no official military rank or status. In effect, they were only the secretaries of the party or *Komsomol* branches in the units to which they were assigned. The title "commissar" was abolished in 1943 and replaced by the title "deputy commander in charge of political affairs."

9. Dobrovolskas, *Lietuviai kariai*, p. 52.

10. Instead of horses, soldiers were sometimes harnessed to haul cannons under enemy fire. See Dobrovolskas, *Lietuviai kariai*, p. 60. "Horses collapsed and human beings continued to march," I. Ehrenburg wrote in his essay, "The Lithuanian Heart." According to J. Kličius, ed., *Žygiai, apkasai, atakos Didzviojo Tevynes Karo dalyviu prisiminimai* (Marches, Entrenchments and Attacks During the Great Patriotic War) (Vilna, 1953), p. 305, there is the following testimony (Steinman, p. 11) as to the fate of the fallen horses: "What a joy it was to find a dead horse to cook in one's pot. But sometimes there was no patience, and the horse was eaten half done." See also Testimonies: Kanfer, p. 23; Meirovitz, p. 15. A detailed description of the sufferings of the participants in this march may be found in Kličius, *Žygiai*, p. 136; J. Viducinski, "In der 16ter Litvisher Diviziye" (In the 16th Lithuanian Division), *Sefer Zikkaron le-Ezor Svenzian* (Memory Book of the Svencian Region) (Tel Aviv, 1965), pp. 1751–52; Z. Arem, *In der Litvisher Diviziye* (In the Lithuanian Division), *Mul ha-Oyev ha-Nazi* (Facing the Nazi Enemy), vol. 1 (Tel Aviv, 1962), pp. 38–40.

11. Because of the primary strategic importance of the Orel-Kursk salient, which the Germans intended to use as a bridgehead, the Germans concentrated twenty infantry divisions and twenty armored divisions (Panther and Tiger tanks and Ferdinand cannons) there. In their effort to

smash the Red Army lines, they let loose everything they had west of Kursk on a 160-mile line, extending from Belgorod to Mtsensk.

12. According to Soviet sources, the Lithuanian Division destroyed 116 German tanks, 50 armored vehicles, 249 cannons, and 152 trucks and took more than 12,000 prisoners. The men of the division were awarded more than 21,000 medals and decorations, including 12 "Hero of the Soviet Union" medals; see Dobrovolskas, *Lietuviai kariai*, p. 137.

13. A. Joffë, ed., *Hitlerine okupacija Lietuvoje* (The Hitlerite occupation of Lithuania) (Vilna, 1959), pp. 420–421, and J. Macijauskas, *Už liaudies laimę*, p. 436, *Tiesa*, October 11, 1946.

14. J. Litvak, "Ha-Diviziyah ha-Litait—Rikuz ha-Lohamim ha-Yehudim ha-Gadol beyoter be-Milhemet ha-Olam ha-Shniyah" (The Lithuanian Division—The Greatest Concentration of Jewish Fighters in World War II) *Gesher* (The Bridge) vols. 23–24 (1960), p. 100.

15. Testimonies: Ben Zvi, III, p. 24: Kanfer, p. 24: Rogalin, p. 7; Meirowitz, p. 7.

16. Estimates as to the number of Jewish casualties in the first engagements in the Alekseyevka region in February 1943 run as high as 4,500. See, for example, Litvak, "Ha-Diviziyah ha-Litait", p. 101, who bases his estimates on the testimony of Rest, p. 5. We read of 5,000 Jewish graves as a result of that battle in L. Heiman, "Ha-Generalim shel Khrushchev" (Kruschev's generals), *Likutim me-Itonut ha-Olam* (Digest from World Newspapers), vol. 28 (1964), p. 3, and a soldier from the 224th Regiment reports: "On the first day of the fighting at Alekseyevka, 930 men were killed, including—so we calculated among ourselves—800 Jews. On the second day we lost more than a thousand, and then we said among ourselves that the division was no longer Jewish." Testimonies: Bick, p. 35. These estimates stem from the fact that most of the losses were in the Second Battalion of the 167th Regiment and other units which had a high percentage of Jews. Testimonies: Niv, p. 3. For example, from the famous Sixth Company, only eighteen men survived. Testimonies: Katz, p. 73; Flaks, p. 6; Weizmann, p. 7; Kantor, II, p. 7; Gurevicz, p. 6.

CHAPTER 5
The Jewish Soldiers: A Cross Section

1. J. Dobrovolskas, *Lietuviai Kariai Didžiojo Tevynes Karo Frontuose* (Lithuanian soldiers on the frontlines of the Great Patriotic War) (Vilna, 1960), p. 49.

2. These findings are based on data gathered from all available sources and apply to 1,000 Jewish veterans of the Lithuanian Division living in Israel, the Soviet Union and elsewhere, as well as to soldiers who were killed in battle or died since the war. Since there were about 5,000 Jewish soldiers in the division, these 1,000 should provide a reasonable, random representative sampling.

3. *Statistikos biuletenis* (Statistical Bulletin), Kovno, 1924.

4. Dobrovolskas, *Lietuviai Kariai*, table 4, p. 51.

5. Testimonies: Bat Ami, p. 18. See also Testimonies: Kantor, II p. 27; Meirovitz, p. 33; Bleimann, pp. 8–9. Some instances are also known of soldiers who informed on strict commanders upon whom they wished to take revenge. In one such instance, Sergeant D. Rom, a former member of the right-wing Zionist-Revisionist organization, was arrested and expelled from the organization. Testimonies: Ben-Eliezer, p. 21; Bleimann, pp. 33, 52.

6. Among the soldiers and officers who were arrested and expelled from the division, some of whom disappeared without trace, were the lawyer Maisel, Volpe, the Shilansky brothers, Pushara, Valberg, and Immerman. Testimonies: Volpe, V, p. 6. See also Testimonies: Verkul, p. 20: Jochelson, p. 45; Schwartz, I, pp. 24–25; Levy, p. 3. It may be assumed that before the division set out for the front in January 1943, veterans of the Spanish Civil War were also among those expelled.

7. David Krivosheyev, born in 1905, was one of the leaders, first, of the Socialist Zionist Students Association and, then, of the Socialist Zionist Party, and manager of the party organ, *Dos Vort* (The Word). In the division, he was a popular and outstanding squad leader who "by his power of persuasion and personal example succeeded in raising the level of his unit so that the 6th Platoon—the Jewish platoon of which he was a member—was famous throughout the battalion," R. Levitan, "Shir ha-Kineret be-Arvot Oryol" (The Story of the Kinneret in the Steppes), *Al ha-Mishmar* (On Guard), September 14, 1958. When his unit was sent to the front without him, they were told by the high command that "he has been transferred to another unit." But when they reached the front, they learned the truth: he had been expelled from the army. It had transpired that "he was not 'reliable.' Someone had informed on him to the effect that he was a Socialist Zionist." *Ibid.* He was sent to hard labor in the coal mines in Siberia, where he died in 1945; R. Chasman, D. Lipetz, I. Kaplan, and R. Rubinsten, eds., *Yahadut Lita* (Lithuanian Jewry), vol. 3, (Tel Aviv: 1967), p. 327. See also R. Levitan, *Diviziyah Adumah im Havai Kahol Lavan* (The Red Division with a Blue and White Tinge), *Be-Mahaneh Nahal* (Fighting Pioneer Youth Camp) (April 7, 1965), p. 13, and Testimonies: Giselevitz, p. 60; Leikovitz II, p. 5; Verkul, pp. 17–18.

8. According to one version, twelve officers, sergeants, and privates were removed from the division because of their Zionist past, Testimonies: Volpe, II p. 13. It may be assumed that the number was greater and that many of these expulsions were kept secret because of "a standing order not to talk about it," Volpe II, p. 14. Among the Jewish soldiers expelled from the division on other political security grounds were Pilviškiai, who was accused of antigovernment statements and who had spent time in Germany before the war, (Testimonies: Ben Eliezer, p. 43); G. Mirvis of Raseiniai, for having been a member of the Lithuanian Nationalist-Military Shooting Club (Testimonies: Meirovitz, p. 31); Bach, for having remarked that "in the war between the Soviet Union and Germany, the United States will win," (Testimonies:

Feigelovitz, p. 22); a former Polish citizen who asked to be transferred to the Polish army (Testimonies: Pupko, pp. 4–5); Friedman, a former resident of Vilna, who refused to pledge allegiance to the Red Army because he was still under pledge to the Polish army (Testimonies: Niv, p. 4); Markson, because his parents had been exiled (Testimonies: Ben Eliezer, p. 21); and Eliyahu Cohen, for the same reason (Testimonies: Ben Hillel, pp. 25–26).

9. An informer was briefed by his Lithuanian chief as follows: "All the Zionist parties without exception represent English interest, but some are more dangerous, some less." After explaining the differences between the major parties ("even *Hashomer Hatzair* (The Young Guard)—the Russia-oriented and the most leftist of the Zionist parties—was dangerous inside Russia"), he explained how to recognize them: "A Zionist Jew tries to sneak in Hebrew words and speaks about the Jewish Brigade," Testimonies: Bick, p. 24, and Bat Ami, p. 18.

10. Levitan, *Shir ha-Kineret.*

CHAPTER 6
The Jewish Soldiers in Various Units

1. When Private B. arrived at Balakhna, the oldtimers there warned him: "Do you know what the infantry is like? Before they send you to get yourself killed, they tear the soul out of you. Tell them you're an artillery-man." Testimonies: Bick, p. 17. Compare: Testimonies: Smoli, II, p. 9; Vistanietzki, II p. 4; Bin, p. 13; Bat Ami, p. 12.

2. Testimonies: Levitan, V. p. 4. Compare; Testimonies: Leikovitz, II p. 1; Verses, p. 34; Kalmanovitz, p. 49; Bat Ami, p. 12.

3. This refers to A. Kolodny, editor of the *Folksblat* (People's Paper) (Testimonies: Giselevitz, p. 31); the engineer Kagan and the theatrical director H. Leikovitz (Testimonies: Leikovitz, II, p. 2). Most of the lawyers, too, were privates, see Testimonies: Rolnik, pp. 1–2.

4. Testimonies: Gurevitz, p. 22. Compare with Testimonies: Smoli, II, p. 10; Niv, II, p. 4.

5. On his own initiative, the lawyer Z. Rolnik, after serving a few months as a private in the 167th Regiment, got an assignment with the rank of lieutenant to make propaganda broadcasts in German for the German troops. He was also employed to interrogate German prisoners and to prepare court briefs in trials of Germans. Testimonies: Z. Rolnik, p. 3. Compare, Testimonies: Levitan, V, p. 24.

6. The following Jews were unit quartermasters, for example: Lt. Gurevitz of the 156th regiment; Lt. Pinkus of the 267th Regiment; Lt. N. Alperovitz and officer Movshovitz of the 249th Regiment. There were also Jewish interpreters: 2nd Lt. H. Rolnik of the 167th Regiment; Lt. Zimon of the 249th Regiment; and an unnamed Russian Jew of the 156th Regiment. Testimonies: S. Gurevitz, p. 3.

7. The chief *politruk* (political leader) of the 156th Regiment was Cap-

tain Wolfson; when he fell, he was succeeded by Major P. Levitatz. There was also Major F. Abramovitz of the 167th; and A. Senior of the 249th. On the company level, in the 167th there were A. B. Sher, Meigel, and Gilis; in the 249th, Lt. S. Atamuk; and in the 224th, H. Kirkel. *Politruks* in other units were V. Mitzelmacher, Y. Karlin, H. B. Chaimovitz, G. Dembo, and S. Kagan.

CHAPTER 7
The Jewish Soldiers in Battle

1. Testimonies: Domb, p. 4.

2. Kličius, Žygiai, *apkasai, atakos* (Marches, entrenchments, and attacks in the Great Patriotic War) (Vilna, 1961), p. 573. Compare Testimonies: Volpe, II, p. 5; Ben Eliezer, p. 3; Zel, p. 11.

3. For details, see pp. 229–30.

4. Born in Nikolayev to parents who had emigrated from Lithuania, Buber served in the Red Army for thirteen years before World War II and was awarded a "Hero's Medal" in the Russo-Finnish war. Wounded in the battle at Orel (Oriol), he did not return to the Lithuanian Division, where he had commanded the 167th Regiment. Later, he was an active participant in the Third Conference of the Jewish Anti-Fascist Committee in Moscow.

5. Testimonies: Niv, III, p. 3. According to a security officer, there were only five instances of self-maiming by Jewish soldiers at Alekseyeva. Testimonies: Mrs. X, pp. 20–21.

6. For example, a Lithuanian squad leader, Dargis, took his squad, which consisted entirely of Jewish soldiers, out on what was ostensibly a patrol close to the German lines and kept them there until they were captured. He survived, but the Jews were later found dead, their corpses mutilated. Testimonies: Rapaport, p. 43. Compare Testimonies: Garbarovitz, p. 5; Ronder, I, p. 28; Niv, IV, p. 2.

7. This took place during the meeting which was held at the headquarters of the 249th Regiment's Second Battalion at the end of 1944. Testimonies: Ben Zvi, I, p. 47.

8. A. Shapiro of Kedainiai was taken prisoner by the Germans during the fighting of the winter of 1943 and afterwards was found with his limbs amputated and his eyes torn out. Testimonies: Ginzburg, pp. 35–36. Lt. A. Marcus, who was captured together with his platoon in White Russia, claimed that he was Armenian, but later he was betrayed by a Lithuanian and tortured to death. Y. Meltzman, "Pegishot im Benei ha-Ayarah ba-Zava ha-Sovieti" (Meetings with Hometown Residents in the Soviet Army), *Ha-Ayarah be-Lehavot* (The Town in Flames) (Tel Aviv, 1962), p. 196.

9. Testimonies: Y. Levy, pp. 18–29. We known of two more such incidents. When Yeshayahu Levin was captured, he identified himself by a Lithuanian name, Yurka Labenas. He was not betrayed by his Lithuanian comrades and he survived (Testimonies: Ben Zvi, II, p. 17). H. Gitlin, a medical orderly in the 249th Regiment's Fifth Company, identified himself as

a Georgian to his German captors and survived the war (Testimonies: Litvin, pp. 22–23).

CHAPTER 8
The Status of the Jewish Soldiers

1. When summoned to put an end to a violent fracas between two soldiers, Macijauskas reacted typically by declining to interfere only when he learned that the two men were of the same nationality. Testimonies: Veber, p. 8.

2. Tashkent had a large concentration of war refugees, mainly Jews, and at the time "fighting in Tashkent" was a popular Soviet term for those who tried to evade front-line service. In the division, anti-Semites generally avoided the use of the epithet *Zhid* (the Slavic equivalent of "kike") and instead used the euphemism *Vash brat* ("your brethren"). In his diary, a Jewish radio operator reported overhearing the following conversation between two Russians:

> A: "The cooks are cowards."
> B: "Top sergeants and cooks."
> A: "Jews are big cowards."
> B: "Top sergeants and Jews—that's the same thing."
> A: "They're also agents of the political section."

3. Diary of the former soldier M. Chaikin in the private archive of the author, entry of October 1, 1944, p. 68. A senior Lithuanian officer described the inter-group relations in the division as follows: "We hate the Germans and don't care for the Jews either, but we can't tolerate the Russians."

4. Testimonies: Bekin, p. 12. For example, a Jewish recruit was greeted in the dining room by a female soldier whose daughter had been his classmate with this salutation: "Eat and make yourself at home." Testimonies, Borkan, p. 23. See also Testimonies: Flaks, p. 20; Shimonov, p. 26; Rogalin, p. 7; Weinberg, p. 23; Bat Ami, p. 7.

5. These words, spoken by a Jewish doctor during the fighting, express the feeling of many others that the Jews of the division had suffered more than their share of casualties. Testimonies: Flaks, pp. 28, 38.

6. Testimonies: Chefetz, p. 14. Compare: Testimonies: Weinberg, p. 40; Verkul, p. 64.

7. Testimonies: Shimonov, p. 12. Compare: Testimonies: Kagan, p. 37; also the diary of M. Chaikin (mentioned above in note 3) entry for April 7, 1944, p. 52.

CHAPTER 9
National Motifs of the Jewish Soldiers

1. Z. Arem, "In der Litvisher diviziye" (In the Lithuanian Division),

vol. 1 (Tel Aviv, 1962), pp. 38, 42. Compare Testimonies: Giselevitz, p. 40, Jochelson, p. 12.

2. Testimonies: Levitan, V, p. 24.

3. Testimonies: Koriski, I, pp. 40–42. Compare: *Eynikayt* (Unity) February 27, 1943, p. 8 (see Testimonies: Ben Eliezer, p. 40; Gordel, p. 2; Bleiman, p. 31. L. Koriski, "Mit Vilne in Hartsn" (With Vilna in Heart), *Bleter Vegn Vilne* (Paper about Vilna) Lodz, 1947, p. 59. For a Jewish rally celebrating the "October Revolution," see Testimonies: Ben Zvi, I, p. 64. On a party celebrating the appearance of a book by Ilya Ehrenburg in Yiddish, see Testimonies: Verses, p. 36. On political lectures in Yiddish in certain units, see Testimonies: Bin, p. 16.

4. Testimonies: Skurkovitz, I, p. 2; Ronder, II, p. 22; Zedak, p. 27; Weinberg, p. 33; Litvin, p. 21. For a description of a party in the chemical plant, see Testimonies: Veber, pp. 10, 14–15.

5. Y. Lehman, "Ha-Hora ha-Bilti Nishkahat" (The Unforgettable Hora Dance), *Mul ha-Oyev ha-Nazi* (Facing the Nazi Enemy), vol. 1, (Tel Aviv, 1962), p. 167. Compare Testimonies: Levitan, V, p. 11.

6. Testimonies: Ben Zvi, I, p. 66.

7. Testimonies: Bick, p. 26. Compare Testimonies: Bat Ami, p. 19; Bekin, pp. 4–5; Bleiman, pp. 47–49. R. Levitan, *"Diviziyah Adumah im Havai Kahol-Lavan"* (The Red Division with a Blue and White Tinge), *Be-Mahaneh Nahal* (In the Fighting Pioneer Youth Camp). April 7, 1965, p. 14.

8. M. Chaikin, *Diary,* entry for August 14, 1943, p. 29, and Testimonies: ABE, p. 3; Kagan, p. 30; Ginzburg, p. 24; Rosenfeld, p. 15; Veber, p. 13; Chaluzin, p. 74; Jochelson, p. 21; Gordel, p. 11.

9. Testimonies: Kanfer, p. 31.

10. Z. Arem, "Ba-Diviziyah ha-Litait" (In the Lithuanian Division), *Mul ha-Oyev ha-Nazi* (Facing the Nazi Enemy) (Tel Aviv, 1967), vol. 2, p. 9 and Testimonies: Veber, p. 16; Verkul, p. 47; Slova, p. 23. A Soviet source reports having heard the Hebrew cry, *Adonay* ("G-d") in battle: Kličius, ed., Žygiai, apkasai, atakos (Marches, Entrenchments, and Attacks) (Vilna, 1961), p. 165.

11. Testimonies: Verkul, pp. 33–38.

12. Testimonies: Ben Zvi, III, appendices: letters of September 21, 1943, November 10, 1943, and December 15, 1944.

13. When a soldier from Kedainiai lost his rifle, for example, his fellow townsfolk supplied him with a replacement; "and even though the serial numbers did not match, they saved the boy." They also smuggled bread to a fellow townsman sitting in the military prison. Testimonies: Ginzburg, p. 27. In another case, a Jewish soldier whose friend had been seriously wounded charged into the dispensary holding a grenade from which he had pulled the safety pin and forced the orderlies to move his friend back to the hospital quickly. Testimonies: Pupko, p. 44.

CHAPTER 10
The Jewish soldiers and other Jews

1. R. Levitan, *Diviziyah Adumah im Havai Kahol-Lavan* (The Red Division with the Blue and White Tinge), *Be-Mahaneh Nahal* (In the Fighting Pioneer Youth Camp), April 7, 1965, p. 14. Compare Testimonies: Ronder II, p. 24; Yaari, II, p. 2.

2. Asked by Commissar Abramovitz why he was writing letters to Palestine, Sergeant Major R. Levitan replied: "I think that Palestine is abroad, and you yourself got us together and asked us to write to people abroad about the Nazi atrocities. So I'm only doing what you asked. Is Palestine somewhere on Mars?" Testimonies: Levitan, V, p. 14. Compare: R. Levitan, *Diviziyah Adumah*, p. 14.

3. The following is a record of some of the letters from Jewish soldiers of the Lithuanian Division that were published in the Hebrew press in Palestine, listed according to the headline under which they appeared and the periodicals in which they were published:

 a. "Yosef: From a Letter from a Soldier in Russia," *Davar* (The Word), January 5, 1943.

 b. "1,700 Jews Survive in Lithuania," *Ha-Mashkif* (The Observer), October 24, 1944.

 c. "Nazi Massacres in Lithuania," *Ha'aretz* (The Homeland), October 24, 1945.

 d. "Baruch Zedak: Let Revenge for us be Your Life's Goal," *Davar* December 10, 1944.

 e. "Hirsh Zadok: The Last Will of the 50,000 Slaughtered Jews of Kovno," *Ha-Zofeh* (The Viewer), January 10, 1945.

 f. "Myriads of Jewish Fallen," *Ha-Boker* (The Morning), February 5, 1945.

 g. "From the Valley of the Slaughter: Letter from a Girl in the Red Army to her Brother in Kibbutz Yagur," *Zror Mikhtavim* [A Package of Letters], Ein Harod, February 27, 1945.

 For letters published in the United States, see "Letters from Lithuania," *Der Litvisher Yid* (The Lithuanian Jew), nos. 5–6 (New York: 1945).

4. Testimonies: Koriski, I, p. 35. Compare Testimonies: Levitan, V, p. 42; Bleiman, p. 42; Ben Hillel, p. 10; B. Gurevitz, p. 15; Dayan, p. 39.

5. From the letter of Baruch Zedak, "Let Revenge for Us Be Your Life's Goal," *Davar* (The Word), December 10, 1944. See also note 3, paragraphs d and e, above.

6. The Karaites are a Jewish sect who accept only the authority of the Bible and not that of the Talmud or any of the other Rabbinic codes. The Nazis did not harm the Karaites of Troki (Trakai), one of the oldest Karaite communities in Lithuania. Testimonies: Kagan, p. 41.

7. R. Levitan, "Kolot mi-Nivkhei ha-Neshama" (Voices from the

Depths of the Soul), *Heykhal Sheshakah* (The Palace that Sank) (Tel Aviv, 1962), p. 160.

8. See note 3, paragraphs d and e above.

9. According to rumors, one Jewish officer ordered his men to shoot German prisoners after he learned what the Nazis had done to his family.

10. See M. Chaikin, *Diary*, entry for July 15, 1944, p. 59, and entry for July 17, 1944, p. 60, and Testimonies: Rosenfeld, p. 50; Kalmanovitz, p. 50; Jochelson, p. 21; Zedak, pp. 21–22; Borkan, p. 69.

11. Testimonies: Chefetz, p. 16; Ben Zvi, III, p. 69; Koriski, II, pp. 6–9; Giselevitz, p. 35; Kantor, I, p. 18; Jochelson, p. 22; Meltzman, p. 28; Schwartz, p. 29; Erlich, p. 41. The Jewish soldier Petlitzky, for instance, committed many acts of revenge. Testimonies: Litvin, p. 18; Chaluzin, pp. 73–74; Isserlis, pp. 26–27.

12. Testimonies: Flaks, p. 41. Compare Testimonies: Chefetz, p. 16; Litvin, p. 16; Ben Zvi, p. 70; Garbarovitz, p. 8; Dersa, p. 4.

13. Testimonies: Ben Zvi, III, p. 69; Levitan, V, p. 12. Compare Testimonies: Giselevitz, p. 38.

14. Testimonies: Meltzman, p. 23. One banned song, *Shtiler, shtiler, lomir shvaygn* (Quiet, Quiet, Let's Be Still) written by S. Kaczerginski (melody by A. Wolkowisky) in the Vilna ghetto, was a lullaby telling of a father who was murdered at a mass execution in Ponary. The text appears in M. Dworzecki, *Yerushalayim di-Lita ba-Meri u-va-Shoah* (The Jerusalem of Lithuania in the Fight and the Holocaust) (Tel Aviv, 1961), p. 259.

15. Testimonies: Chefetz, p. 16; B. Gurevitz, p. 17. Compare Testimonies: Ben Zvi, III, p. 63; Schwartz, p. 21; Isserlis, p. 26; B. Smoli, II p. 33; Meltzman, p. 28; Zedak, p. 24.

16. Testimonies: Ben Zvi, appendices: letter of August 14, 1944. Compare Y. Viducinski, "In der 16ter Litvisher Diviziye" (In the 16th Lithuanian Division) *Sefer Zikkaron le-Ezor Svenzian* (Memory Book of the Svencian Region) (Tel Aviv, 1965), pp. 1745–62.

CHAPTER 11
Jewish Soldiers in Other Military Units

1. The difficulties involved in accurately estimating the number of Lithuanian Jews in Soviet army units is attested to by the vast gap between official figures on the number of Lithuanians serving in these units in 1944 and 1945. P. Štaras, *Partizaninis judejimas Lietuvoje* (The Partisan Movement in Lithuania) (Vilna, 1966), p. 235, gives a figure of 108,378, while J. Žiugzda, ed., *Lietuvos TSR Istoria* (The History of the Lithuanian SSR) (Vilna, 1958), p. 440, puts it at around 200,000.

2. M. Blitt, a young writer of the Vilna *Yungvald* (Young Forest) group, reached Berlin with the Red Army; when he was honorably discharged in 1947, he was an officer. Testimonies: Rabinovitz, p. 4. Y. Yevzerov, of Vilna, completed his service in the Soviet navy as postwar governor of Altaisk with the rank of major. Testimonies: Verses, p. 22. S. Rudnicki, also of Vilna, was

sent to the Far East and participated in the conquest of South Sakhalin. Testimonies: Rudnicki, p. 11. For an account of Moshe Krupnik, also of Vilna, and who also served in the Far East, see M. Chaikin, *Diary,* entry for April 9, 1945, p. 93.

3. Testimonies: Yashpan, II, pp. 1–4.

4. This is how, for example, the son of a Jewish member of the Lithuanian Division got into a Russian unit in 1944, where he served until 1946. Testimonies: Oranski, p. 60. For the story of young fugitives from the Kovno ghetto who roamed the countryside and the forests until the liberation and then joined security units, see Testimonies: Tarshish, p. 44; Isserlis, p. 25; Chaluzin, p. 57. A young man from the Vilna ghetto who also spent time in concentration camps was mobilized into a Soviet army penal battalion immediately after his liberation. Testimonies: Zak, p. 25. A girl from the Kovno ghetto was taken on by the NKVD as an interpreter after her liberation from the Stutthof concentration camp. Testimonies: Luba Fish, p. 2.

5. A few of the prisoners who survived later joined partisan units in Lithuania and White Russia. Among these were N. Kaganovitz and M. Solz; Solz had fought with the Red Army at Minsk in June 1941.

6. "We've got too many Jews without you," one would-be recruit was told at the Polish recruitment office at Guzari. Y. Kressel, "Levadi" (Alone) *Mul ha-Oyev ha-Nazi* (Facing the Nazi Enemy), vol. 2, p. 163. "We don't need you just now," a Jewish officer from Vilna was told at the Polish army reception center at Buzoluk. Testimonies: M. Levin, p. 23. Some Jews were rejected or discharged soon after being accepted on the grounds that "Vilna belongs to Lithuania." Testimonies: Kalmanovitz, p. 2. Compare E. Rudnicki, *Shana be-Rusia* (A Year in Russia) (Tel Aviv, 1945), p. 211.

7. Jews from the Vilna area who served in General Anders's army included Dr. Slovas (chief dentist), the lawyer Y. Shapiro, Y. Pumpianski, Rozin, L. Levin, Y. Tilevitz, Gershonovitz, S. Gordon, E. Rudnicki, and M. Sheskin. The latter was among those who fought for the establishment of all-Jewish units in General Anders's army. See D. Levin, "Yehidot Yehudiot be-Zava ha-Adom" (Jewish Units in the Red Army), *Ha-Umah* (The Nation) no. 19 (1967), pp. 415–17.

8. Testimonies: Yoram, pp. 17, 19.

9. Testimonies: Pumpianski, pp. 17–20. Compare: Y. Grubner, "Ha-Pzuim Zoakim le-Ezra" *(The Wounded Cry for Help), Mul ha-Oyev ha-Nazi* (Facing the Nazi Enemy), vol. 2, pp. 34–35.

10. Testimonies: Mushkat, p. 28. See also Testimonies: Klibanski, p. 3.

CHAPTER 12
The Background and Development

1. When for example, the Germans entered Raseiniai on June 28, they found that the Lithuanians had already murdered Jews in the streets and pillaged their possessions, just as, when they entered Rokiskis on June 25, they found that the local Jews had been attacked on the previous day;

E. Oshry, *Khurbn Lite* (The Ruins of Lithuania) (New York, 1953), pp. 318 and 322. See also S. Neshamit: *Mi Razah et Yehudei Lita* (Who Murdered the Jews of Lithuania?), *Lamerhav* (To the Open Spaces) (Tel Aviv, September 23, 1943) and E. Yerushalmi, *Umkum fun Yidn in Shavler Geto un Arumike Shtetlekh*, (The Destruction of the Jews in the Shavlian Ghetto and the Adjacent Towns) (Lithuania) vol. I, ed. M. Sudarsky (New York, 1951), p. 1828.

2. From a report by Stahlecker to Heydrich of October 15, 1941, Nuremberg Document No. L-180. The *Einsatzgruppen* of the Nazi Security Police were established in Germany before the outbreak of the Soviet-German war and were designed to purge each area as soon as it had been conquered. According to an agreement with the army of March 26, 1941, with respect to "implementation, execution, command and jurisdiction," four such formations, numbering some nine hundred men, were attached to the main body of troops which invaded the Soviet Union. *Einsatzgruppe A*, under the command of F. Stahlecker, was attached to the northern regiment, which occupied Lithuania, among other places, and was composed of three secondary units *(Einsatzkommandos)* of which the first operated mainly in Estonia, the second in Latvia; and the third in Lithuania. *Einsatzkommando 3* was commanded by K. Jäger who was also head of the Security Police *(Sipo)* and the Security Service (SD) in Lithuania.

3. From a report by Stahlecker on the state of affairs until October 15, Nuremberg Document No. L-180.

4. According to the protocol of the Wannsee Conference dealing with the continued extermination of European Jewry (January 20, 1942), 34,000 Jews remained in Lithuania at the time (Nuremberg Document, No. 2586-G). This number is presumably the total for the three large ghettos alone, although the Svencian ghetto and some small labor camps were at this time still in existence.

5. E. Yerushalmi, *Pinkas Shavli, Yoman mi-Geto Litai 1941–1945*, (The Book of Shavli, Diary from the Lithuanian Ghetto) Jerusalem, 1958, p. 117.

6. Characteristic of this general mood was the motto of the Vilna ghetto leadership, "Jews of the ghetto, remember: Work saves blood." *Geto Yedies* (Ghetto News), August 24, 1942. A leading article in the July 15, 1943, edition of the same newspaper stated that "once again, the truth of what we have so indefatigably taught has been proved correct: there is only one factor which will enable us to survive—our work."

7. From a report of August 1943, on the situation in Lithuania by the head of the *Sipo*-SD in Lithuania, sent to the Head Security Office in Berlin; B. Baranauskas and E. Rozauskas (ed.), *Masines žudynes Lietuvoie 1941–1945* (Mass Murders in Lithuania, 1941–1945) (Vilna, 1945), p. 243.

8. See M. Dworzecki, *Yerushalayim de-Lita ba-Meri u-va-Shoah* (The Jerusalem of Lithuania in the Fight and the Holocaust), Tel Aviv, 1951), pp. 215–41, 253–82; A. Z. Brown and D. Levin, *Toldotehah shel Mahteret—ha-Irgun ha-Lohem shel Yehudei Kovna be-Milhemet ha-Olam ha-Shniyah* (The Story of an Underground—The Resistance of the Jews of Kovno in the Second World War), Jerusalem, 1962, pp. 51–59; Jerushalmi, Umkum fun Yidn, pp. 137–38.

9. Protocol from a consultation between the ghetto leaders and an obstetrician, Dr. Peisachovich, held on March 24, 1943, when it was decided to induce labor and not to notify the German authorities; see Yerushalmi, pp. 188–200. See also A. Peretz, *Be-Mahanot Lo Bakhu—Mi-Reshimotav shel Rofe* (In the Camps No One Cried—From the Lists of a Doctor) (Tel Aviv, 1960), pp. 36–37.

10. M. Yellin and D. Gelpern, *Partizaner fun Kaunaser Geto* (Partisans from the Kovno Ghetto) (Moscow, 1948), pp. 110–12. Underground member Malka Pugatzki ("Smoli") alone smuggled out seventeen children, twelve of whom were saved; the fate of the others is unknown. M. Gefen *et al.*, eds., *Sefer ha-Partizahim* (Book of the Jewish Partisans) (Merhavia, 1958), pp. 231–32.

11. C. Lazar (Litai), *Hurban u-Mered* (Destruction and Revolt) (Tel Aviv, 1950), pp. 268.

12. See the memoirs of one of the escapees, Z. Matzkin, in *Sefer Zikkaron le-Ezor Svenzian* (Memory Book of the Svenzian Region), ed. S. Kanz (Tel Aviv, 1965), pp. 613–28; compare S. Farber, *Ha-Ayarah be-Lehavot* (The Town in Flames) (Tel Aviv, 1962), pp. 203–205.

13. See minutes of the escapees, plate 18, Hebrew edition.

14. J. Gar, *Umkum fun der Yidisher Kovne* (Destruction of the Jewish Kovno) (Munich, 1948), pp. 116–68. Apparently from the Hebrew, *melunah*, the term *maline* was known in Vilna before the war, but became very widely used during the Holocaust, especially among the Jews of Lithuania.

15. S. Grinhaus, *Fun Letzten Khurbn* (From the Last Destruction) 7, p. 36. See also L. Garfunkel, *Kovnah ha-Yehudit be- Hurbanah* (The Destruction of Kovno's Jewry) (Jerusalem, 1959) p. 197 and *see also* Testimonies: J. Verbovski, p. 4. Chaim Schneider survived.

16. Section 36 of the FPO regulations, Moreshet Archives, D.1360.

17. From directive no. 3 of the "military program" of the Anti-Fascist Organization in the Kovno ghetto, Yellin and Gelpern, *Partizaner fun Kaunaser Geto*, pp. 49–50.

18. Apparently, this principle of "internal responsibility" was one reason why there were so few clashes with the Germans, despite opportunities for fighting; see Testimonies: B. Zak, p. 7. One of the few exceptions was the case of N. Mak, the watchmaker, who attempted to escape through the fence of the Kovno ghetto on November 15, 1942, intending later to flee the country. Caught in the act by a German guard, Mak drew his revolver, fired, but missed. He was seized on the spot and handed over to the Gestapo. On their orders, he was hanged in the center of the ghetto; see Garfunkel, *Kovnah ha-Yehudit be-Hurbanah*, pp. 135–38; Gar, *Unkum fun der Yidisher Kovne*, pp. 130–33.

19. E. Reif, *Keyzad Hushmadah Shkud, Kehillat Shkud* (How Skuodas Was Annihilated—The Community of Shkud) (Tel Aviv, 1958), pp. 45–46. See also Testimonies: Factor, p. 16.

20. E. Oshry, *Khurbn Lite*, p. 291. After the war, this incident was reported in the press in an attempt to identify the name of the Lithuanian or

German who was killed by Shlapobersky. See *Tiesa*, Vilna, January 23, 1965, and April 11, 1965.

21. Nuremberg Document No. PS-3279. See also B. Baranauskas and E. Rozauskas, *Masines Žudynes Lietuvoje*, (Mass Murders in Lithuania), Document No. 115, p. 135 (from Jäger's report of December 1, 1941), for additional details. This source says, "In all, 2,236 Jews were taken away from Žagaré to be killed (633 men, 1,107 women, 496 children), 150 Jews were shot on the spot while the rebellion was being quelled, and seven Lithuanians (according to the Germans "partisans") were wounded. According to an eye-witness, it was Alter Zhagorsky who called upon the Jews to flee and who stabbed a Lithuanian guard to death. Avraham Ackerman attacked another guard and bit his throat; Testimonies: Ber Peretzman, p. 2.

22. For the text (and Hebrew translation) of the song *Arois iz in Vilne a Nayer Bafel* (A new command has come out in Vilna) see M. Dworzecki, *Yerushalayim de-Lita*, pp. 353–60. See also Table 27.

23. In the Shavli ghetto, the children (age 18 and younger) formed only 30 percent of the total ghetto population at the beginning of January 1943, while most of the remaining 70 percent were middle-aged. E. Yerushalmi, *Pinkas Shavli* (The Book of Shavli) (Jerusalem, 1958), p. 152. By April 1943, the proportion of adults in the Kovno ghetto was above 77 percent, while 63 percent were fit for work. *Ibid.*, p. 193. See also L. Garfunkel, *Kovnah ha-Yehudit be-Hurbanah*, p. 83.

24. In April 1943, 59 percent of the population of the Vilna ghetto was female, and 41 percent was male. H. Kruk, *Togbukh fun Vilner Geto* (Diary from Vilna Ghetto), April 26, 1943), p. 254. During the same period in the Kovno ghetto, 56 percent of the population were women, and 44 percent were men: *Yerushalmi, Pinkas Shavli*, April 9, 1943, p. 193. In Shavli, the proportion of women was as high as 66 percent. *Lite*, vol. 1, p. 1779.

25. The members of the Kovno *Ältestenrat* (Council of Elders) who were imprisoned during the Soviet regime were L. Garfunkel, J. Goldberg, Rabbi S. A. Snieg and Z. Levin. The chairman of the Jewish Council in the Shavli ghetto, M. Leibovitz, was active in the Union of Front Line Jewish Fighters and was thus liable to imprisonment and expulsion during the Soviet regime; the same was true of the head of the Vilna ghetto, J. Gens.

26. On the spontaneous organization of Jewish men to overcome Lithuanian rioters in Kovno in 1923, see L. Chein-Shimoni, *Nekhtn* (Yesterday) Buenos Aires, 1959, p. 79. When Y. Olshanski, the commander of the Haganah in Tel Aviv in 1921–22, visited his native Lithuania, he participated then in a number of secret meetings held by a small number of men who established this organization. Testimonies: Y. Olshan (Olshanski), p. 1.

27. During one of the clashes that took place in Vilna on November 10, 1931, between Polish students and their Jewish colleagues who were greatly helped by the well-known Jewish "strong men" *(Di Shtarke)* from the Novogrudek district, a Polish student named Watzlawski was killed. From then on until the outbreak of World War II, the anniversary of his death was an

occasion for clashes between students and Jews in Poland. On these events, see newspapers from that period, "Di Nekhtike un Hayntike Ekstzesen in Vilne," (The Riots of today and yesterday in Vilna), in *Di Yidishe Shtime* (The Jewish Voice) November 12, 1931. See also testimonies of those involved in the fighting: M. Levin, pp. 2–5; A. Rindzunski, pp. 2–3; Libo, p. 11; M. Dworzecki, I, p. 2.

28. On self-defense operations organized by Jewish soldiers against Cossack rioters in September 1915 in Smorgon, see: *Yehadut Lita* (Lithuanian Jewry), vol. 1 (Tel Aviv, 1960), p. 120. On active participation by Jews in fighting to defend the Bolshevist regime in Vilna in 1918–1919, see Testimonies: Antubil, p. 10; Kaplan, II, pp. 8–9; Shafriri, pp. 3–4; Dworzecki, I. pp. 1–2. On self-defense organized by the Jewish Fire Brigade in the small town of Adutiškis during the changeover from Polish to Soviet rule in September 1939, see: A. Bak, *Sefer Zikkaron le-Ezor Svenzian* (Memory Book of the Svenzian Region) ed. S. Kanz (Tel Aviv, 1965) p. 322. On the bloody encounters between the self-defense group and rioters in Daugeliškis at that time, see also: *Di Geshikhte fun Shtetl* 1965 (The Story of the Town) p. 1171.

CHAPTER 13
In the Large Ghettos—Vilna and Kovno

1. "Let favorable mention be made here of Anton Schmidt," wrote Mordechai Tenenbaum in April 1943, "a German sergeant from Vienna, and one of the Righteous Gentiles, who risked his life to save hundreds of Jews from the Vilna ghetto and was a faithful friend of the movement and the writer. [He was] killed by the gendarmerie because of his connections with us." M. Tenenbaum-Tamaroff, *Dappim min ha-Dleykah* (Pages from the Conflagration) (Tel Aviv, 1947), p. 124.

2. For a photograph of this proclamation, see fig. B1.

3. Itzik (Yitzchak) Wittenberg was born in Vilna in 1907 into a working-class family. He became a tailor and from the age of twenty-one was a member of the illegal Communist party. He was particularly active in the trade unions. In 1936, he was elected chairman of the illegal Leather Workers' Union. At the end of 1939, he was among those who left Vilna for Byelorussia with the Red Army. During the Soviet regime in Lithuania (1940–1941), he returned to Vilna and reassumed his position of chairman of the Leather Workers' Union. See fig. C5.

4. This quotation is in accordance with the Hebrew translation found in R. Korczak, *Lehavot ba-Efer* (Flames in Ashes), 3rd edition (Merhavia, 1965), pp. 62–63. Compare Lazar, *Hurban u-Mered* (Destruction and Revolt) (Tel Aviv, 1950), p. 61. According to Lazar, Major Frucht was also a representative of the Revisionists. See also H. Seidel, *Adam ba-Mivhan* (The Test of a Man) (Tel Aviv, 1971), p. 56.

5. M. Dworzecki, *Yerushalayim de-Lita ba-Meri u-va-Shoah* (Jerusalem of Lithuania in Struggle and Holocaust) (Tel Aviv, 1951), p. 205. According to the

testimony of one of the leaders of the organization, its members called themselves "forest partisans," Testimonies: Brand, p. 19.

6. While FPO sources estimate that the number of *Yechiel* members at the time of the union was only a few dozen (Testimonies: Kovner, p. 53; Lazar, p. 28), *Yechiel* sources note that its members numbered more than two hundred, (Dworzecki, *Yerushalayim de-Lita*, p. 205; collective interview, Vilna, pp. 72–74). Auxiliary data can be found in the numbers of the groups which were either sent to the forest by *Yechiel* or enjoyed the organization's protection; there were eight in Friedman's group, twenty-five in Leibl Bass's group, twenty in the Grodno group, and seventy in the three groups that were sent to the Rudninkai forests—in all, some 130 persons; Dworzecki, pp. 403–407.

7. Quotation from Korczak, *Lehavot ba-Efer*, p. 169. For detailed descriptions of the surrender of Wittenberg, see Korczak, pp. 160–69; Lazar, pp. 122–30; *Der Wittenberg Tog in Vilner Geto* (The Wittenberg Day in Vilna Ghetto) *YIVO Bleter* (YIVO Pages) 30, pp. 188–213. On the role played by Wittenberg's Communist comrades in convincing him to surrender to the Gestapo, see Testimonies: Sutzkever, p. 1; Reznik, p. 32; Rindzunski, pp. 93–95; Krizhevski, pp. 49–55, 57–58. On the part played by the members of the Jewish Police and Jewish Gestapo agents in Wittenberg's surrender, see testimonies taken in 1944 from A. Gontovnik and F. Dondes in *Masines Žudynes Lietuvoje* (Mass Murders in Lithuania), pp. 173–76. On the atmosphere prevalent among various sections of the population after Wittenberg's surrender, who felt relieved that the ghetto had been saved and admired a personality who had the strength to sacrifice himself. See Z. Kalmanovitch, *A Togbukh fun Vilner Geto* (A Diary from the Ghetto in the Nazi Vilna), *YIVO Bleter* (YIVO Pages), vol. 15, p. 75; H. Seidel, *Adam ba-Mivhan*, p. 55; M. Rolnik, *Ani Hayevet le-Saper* (I Must Tell) (Jerusalem, 1965), pp. 89–91; M. Balberyszki, *Starker fun Aizen* (Stronger than Iron) (Tel Aviv, 1967), pp. 458–466; A. Kovner, "Mifgash me-Ever la-Hasheykhah" (Meeting on the Other Side of Darkness) *Yalkut Moreshet* (Anthology of a Heritage), vol. 17 (1974), p. 24; A. Kovner, "Nissayon Rishon le Haggid" (The First Temptation to Tell) *Yalkut Moreshet* (Anthology of a Heritage), vol. 16 (1973), pp. 11–13.

8. "I remember that Chvojnik was with us," relates one FPO member, who saw Wittenberg going to surrender, in his testimony, "and that as a member of the command (of the FPO), he warned us that anyone who tried to attack the police and free the commander would be regarded as a traitor and shot. Why? The members of the FPO were generally against Wittenberg's surrender." Testimonies: Rindzunski, p. 97.

9. For the text of the proclamation, see Plate 21 in Hebrew edition.

10. Upon the arrival of the third group from Kailis, the following was recorded in the operational diary of the "Avenger" detachment on September 2, 1943: "Sixty men were brought to the partisans from Vilna. Vitka Kempner and Chayaleh brought the group. The group arrived safely." Moreshet Archives, D.1.524. A Hebrew translation of this quote is in *Yalkut Moreshet*, vol. 2, 112. See also: Lazar, *Hurban u-Mered*, p. 225 and Korczak, *Lehavot ba-Efer*, p. 258. For an extract from this diary, see Plate 25, Hebrew edition.

11. According to Soviet sources, the entire partisan movement (including sabotage groups and underground organizations) numbered approximately seven thousand persons between 1941 and 1944.

12. M. Dworzecki, *Mahanot ha-Yehudim be-Estonia, 1942–1944* (Jewish Camps in Estonia) (Jerusalem, 1970, pp. 307–308. For a description of the first meeting between Goldstein, and Zipelevicz and the continued contact between them, see Testimonies: B. Goldstein, pp. 36–39.

13. H. Kruk, *Min ha-Gnizah ha-Estonit* (From the Estonian Archives) *Yalkut Moreshet*, vol. 2, 54. On the impressions of the unorganized elements from this group in the camp, see Balberyszki, *Starker fun Aizen*, pp. 543–44. On attempts by an underground group to obtain arms and to organize escapes, see Seidel, *Adam ba-Mivhan*, pp. 73–82.

14. See certificate of platoon commander B. Goldstein endorsed by the partisan command, Korczak, *Lehavot ba-Efer*, p. 81.

15. Born in Vilkija near Kovno in 1912, during World War I, Chaim Yellin lived with his family in Voronezh in Russia. In 1932, he completed his studies at the Hebrew gymnasium in Kovno with distinction. He studied at the Kovno university and received a degree in economics. In 1936, he began to publish articles and reports in the daily *Folksblat*, (People's Paper) and in literary collections. As an active member of the Communist party, he was appointed director of the government printing press during the Soviet regime (1940–41) and a member of cultural and party councils and institutions. He attempted to flee to Russia when Lithuania was invaded by the Nazis, but the Germans forestalled him. In the ghetto, he lived under an assumed name, Kadison, as he feared the secret police who were hunting him as a Communist and well-known figure. See Oleyski et al. (eds.), *Chaim Yellin—Lohem ha-Geto veha-Sofer* (The Ghetto Fighter and the Writer) (Tel Aviv, 1980).

16. A number of Jewish Communists in the Kovno ghetto made preparations to join a group of Soviet citizens and prisoners who were hiding in the forest. The group was nicknamed the "Red Partisans." On November 17, 1941, when the group was about to leave for the forests along with a number of people from the ghetto, they learned that the Gestapo was on their trail, and were forced to postpone their departure without informing the other Jewish Communists in the ghetto. It was later learned that the entire group had been killed in a police ambush.

17. The following people participated in the negotiations: C. D. Rattner and D. Gelpern for the Communists; Z. Levin, one of the leaders of the Revisionists in Lithuania and a member of the Ältestenrat in the Kovno ghetto, and A. Srebnitzki, one of the Socialist Zionist leaders and manager of the ghetto pharmacy, for *Matzok*. Chaim Yellin and Dr. R. Volsonok, a military commentator who joined the Communists in the ghetto, occasionally participated in the discussions. Another participant, A. Golub from *Matzok*, resigned after his suggestion had been rejected that the negotiations be stopped on account of national political problems. Testimonies: Tori, p. 37ff.

18. In a list which included the vast majority of the members of the resistance movements in the Kovno ghetto, 505 names are mentioned, among

them 224 who left the ghetto for the forest with weapons; eighty of these perished. Z. A. Brown and D. Levin, *Toldotehah shel Mahteret—ha-Irgun ha-Lohem shel Yehudei be-Milhemet ha-Olam ha-Shniyah* (The Story of an Underground—The Resistance of the Jews of Kovno in the Second World War) (Jerusalem, 1962), pp. 393–400. According to a Soviet-Lithuanian source, the united organization which was called the Anti-Fascist Union of the Ghetto had 463 members, including forty members of the Communist party and thirty-two members of the *Komsomol*. P. Štaras, *Partizaninis judėjimas Lietuvoje* (Partisan Movement in Lithuania) (Vilna, 1966), p. 271.

19. The first group, which left on August 5, 1943, included Y. Milstein, J. Davidov, B. Yoffe, M. Slovianski, and Y. Teitl. All of them perished. The leader of the group, Milstein, was awarded the "Red Star," according to an order issued by the Praesidium of the Supreme Soviet on July 1, 1958; A. Viršulis, *Didvyriu Kelias* (The Road of the Heroes) (Vilna, 1959), pp. 18, 63. The second group left at the end of August and was led by A. Vilentshuk. It reached the Jeznas forests and returned safely to the ghetto. The third group left at the beginning of September and included M. Lipkokvitz, M. Stern, and Z. Borodavka. They all perished between Jonava and Ukmergė. An additional group led by Ch. Padison, surveyed the area around Jonava, and another, under the leadership of H. Gutman, investigated the Garliava area. Both of these returned safely to the ghetto. Yellin and Gelpern, *Partisaner fun Kaunaner Geto* (Partisans from Kovno Ghetto) (Moscow, 1948), p. 123.

20. Gessia Glezer was born in Shavli in 1905. Her Communist activities led to her internment in various prisons, including Fort Nine in Kovno. When the Red Army entered Lithuania in 1940, she was appointed party representative in the "Silva" factory in Kovno. During the Nazi invasion, she fled with the Communist activists to Kirov in the Soviet Union. In 1942, she volunteered for the Lithuanian Division and was trained in the "Special Company." In the summer of 1943, she was parachuted into Eastern Lithuania and met with FPO members in Vilna. In Kovno, she lived in the house of a Lithuanian doctor, Elena Kutorgienė, until February 1944. She died in May 1944 while working for the Communist Party. For details, see D. Levin, *Ele Shelo Zakhu le-Kanfei Zanhan* (Those Who Were Not Decorated), *Yalkut Moreshet*, vol. 4, 39–42.

21. For an exact description of their perilous journey to Augustov, see N. Endlin, *Oif di Vegn fun Partizaner Kamf—Zichroines* (Memories of a Jewish Guerrilla Fighter) (Tel Aviv, 1980), pp. 117–165.

22. The special section which executed orders and decisions in matters of internal security (including death sentences) and also acted as a mediator with arms dealers on the black market, was known in the ghetto as the "Black Staff."

23. Brown and Levin, *Toldotehah shel Mahteret*, pp. 356–57. See also Yellin and Gelpern, pp. 117–19; R. Ben Eliezer, "Kamfs Bavegung in Kovner Geto," (Struggle Movement in Kovno Ghetto) *Fun Letztn Khurbn* (From the Last Destruction), 10, 8; Gar, *Umkum fun Yidisher Kovne* (Destruction of the Jewish

Kovno) (Munich, 1948), p. 226. For echoes of the controversy over the causes of Yelin's death, see D. Levin, "Hishtakfut Ma'avakah shel Kehila Yehudit be-Gilgulei be-Sefer Sovieti" (The Reflection of a Struggle of a Jewish Community—In a Soviet Book), Moreshet, Vol. 13, (1971) pp. 180–84.

24. Brown and Levin, *Toldotehah Shel Mahteret*, pp. 357–58. Compare Yellin and Gelpern, p. 126; Z. Brown, "Di Shlakht baim Breg Taykh," *Nayvelt* (Tel Aviv, May 15, 1950); Ben Eliezer, "Kamfs Bavegung in Kovner Ghetto," p. 10.

25. M. Segalson, *Di Likvidatziye fun Kovner Geto* (The Liquidation of the Kovno Ghetto) (Landsberg an Lach, 1945), p. 5 (mimeographed).

26. Z. Grinberg, "Shuhrarnu mi-Dachau" (We were Liberated from Dachau) *Kamah*, vol. 1 (Jerusalem, 1948) p. 196.

27. *Nitzotz*, which was founded in 1940 under the Soviet regime and appeared in the Kovno ghetto, was circulated in the Dachau–Kaufering concentration camp in Bavaria in the form of a notebook containing fifteen to twenty handwritten pages. The paper usually appeared before festivals and special events; for example, no. 3 (38) appeared on Hanukah, 1945, no. 4 (39) on *Tu bi-Shvat*; no. 5 (40) on Purim; no. 6 (41) on Pesah; no. 7 (42) before the imminent liberation, with forty-two numbers in all appearing between 1940 and the liberation (April 25, 1945). Original editions are in Yad Va-shem Archives, B/5-2. Concerning the Origins of Nitzotz, see note 7, chap. 2.

CHAPTER 14
In the Small Ghettos—Shavli and Svencian

1. E. Yerushalmi, *Pinkas Shavli*, pp. 174–75, 5n.

2. The background to the threats of division was the "revolt of the youth against culturism and their desire for practical measures." A group of Betarites delivered long daggers to the *Massadah* leadership in order to have handles fitted onto them. When they received them back, the daggers had actually been cut down, on the grounds that "one cannot rely on you Beta-rites. If a drunken peasant comes into the ghetto and starts to fool around, you'll bayonet him on the spot." Testimonies: D. Shilansky, p. 15. See also Testimonies: S. Shapiro, p. 10.

3. The reference is particularly to spiritualist seances that became especially popular after the children's *Aktion*. "People in the Shavli ghetto have developed a craze for table-turning. They put their hands on a table and ask it questions. Knocks are heard coming from the table and those present count them and believe in them. The questions are, of course, mainly about the old people and children who were taken away. . . . all the tables say that the children are still alive and that their parents will see them again, and the poor wretches are comforted by this." E. Yerushalmi, *Pinkas Shavli* p. 321. See also Testimonies: Pur, p. 16 and Leshtchinsky, p. 15.

4. M. Shutan, in *Sefer Zikkaron le-Ezor Svenzian* (Memory Book of the Svencian Region), ed. S. Kanz (Tel Aviv, 1962), p. 1663.

5. We have the names cf fifty-two people who left the Švenčionys ghetto for the forest. For a list of these names, see S. Bushkanitz, "Di Geshikhte fun Svenzian" (The Story of Svencian) in *Sefer Zikkaron le-Ezor Svenzian*, p. 173. Bushkanitz estimates that a total of one hundred people left Svencian for the forest. Testimonies: Bushkanitz, pp. 14–16. See also Testimonies: N. Svirski, pp. 9–14. p. 173.

6. For a reconstruction of the emissaries' conversations with FPO Commander Wittenberg and with the leader of the ghetto, Jacob Gens, see M. Shutan, "Shtei Pegishot" (Two Meetings), Pirsumei Muzeyon ha-Lohamim ve-ha-Partizanim (Publications of the Museum of the Combatants and Partisans) vol. 5, pp. 11–14. Compare Moshe Shutan "Mit gever in di Hent" (With Arms in the Hands), in Sefer Zikkaron le-Ezor Svencian, pp. 1668–70. M. Shutan was himself one of the emissaries.

CHAPTER 15
Social and Ideological Bases

1. Testimonies: N. Reznik, p. 19.

2. Reznik, p. 42.

3. Reznik, p. 22. See also the FPO order to increase its numbers, Moreshet Archives, D.1.383. On the basis of an order to "attract everyone suitable to the FPO," the poet S. Kaczerginski, who belonged to one of the movement's cells, suggested that Itzik Wittenberg be accepted into the FPO, without realizing that the latter was at that time commander-in-chief of the organization. S. Kaczerginski, *Ikh Bin Geven a Partizan—di Grine Legende* (I Was a Partisan—The Green Legend) (Buenos Aires, 1952), p. 34.

4. In the original document, in Yiddish, which is in the Moreshet Archives, D.1.360, the sections quoted are numbered from six to fifteen in the regulations. In actual fact, a platoon was four squads (groups of five). R. Korczak, *Lehavot ba-Efar*, p. 86. See also, *Hurban u-Mered*, C. Lazar, p. 64. For a photograph of the first page of the regulations, see plate 14, Hebrew edition.

5. For instance, the commander of the FPO, Itzik Wittenberg, was called "Leon"; the detachment commander, Glazman, "Avraham"; the detachment commander Kovner, "Uri"; Yellin, one of the JFO commanders in Kovno, "Vladas." Even the writer S. Kaczerginsky who knew many left-wing sympathizers including Wittenberg, did not identify Wittenberg with the commander "Leon." "I was sure that he ("Leon") was a strategist or elderly lieutenant-colonel, who had been sent to us from the other side of the front." *Shmerke Kaczerginski Ondenk Bukh* (Memory Book of Shmerke Kaczerginski) (Buenos Aires, 1955), p. 189. He even tried to recruit Wittenberg into the FPO. (See note 3.)

6. D. Gottesfurcht *et. al.* eds., Sefer Deror, (Ein Harod, 1947), p. 392. A Polish refugee who was sent from the Kovno ghetto to the forest spontaneously rejected an enticing offer from the partisans to join up with them "because he felt tied to the ghetto and his movement." Zvi A. Brown, *Zik-*

hronot [Memories] private archives; see also Z. A. Brown and D. Levin, *Toldotehah shel Mahteret—ha-Irgun ha-Lohem shel Yehudei be-Milhemet ha-Olam ha-Shniyah* (The Story of an Underground—The Resistance of the Jews of Kovno in the Second World War) (Jerusalem, 1962), p. 95.

7. The following groups were active in the Kovno ghetto: *Bar Giora; Zorg—Zelbstshutz Organizatsiye* (Self-Defense Organization); *Zelbstshutz Komitet* (Self-Defense Committee); the Kėdainiai group, which was active in the labor camp in the Kedainiai district, which was a branch of the Kovno ghetto; and a group of activists in the Kaišiadorys labor camp, affiliated with the Kovno ghetto. In the Vilna ghetto, the following groups were active: "Grodnoites" (refugees from Grodno); a group from Svencian and nearby towns; a group from Bezdany (a labor camp near Vilna); the Urbanovicz group, and others. Nonpolitical groups were organized in the Daugeliai and Linkaičiai labor camps near the Shavli ghetto.

8. From the commentary to the FPO regulations, published in April 1943 in the Vilna ghetto. Moreshet Archives, D.1.386, translated from the Hebrew as found in Korczak, *Lehavot ba-Efer,* p. 146.

9. *Ibid.,* p. 182. For the original proclamation, see Moreshet Archives, D.1.382; for a photograph of the proclamation, see plate 21, Hebrew edition.

10. M. Dworzecki, *Yerushalayim de-Lita ba-Meri u-va-Shoah* (Jerusalem of Lithuania in Struggle and Holocaust) (Tel Aviv, 1950), pp. 196–97.

11. M. Yellin and D. Gelpern, *Partizaner fun Kaunaser Geto* (Partisans of the Kovno Ghetto) (Moscow, 1948), p. 83. The program was apparently changed later on, in order to place more emphasis on fighting in the forest.

12. The original will (in Hebrew) is in the Yad Vashem Archives, B/5-2. A photograph of the certificate can be found in Brown and Levin, *Toldotehah shel Mahteret,* p. 73.

CHAPTER 16
"Routine" Underground Activities

1. Mention should be made here of Baruch Goldstein, who distinguished himself in "removing" arms for the FPO from a *Beutenlager* in the Vilna area. Concealing them on his person, he managed to remove and smuggle three machine guns, six rifles, and ten submachineguns into the ghetto. R. Korczak, *Lehavot ba-Efer* (Flames in Ashes), 3rd edition (Merhavia, 1965), pp. 84–85; See also, Testimonies: Goldstein, pp. 14–25.

2. The price of "Parabellum" pistols in the Kovno area fluctuated between 1,500 and 9,000 Reichsmarks; Z. A. Brown and D. Levin, *Toldotehah shel Mahteret* (The Story of an Underground) (Jerusalem, 1962), pp. 214–222. The price of rifles in the Vilna ghetto rose from 1,500–9,000 *Reichsmarks* to 10,000–15,000 *RM.* I. Kowalski, *A Secret Press in Nazi Europe: The Story of a Jewish United Partisan Organization* (New York, 1978), p. 85. See also Testimonies: Karapans, p. 1; Shin, p. 24, and Z. Lifshitz, p. 7.

3. Together, the FPO and *Yechiel* apparently owned no more than

twenty-five rifles, four or five machineguns, and some fifty pistols. A description of an FPO arms depot mentions "hand grenades, pistols, ammunition, and a Diyakhterev machinegun." Korczak, *Lehavot ba-Efer,* p. 150; Testimonies: Charmatz, p. 9 and Goldstein, p. 15. Even the FPO group that left for the forests on July 24, 1943 (the twenty-one people led by Joseph Glazman), a "very important group" with whom "they wished to create an impression" in the forest, possessed only a relatively small amount of weapons: one machine gun, two submachineguns, and for the rest, home-made pistols and hand grenades. The quality of arms in the possession of the FPO groups that reached the forests afterwards was even smaller.

4. The original list is in the Moreshet Archives, D. 1.4631. The Hebrew translation is in *"Reshimat ha-Neshek li-Kevuzah Lohemet shel FPO"* (List of Arms of a Fighting Group in FPO), *Yalkut Moreshet,* vol. 2, p. 110.

5. Collective interview with former Underground members in the Shavli Ghetto, pp. 6, 30–31, 32, 36. See also Testimonies: Rozhanski, p. 6; Shilansky, pp. 12, 42–43; Pick, p. 9; Pur, p. 13; Yisraeli, p. 19, and Erelis, pp. 1–2.

6. Yellin and Gelpern, *Partizaner fun Kaunaser Geto* (Partisans of the Kovno Ghetto) (Moscow, 1948), pp. 42–43.

7. Brown and Levin, *Toldotehah Shel Mahteret,* p. 91. Compare also Testimonies: Y. Rochman, p. 8.

8. Korczkak, *Lehavot ba-Efer,* p. 117. See also Testimonies: A. Kovner, p. 30.

9. Despite the great desire that information reach the *Yishuv* (the Jewish community) in Palestine, and worry over the question "why does the *Yishuv* in Palestine not help . . . is the world indifferent to our plight?" (Testimonies: Pur, p. 27), it seems that until the end of 1942 at least, the Yishuv in Palestine did not have "any direct contact with the Jews in the border areas (Vilna district) or the Jews in the Baltic countries." M. Noystadt, "Tenuatenu be-Zippornei ha-Nazim" (In the Claws of the Nazis), *Ha-Noar be-Mahteret* (The Youth in the Underground) (Tel Aviv, 1942), p. 8. A slight change for the better took place during the second half of 1943, when contact was established by way of Moscow through partisan units in Eastern Lithuania.

10. Resolution No. 2 made at a meeting of the *Hashomer Hatza'ir* leadership at the beginning of December 1941 in a Benedictine convent near Vilna; see Korczak, *Lehavot ba-Efer,* p. 46. Compare Resolution No. 6 from the FPO's founding meeting on January 21, 1942: "The organization will inculcate the other ghettos with the idea of resistance, and will establish contact with fighting forces outside the ghetto." *Ibid.,* p. 62; Lazar, *Hurban u-Mered,* Tel Aviv, 1940, p. 61.

11. Y. Zuckerman, *Ha-Irgun ha-Yehudi ha-Lohem: Hakamato ve-Hitpathuto* (The Jewish Fighting Organization: Its Creation and Development) (Warsaw, March 1944): *Ha-Meri ve-ha-Mered be-Geto Varsha* (Struggle and Revolt in the

Warsaw Ghetto) (Jerusalem, 1965), no. 38, p. 108. Compare *Sefer ha-Partizanim* (Book of the Partisans), vol. 1, p. 14; *Yerushalayim de-Lita*, p. 154.

12. From the first proclamation, "Let us not go like sheep to the slaughter," composed by Abba Kovner at the end of December 1941. See fig. B1.

13. Testimonies: Kovner, p. 21. This proclamation was a second edition of the first, and was specially modified for use in other ghettos. It was taken to Bialystok and Grodno by Tossia Altman: *Ibid.*, p. 10.

14. The following is an example of the contents of leaflet no. 27, dated June 30, 1942: "London: the German offensive near Kursk was supported by tanks: according to Moscow, the attack was repulsed. Orel continues to ward off all attacks. The Germans advanced slightly on one of the sectors of the Sevastopol front by means of a decisive concentration of reserve forces. In other sectors—no important changes. The British Air Force has bombed northern Germany."

15. The *Ha-Tehiyah* newspaper was edited and written almost entirely by Y. Virbalinski. Testimonies: Shapira, pp. 2 and 6. The *Massadah* appeared at least six times in five hand-written copies since "there was not even any carbon paper." Those who copied the text were D. Srolovitz, Z. Levinson, S. Shapiro, C. Sverdiyol, and D. Shilansky. Testimonies: Lavi, p. 16; Faktor, p. 6; Shalit, p. 254. See also: L. Shalitan, "Mi-Yoman Saruf le-Zekher Tenuat ha-Mahteret mi-Geto Shavli" (From a Burned Diary in Memory of the Underground Movement in Shavli Ghetto), *Nitzotz*, 2 (47), October 15, 1945, private archives. The bulletin *Hashkem* [Rise Early], which was issued according to the advice of the veteran teacher and author Aharon Frank, was dedicated to problems of weapons and defense. Its slogan was *Ha-Ba le-Hargekha Hashkem le-Horgo* (If someone wants to kill you, kill him first). It was edited by L. Shalitan, *Azoy Zainen mir Geshtorbn* [So We Died], p. 211. *Mi-Ma'amakim* [From the Depths], the *Netzah* bulletin, generally appeared for festivals and anniversaries (three or four times a year). In all, it appeared about eight times; Testimonies of S. Shapira, p. 2. Two editions of *Yediot* (circulars written by members of *Hehalutz* from Poland who had been incarcerated in the Shavli ghetto) also appeared.

16. Shalit, So We Died, pp. 222–23. According to the Shalit, the bulletins were written by Dr. Faktor and S. Katz and were pasted on bulletin boards in the city by a Jew whom the municipality employed to paste up official announcements. It should be noted that this fact is not confirmed by any other source in our hands.

17. Testimonies: Lavi, p. 7.

CHAPTER 17
Major Resistance Plans and Their Execution

1. Testimonies: Shilansky p. 11 and Lavi, p. 20. On the general conference on February 5, 1943, where the question whether to "prepare for resist-

ance immediately or to wait" was raised, see E. Yerushalmi, *Pinkas Shavli* (The Shavli Book) (Tel Aviv, 1958), p. 174, 5n. See also note 3 below.

2. Sections of a "military plan for defending the ghetto" were found after the war in archives hidden by the Anti-Fascist Organization, M. Yellin and D. Gelpern, *Partizaner fun Kaunaser Geto* (Partisans from the Kovno Ghetto) (Moscow, 1948). Part of the document cited below is quoted in this source. *Ibid.*, pp. 63–65.

3. Testimonies: Shilansky, p. 21. A teacher named Kasin proposed a plan to "set fire to the ghetto, whosoever can will escape." L. Shalitan, *Azoy Zainen mir Geshtorbn* (So We Died) (Munich, 1948), p. 213. According to Yerushalmi, M. Leibovitz, the chairman of the Jewish Council, suggested at a conference with other public figures and members of the underground at the time of the fall of Stalingrad (February 5, 1943) that they "set the entire ghetto on fire as soon as there is any danger and blaze a trail to the forest," E. Yerushalmi, *Pinkas Shavli*, pp. 174–75, 5n.

4. D. Shilansky, *Be-Keleh Ivri* (In a Hebrew Jail) (Tel Aviv, 1955), p. 15. See also: D. Shilansky, "Hiyukh mi-Mromei ha-Gardom" (A Smile from the Scaffold) *Pirsumei Muzeyon ha-Lohamim ve-ha-Partizanim*, vol. 14 (1972), 5–6. According to one plan, they would saw through the frame of the gallows. Shalitan, *Azoy Zainen mir Geshtorbn*, p. 221. Compare Testimonies; Lavi, p. 21 and Erlich, p. 19.

5. Testimonies: Erlich, pp. 13–16. See also Testimonies: Pur, p. 13.

6. For preparations to escape from Daugeliai and the results, see below, p. 171. See also D. Shilansky, *Be-Keleh Ivri*, p. 18; E. Yerushalmi, *Pinkas Shavli*, appendices: p. 384, L. Shalitan, *Azoy Zainen mir Gestorbn*, pp. 229–30; Testimonies: Goz, pp. 1–4; Shilansky, pp. 44–52, and Reuveni, pp. 24–35.

CHAPTER 18
Relations with Ghetto Authorities and Communists

1. L. Garfunkel, *Kovna ha-Yehudit be-Hurbanah* (The Destruction of Kovno's Jewry) (Jerusalem, 1959), p. 263. Compare the words of the head of the Vilna ghetto in a conversation with a partisan emissary: "It is our duty to hold out as long as we can. . . . We may not shorten the ghetto's existence by even one day. I shall fight for each day and history will judge me accordingly,", M. Shutan, "Mit Gever in di Hent" (With Arms in the Hands), *Sefer Zikkaron le-Ezor Svencian* (Memory Book of the Svencian Region), ed. S. Kanz (Tel Aviv, 1965) p. 1668.

2. Yellin and Gelpern, *Partisaner fun Kaunaser Geto* (Partisans of the Kovno Ghetto) (Moscow, 1948), pp. 42–43. In other Soviet sources, Z. Levin, a member of the Ältestenrat, and police officers M. Levin, Y. Zupovitz, and I. Greenberg, are also favorably mentioned. See M. Elinas, D. Gelpernas, *Kauno getas ir jo Kovotojai* (The Kovno Ghetto and Its Fighters) (Vilna, 1969), pp. 119 and 163.

3. From a speech by Gens, quoted in Korczak, *Lehavot be-Efer* (Flames in

Ashes) (Merhavia, 1965) p. 126. See also C. Lazar, *Hurban u-Mered* (Destruction and Revolt) (Tel Aviv, 1950), pp. 79–80.

4. For various versions of these agreements, see: Lazar, *Hurban u-Mered*, pp. 156, 161, 172–74, 1 179 and M. Balberyszki, *Starker fur Aizen* (Stronger than Iron) (Tel Aviv, 1967) pp. 473–74; See also, Testimonies: Brand, p. 31; Magid, p. 35, Krizhevski, pp. 62–67 and Burgin, p. 41. Compare also Korczak, *Lehavot be-Efer* (Flames in Ashes) (Merhavia, 1965) p. 184.

5. Shutan, "Mit Gever in di Hent," pp. 1668–69.

6. Hayoez Ha-Mishpati la-Memshalah neged Adolf Eichmann (The Attorney General v. Adolph Eichmann), Testimonies: Eiduyot, A. (Jerusalem, 1963); Testimonies: Kovner, p. 340. On the FPO's negative answer to Stankiewicz's emissaries, despite internal FPO dissension, see Testimonies: Rogovski, p. 14 and Ziamka, pp. 9–10. This was the same Jewish police commander who, in the Svencian ghetto, once tried to destroy the weapons of an underground group, condemning them as "murderers of the tiny remnant of Jews left in the ghetto." Shutan, "Azoy hobn mer gekemft" [So We Fought], *Sefer Zikkaron le-Ezor Svencian* (Memory Book of the Svencian Region) (Tel Aviv, 1965), p. 1684. See also above, p. 130.

7. Testimony of R. Korczak in Testimonies: Kovner, p. 27. This fact is also recognized by Soviet sources. See: P. Štaras, *Partizanis Judejimas Lietuvoje* (Partisan Movement in Lithuania) (Vilna, 1966), p. 106. Compare also: Testimonies: Rindzunski, p. 29 and Kovner, p. 8.

8. Yellin and Gelpern, p. 78.

9. These declarations were made at the beginning of March 1944, at a farewell party for a group (the seventh) that was about to leave for the forest. Z. A. Brown and D. Levin, *Toldotehah Shel Mahteret* (The Story of an Underground) (Jerusalem, 1962) p. 207.

10. "There was complete faith (in Wittenberg) and this faith was justified." Testimonies: Kovner, p. 31. On the opinion that the Communist members of the FPO were influenced ideologically to a great extent by their Zionist comrades, see Testimonies: B. Goldstein, p. 27; Reznik, p. 31, and Kovner, p. 21. An example of Wittenberg's great personal friendliness is the statement in the testimony of a leader of *Betar* that Wittenberg agreed to toast the State of Israel. Testimonies: Lazar, p. 22. In the Kovno ghetto, too, close relationships developed between *Matzok* representatives Zvi Levin and A. Srebnitzki of the underground command and Chaim Yellin, but this was not the case with the others. Testimonies; Z. Levin, II, p. 16.

11. In addition to the organizational help which the FPO extended to the Lithuanian Communist underground in Vilna, the former also transferred two pistols to them "in order to equip them with basic weapons." Testimonies: Kovner, p. 34. The JPO transferred four rifles to an ally outside the ghetto: Testimonies: Endlin, p. 3.

12. R. Korczak, *Lehavot be-Efer*, p. 180.

13. Konstantin Telyatnikov, "Mingle with the People," *Soviet Life*, no. 8 (1979): 30–36. Compare also: D. Levin, "Fact and Fiction," *Yad Vashem News*, 1973, pp. 21–23.

CHAPTER 19
Departure for the Forests

1. E. Yerushalmi, *Pinkas Shavli* (The Book of Shavli) (Jerusalem, 1958) appendices, p. 381. See also Shalit, *Azoy Zaynen mir Gestorben* (So We Died) (Munich, 1948), p. 220. Testimonies: Lestschinsky, p. 8; Shilansky, p. 39, and Rozhanski, p. 11.

2. In a letter from Narocz to the FPO headquarters Joseph Glazman wrote: "If all the FPO fighters were here with their weapons, we should be able to establish a strong Jewish fighting unit." Quoted in R. Korczak, *Lehavot be-Efer* (Flames in Ashes) (Merhavia, 1965), p. 174. See also the quotation of the same sentence in C. Lazar, *Hurban u-Mered* (Destruction and Revolt) (Tel Aviv, 1950) p. 179.

3. Testimonies: Tori, p. 42.

4. Lazar, *Hurban u-Mered*, p. 192. Compare Testimonies: Feiga Milstein, p. 24; and Brand, p. 57. On a hitch in the departure of members of Akiva through the sewers, see H. Seidel, *Adam ba-Mivhan* (Tel Aviv: 1971), p. 65. Compare also H. Seidel, *Havrei Kevuzat Akiva be-Derekh lo Derekh* [Members of Akiva Group on a Winding Way], *Massuah*, vol. I (Tel Yitzhak–Tel Aviv, 1973), p. 49. For a description of the departure A, see appendix account of A. L. Sapirstein.

5. Testimonies: Erelis, p. 4.

6. On a discussion between S. Madeysker, an FPO activist and a Jewish guide who wished to include members of his family in his group, see Testimonies: Shutan, p. 32.

7. *Leksikon ha-Gevurah—Partizanim ve-Lohamei Mahteret Yehudi'im be-Ezorim ha-Ma'aravi'im shel Berit ha-Mòatzot* [Biographical Dictionary of Jewish Resistance] Y. Granatstein and M. Kahanovich, eds., vol. 1, parts 1–2 (Jerusalem: 1965).

CHAPTER 20
The Partisan Units

1. One of them was Chaim Gamer from the hamlet of Zarasai, who was born in 1919, graduated from a training school for paratroopers, and was parachuted into the Leningrad front.

2. See Plate 18 in the Hebrew edition.

3. According to Soviet sources, the number of partisan groups and units in Lithuania as a whole in 1944 was sixty-seven, with a total of 8,163 fighters, as opposed to fifty-six units with 4,660 fighters in 1943. See Štaras, *Partizaninis judejimas Lietuvoje* (Partisan Movement in Lithuania) (Vilna, 1966), p. 233.

4. According to a Polish source, the armed forces of the Armia Krajowa in the Rudninkai forests totaled some 1,300 fighters under the command of General Wilk. *Polskie sily zbroine, w drugiej wojnie swiatowej*, (Polish Armed

Forces in the Second World War) vol. 3, *Armia Krajowa* (Home Army) (London, 1959), p. 600. On the activities of the "White Poles' in eastern Lithuania and their brutal attitude toward partisans in general and Jewish fighters in particular, see *Sefer ha-Partizanim*, vol. 1, pp. 141, 256; C. Lazar, *Hurban u-Mered* (Destruction and Revolt) (Tel Aviv, 1950), pp. 238, 361.

5. Testimonies: Rogovski, p. 5.

6. According to another source, the number of losses sustained by the Jews during the siege was 130. R. Korczak, *Lehavot be-Efer;* (Flames in Ashes) (Merhavia, 1965), p. 244, note.

7. One girl who was accepted, "after petitions and entreaties," into the *Parkhomenko* detachment was killed by a non-Jewish partisan. Seven former FPO members were robbed of their weapons while searching for a unit that would agree to accept them as members. Afterwards, all but one were beheaded by peasants armed with axes. Korczak, *Lehavot be-Efer,* pp. 246 and 248.

8. A member of the FPO staff, N. Reznik, who negotiated with him said: "He [Šumauskas] explained to us that the Lithuanians were accusing him of allowing the Lithuanian Brigade to become Jewish. I said to him that we are Lithuanian citizens and we worked under your command in the ghetto; you transmitted orders to us and we carried out spying operations and diversionary tactics; therefore, you are obliged to take care of us." Testimonies: Reznik, p. 28. N. Reznik, *Ha-Tenuah ba-Geto u-ve-Ya'arot Lita* [The Movement in Ghetto and forests of Lithuania], *Massuah,* vol. 1 (Tel Yitzhak–Tel Aviv, 1973), p. 49.

9. Of the thirty Jewish paratroopers (including three women) about whom information is available, seven died while being parachuted down or shortly afterwards. Many of the others were employed in directing communications centers and in radioing to the partisan command in Moscow from partisan bases. Others participated in military activities, and eight (some of whom are mentioned above) occupied high-ranking positions in the military and political command.

10. Testimonies: Magid, p. 3.

11. The names of the commanders and commissars in the four Jewish detachments were as follows: 1. Abba Kovner; I. Schmidt; 2. S. Kaplinski; Chyena Borovska; 3. J. Prener; B. Shereshnevski; 4. A. Aharonovicz, B. Shereshnevski.

12. The Lithuanian paratrooper, S. Maziliauskas ("Krauklis") was appointed in place of the Jewish commander to the "Death of Fascism" detachment and the Lithuanian paratrooper Vainutis ("Šilas") took the place of the Jewish commander of the "Struggle" ("Borba") detachment. Vainutis later resumed his position as commander of the "Thunder" ("Perkūnas") detachment, and Captain Ivan (or Nikolai) Vasilenko, a prisoner who had escaped from Fort Nine in Kovno with members of the JFO, replaced him. The latter posed as a Ukrainian and only isolated individuals in the forest knew of his

Jewish origins (his real name was Israel Veselnitzki). See below, p. 000 and Korczak, *Lehavot be-Efer*, p. 244.

13. The Lithuanian commander, paratrooper J. Simanavičius ("Petraitis"), was replaced when the commanders and commissars of the first and second detachments were dismissed pursuant to accusations that they allowed partisans under their command to remove weapons that had been parachuted in. During these changes of command, the commander of the second detachment, S. Kaplinski, was replaced by A. Rassel (Sabrin), and Chyena Borovska, the detachment's commissar, was replaced by J. Charmatz. See Korczak, *Lehavot be-Efer*, p. 194; compare: Lazar, *Shoah Va-Mered* pp. 336–337.

14. Eva Rivlin from Vilna was parachuted into Cracow, Poland, in the spring of 1944 and her fate is unknown. J. Bunk from Vilna was parachuted into the Vilna area in 1942, sent back to the Soviet Union, and sent out again in 1943 to head the Communist underground in the Bialystok area. On his way to the forest, he was surrounded by Germans and committed suicide after running out of ammunition. M. Klibanski was parachuted into the Naliboki area of Byelorussia in December 1943, and also worked in the Lida Novogrudok area.

15. Testimonies; Chaluzin, pp. 48, 50, 60, and Isserlis, pp. 5–6. On the activities of the Kestutis detachment under the command of a paratrooper named Stalonis, see P. Štaras, *Partizaninis judejimas Lietuvoje*, pp. 9, 132, 139, 254.

16. See Aba Gefen, *Unholy Alliance* (Jerusalem, 1973), pp. 15–66.

17. Y. Granatstein and M. Kahanovich, *Leksikon ha-Gevurah* [Biographical Dictionary of Jewish Resistance] (Jerusalem, Yad Vashem, 1965), vol. 1, p. 196. According to a Soviet-Lithuanian source, 1,422 persons, that is, 15.4 percent of the 9,187 partisans who fought in Lithuania, were killed. Štaras, *Partizaninis judejimas Lietuvoje*, p. 233.

18. The Soviet Lithuanian source which states that the number of Jewish detachment commanders was four, mentions the names of the following Jews in its list of detachment commanders: A. Meskup, S. Kaplinski, A. Vasilenko, and Ch. Borovska. Štaras, *Partizaninis judejimas Lietuvoje* pp. 247–248. This source makes no mention of the others: A. Kovner, J. Prener, A. Rassel, (Sabrin) and A. Aharonovicz.

19. A list of their names appears at the end of Lazar, *Hurban u-Mered*. pp. 404–409.

CHAPTER 21
The Jewish Partisans in Action

1. H. Solz, L. Katz from Valkininkai (Olkeniki), the Osner brothers from Nacza, B. Yochai from Svencian, M. Chodosh from Kubilnik, S. Valonas from Jovana, L. Walk from Stojaciszki, and B. Rogovski from Radun are the names of a few.

2. A photostat of this speech (in Russian) appeared in the newspaper *Sovietskaya Litva* on July 9, 1944. See *Sefer ha-Partizanim* (Book of the Partisans), vol. 1, p. 158. This speech appeared also in the newspaper *Tiesa* (Truth) on July 9, 1945. For the English translation of this speech, see I. Kowalski, *A Secret Press in Nazi Europe* (New York, 1979), p. 322.

3. Quoted in Štaras, *Partizaninis judejimas Lietuvoje* (The Partisan Movement in Lithuania) (Vilnius, 1966), p. 299.

4. Quoted in Štaras, *Lietuvos partizanai* (The Partisans of Lithuania) (Vilnius, 1967), p. 7.

5. This diary, written in Russian, was donated by Dov Levin and Zvi Brown to the *Moreshet* Archives, where it is catalogued under D.1.254. The Hebrew translation by A. Baram was published in the *Yalkut Moreshet*, vol. 2, 1964, pp. 111–26. According to the editor, M. Neriyah, compared with other sources, this diary does not include all the operations carried out by the "Avenger" detachment, and was apparently a concise report drawn up for a specific purpose. A photostated extract from the diary is in plate 25.

6. Quoted in Štaras, *Partizaninis judejimas Lietuvoje*, p. 231. According to another Soviet source, sixteen trains were derailed; 315 railway tracks were blown up; four enemy garrisons were destroyed; a few hundred Soviets were rescued from slaughter or deportation to Germany, and the Red Army was assisted in the liberation of Vilna: *Mažoji Tarybine Lietuviskoji Enciklopedija*, vol. 2, ed. J. Matulis (Vilnius, 1966), p. 607.

7. For details, see Y. Arad's testimony, pp. 240–243.

8. C. Lazar, *Hurban u-Mered* (Destruction and Revolt) (Tel Aviv, 1950), p. 240.

9. Testimonies: M. Yitzhaki (Gelbtrunk), Yad Vashem Archives, p. 36.

CHAPTER 22
The Jewish Motif

1. An opposing view claims that the delay was due to the fact that the order from the partisan command to leave for the Rudninkai forests did not reach the ghetto in time because "it was lying for a week in the pocket of one of the members of the underground committee in the city." R. Korczak, *Lehavot be-Efer* (Flames in Ashes) (Merhavia, 1965), p. 195, note.

2. M. Kahanovich, *Milhemet ha-Partizanim ha-Yehudim be-Mizrah Eiropa (The Fighting of the Jewish Partisans in Eastern Europe)* (Tel Aviv, 1954), p. 141; see also J. Greenstein, *Ud mi-Kikar Hayovel* (Fire from the Jubilee Square) (Tel Aviv, 1960), pp. 116–18. On the disbanding of the *Kosciuszko* unit, see T. and Z. Belski, *Yehudei Ya'ar* (Jews of the Forest) (Tel Aviv, 1946), p. 172.

3. *Sefer ha-Partizanim* (The Book of the Partisans), p. 70.

4. The Jewish Communists who were in favor of disbanding the Jewish units claimed that the Jews had no need to isolate themselves and that they were obliged to show their loyalty to the Revolution by being the first to obliterate ethnic distinctions. Their opponents argued that the very existence

of separate Jewish camps increased the possibilities of attracting the Jewish populace to Communism, since in mixed units, where the command was sometimes anti-Semitic, Jews were driven away from Communism.

5. *Sefer ha-Partizanim,* p. 184; see also Testimonies: Rivkah Gurvicz, p. 25.

6. C. Lazar, *Hurban u-Mered* (Destruction and Revolt) (Tel Aviv, 1950), p. 216; compare these statements from testimonies: "We went, as it were, from the frying pan into the fire," Testimonies: R. Gurvicz, p. 19; "We felt once again as though we were with the Germans," Testimonies: R. Gordon, p. 33. See also Testimonies: Mozes, p. 21.

7. Testimonies: Burgin, p. 31. H. M. Basok, "Nerot Hanuka Beyn ha-Partizanim" (Hanukka Candles among the Partisans) *Mahanayim*, vol. 24 (1966), 63.

8. See Z. A. Brown and D. Levin, *Toldotehah shel Mahteret* (The Story of an Underground) (Jerusalem, 1962), pp. 152, 282, 294; see also Testimonies: Endlin, pp. 63–67.

9. The former policemen were Itzkovicz, Kvas, Salzwasser, Salzstein, Ring, and Schwarzbard; *Sefer ha-Partizanim,* vol. 1, p. 114. See also Lazar, pp. 253, 260–265, 281–284; I. Kowalski, *A Secret Press in Nazi Europe* (N.Y., 1978), pp. 109–111; Testimonies: Shin, pp. 501–51; Brand, pp. 33–34; Rindzunski, p. 72; Kovner, p. 49; Charmatz, p. 34, and Krizhevski pp. 26–27.

10. For more details on accusations of domination in the Jewish camp, searches for gold, the confiscation of valuables, and the danger of a split which threatened the Jewish camp, see: Lazar, pp. 244, 294, 235–36. Testimonies: Brand, pp. 32, 39–43, and D. and B. Svirski, pp. 32–42 (from the *Yechiel* group). For the command's version of these accusations, see *Sefer ha-Partizanim,* vol. 1, pp. 61–62, 100–109 and Testimonies: Charmatz, p. 35; Kaganovicz, p. 2; Rindzunski, p. 68.

11. Lazar, pp. 267–335. Testimonies: D. Svirski, pp. 44–45 and Milstein, pp. 25–26; see also *Sefer ha-Partizanim,* vol. 1, pp. 109–110. Compare also, the social problem of accepting unarmed Jews who were unqualified to fight into the Jewish *Belski* detachments (the *Kalinin* Brigade), where they were nicknamed "stuffed dummies." Testimonies: Geller, p. 61. See also, L. Engelstern, *In Getos un Velder* (In Ghettos and Forests) (Tel Aviv, 1972), p. 200.

12. A few words of Russian origin received Jewish suffixes. For example, from the Russian word *Bombiozhka* ("bombing"), which was used colloquially to mean "seize," they created the verb *bombiren.* At times, they even ignored the password of the day, and when they were sure that they had to identify themselves to Jews, they said *Shema Yisrael* (Hear, O Israel).

13. Among the most popular Hebrew songs in the "Death to the Conquerors" detachment, songs which were also sung by the Russians, were *"He Harmonika Nagni Li"* (Hey, Harmonica, Play for Me) and *"Sovevuni Lahat Esh Boeret"* (Flame of the Burning Fire, Encircle Me). These songs were brought from the ghetto by members of *Hashomer Hatzair* and *Deror.*

14. For a description of a Hanukkah party held in the forest in the winter

of 1943, in the hut of N. Reznik, a former FPO staff member, see Basok, "Nerot Hanukka Beyn ha-Partizanim," pp. 62–64; compare *Sefer ha-Partizanim*, vol. 1, p. 189.

15. On the beginnings of the movement for illegal immigration to Palestine from Vilna, on the basis of a program drawn up in the forest, see: Y. Bauer, "Reshit ha-Berihah," (The Beginning of the Flight), *Yalkut Moreshet*, 4 (1965), 95–100. D. Levin, *Levatei Shihrur, Shevut*, vol. 2, 1974, 64–73.

16. For a photostat of an extract from this letter, see Plate 28.

17. M. Yellin and D. Gelpern, *Partizaner fun Kaunaser Geto* (Partisans of the Kovno Ghetto) (Moscow), 1948), p. 55.

18. In a letter written in Yiddish on April 8, 1944, Abba Kovner concentrated on the following three points: 1. A promise to take steps to bring Sutzkever's sister-in-law out of the HKP camp; 2. A reminder to Sutzkever to talk to a large number of people about the Vilna ghetto and Lithuanian Jewry; 3. A request that Sutzkever urge the appropriate authorities to supply arms for the Jewish "Avenger" detachment. The fourth paragraph was apparently cut by the Soviet censor. The original letter is in A. Sutzkever's private collection in Tel Aviv.

19. *Ha'aretz*, September 1, 1944; May 5, 1961, p. 1. Compare: "Ha-Yoetz ha-Mishpati la-Memshalah Neged Adolf Eichmann" (The Attorney General of the Government *v.* Adolf Eichmann) *Eduyot* (Testimonies), vol. 1 (Jerusalem, 1963), p. 347.

CHAPTER 23
Portrait of the "Struggle" Unit

1. One of the subjects of dissent between them was apparently the continued existence of the Vilna detachments as exclusively Jewish entities. See: C. Lazar, *Hurban u-Mered* (Destruction and Revolt) (Tel Aviv, 1950), pp. 257–58. Compare above, pp. 000. See also Testimonies: Brand, pp. 48–50.

2. For details of this miserable journey and the depression of those who took part in it, see: Lazar, *Hurban u-Mered*, pp. 270–94 and Testimonies: Brand, pp. 47–49.

3. Some of the commanders who remained were even of the opinion that they should break through to occupied Soviet territory by way of the front, so unwilling were they to return to the Rudninkai forests. Testimonies: Brand, pp. 51–52.

4. Nahum Kaganovicz was born in Vilna in 1913. He studied in a technical institute, served in the Polish army, and took part in the battles near Warsaw in September 1939, for which he was decorated for bravery. He was one of the leading members of the FPO in the Vilna ghetto and was instructed to take a group of prisoners from the Kailis labor camp to the forest on September 27, 1943. He served alternately as squad commander and deputy commander of the "Struggle" detachment. After having been wounded in the hand in the summer of 1944, he was promoted to the rank of sergeant-major.

5. Testimonies: Telerant, p. 24; Solz, p. 1. See also R. Korczak, *Lehavot be-Efer* (Flames in Ashes) (Merhavia, 1965), p. 275.

6. Captain Nikolai Leonovich Vasilenko, who was commonly believed to be a non-Jew (his nationality was described in an official document as Ukrainian) was born in 1906 into a traditional Jewish family in a Jewish village in the Kherson district of the Ukraine. He worked as an engineer until the outbreak of war, when he helped to build fortifications in Simferopol. He did not hide his Jewish origins from the fighters in the Kovno ghetto who fled with him from Fort Nine. For details, see Z. A. Brown and D. Levin, *Toldotehah shel Mahteret* (Jerusalem: 1962), pp. 155, 160, 163–64, 169–72, 291; Korczak, *Lehavot be-Efer*, pp. 276–77; Testimonies: Kaganovicz, p. 3 and Telerant, p. 39. See also note 12 of Chapter 20.

7. One of the sources states that Vasilenko remained at a great distance from the fighters and treated them severely. According to this source, he introduced ironclad discipline in the unit. He was wont to dispatch groups to operations with the following words: "Remember, if you don't succeed, there'll be serious consequences." R. Korczak, *Lehavot be-Efer*, p. 277. A similar opinion is expressed in another source: "In order to prove that he isn't a Jew, he treats the Jews harshly." Lazar, *Hurban u-Mered*, p. 318. See also Testimonies: Solz, pp. 36–37 and Gelpern, p. 3. On the other hand, others claim that he was a typical soldier and thus expected discipline and compliance with orders from the partisans, regardless of their national origins. Testimonies: Telerant, p. 28 and Kaganovicz, p. 3.

8. The presence of women in the forest, and particularly married couples, did indeed become a social problem, but the Jewish command of the Vilna detachments did not go so far as to separate them. See: Brown and Levin, *Toldotehah shel Mahteret* (The Story of an Underground) (Jerusalem, 1962), pp. 284–86. See also, Korczak, *Lehavot be-Efer*, p. 272; Kahanovich M. Kahanovich, *Milhemet ha-Partizanim ha-Yehudim be-Mizrah Eiropa* [The Fighting of Jewish Partisans in Eastern Europe] (Tel Aviv, 1954), pp. 227, 324, 339.

9. For a description of the discovery of Major Kolosov's treachery and his dramatic arrest, see: Korczak, p. 277; N. Kaganovicz, *Zikhronot me-Hayei ha-Partizanim be-Ya'arot Rudniki* [Memories from the Life of the Partisans in the Rudniki Forests] (manuscript in Yiddish), in the author's private archives, pp. 27–28.

10. A characteristic expression of this opinion can be seen in the words of the Jewish fighter L., who, on his return from an arms acquisition operation, remarked to some friends: "We could go out less (on operations) and spare ourselves losses in heads (*viz.* sacrifices)." Kaganovicz, *Zikhronot*, p. 16. Just before their departure from the forests, the Jewish fighter B. remarked to his squad commander, who suggested attacking an enemy convey that had crossed their path: "There is no need: won't we soon be liberated?" Testimonies: Telerant, p. 47. See also Testimonies: Solz, pp. 29–30.

11. Kaganovicz, *Zikhronot* pp. 34–36. Until arms were finally parachuted

in to them, the two Jewish battalions, "Death to Fascism" and "Struggle" possessed no more than thirty-seven weapons.

12. Testimonies: Telerant, pp. 32, 58–59. Apparently, Vasilenko, too, did not have great faith in the former prisoners of war, and according to a hearsay witness, even said to them: "I would shoot you with my own hands, but you are not under my command." Testimonies. Kaganovicz, *Zikhronot,* p. 3. After leaving the forest, nearly all the former prisoners were sent to the front in the "punishment battalions."

CHAPTER 24
Summing Up

1. Moshe Segalson, *Partizaner Bavegung in Kovner Geto* (Partisan Movement in the Kovno Ghetto) (Landsberg, 1945), mimeographed.

BIBLIOGRAPHY

DOCUMENTS

From Moreshet, the Anielewicz Museum in Memory of the Commander of the Warsaw Ghetto Uprising, Givat Havivah

The Hermann Kruk Collection, D.2.45, D.2.43–2.16 (Yiddish, 1941–1944)

Proclamation founding the FPO, D.1.4630 (Yiddish, January 1, 1942)

FPO code of behavior, D.1.360 (Yiddish, March 1943)

Arms list of an FPO fighting group, D.1.4631 (Yiddish, 1942)

Thirteen news bulletins for FPO members, D.1.365–77 (Yiddish, 1942)

Instructions to FPO commanders, D.1.378–81 (Yiddish, 1942)

Letter from an FPO commander ("Uri") to the commander of a partisan brigade (F. G. Markov), D.1.395 (Russian, 1943)

Order from the commander of the first FPO battalion condemning communications offenses, D.1.385 (Yiddish, June 24, 1943)

FPO proclamations in various languages, D.1.387–91 (Polish, Russian, German, 1943)

Order from an FPO commander ("Uri") concerning the care of weapons, D.1.384

Proclamation announcing the uprising to the Jews of the Vilna ghetto, D.1.382 (Yiddish, September 1, 1943)

Comments *(Komentaren)* on the FPO code, D.1.386 (Yiddish, 1943)

Diary of the staff of the *Mestitel* ("Avenger") battalion in the Rudninkai forests, D.1.4650 (Russian, October 7, 1943–August 8, 1944)

Underground bulletin *Za Wolnosc* ("For Freedom"), D.393 (Polish, 1944)

Letter to *Hashomer Hatza'ir* members in the Rudninkai forests, D.2.15 (Hebrew and Yiddish, March 1944)

Testimonies of Jewish partisans in the Rudninkai forests, D.1.4.1.5.

Testimonies of Jewish partisans in the Narocz forests, D.1.4.1.11

Short annotated diary by Abba Kovner, D.2.102

Material concerning Jewish soldiers in the Lithuanian Division, D.1.6.14

From the Yad Vashem Archives, Jerusalem

Report of October 15, 1941, operation against the Partisans, Nuremberg Doc. L-180

Report of the head of the German security services in Lithuania concerning the extermination of the Jews (microfilm) JM/2910 (German, 1941)

Testament of a member of the IBZ command from the Kovno ghetto to his comrades, B/5-2 (Hebrew, 1944)

Editions of *Nitzotz* from the Kovno ghetto, B/12-5 (Hebrew, 1942–1944)

An appeal by A. Sutzkever and S. Kaczerginski on behalf of Jewish partisans to the commander of the Markov brigade, 0–43 N/2a–1 (Russian, October 9, 1943)

Collection of testimonies from the Central Historical Commission under the auspices of the liberated Jews in the American zone, Munich, M-I/E

Collection of historical questionnaires issued by the Central Historical Commission, Munich, M-I/Q

The collection on displaced persons of the Central Historical Commission, Munich, M–I/P

The Mersik–Tenenbaum underground collection from the Bialystok ghetto, M–11

The Dr. E. Yerushalmi collection on the destruction of the Jews of Shavli, P–4

The Íssak Stone collection: Nazi documents, 0–18

A collection of documents from the YIVO archives concerning the Vilna ghetto (Sutzkever–Kaczerginsky), 0–43 JM/1195 (Microfilm)

Collection of documents from the *Ha-Kibbutz ha-Arzi* archives concerning the Holocaust period, 0–46/JM/1177

Collection concerning the Klooga concentration camp in Estonia, 0–47, JM/2000–2798

Eichmann Trial, TR–3

Einsatzgruppen Case, N–IX

High Command Case, N–XII

Ereignismeldungen UdSSR, Meldungen aus den besetzten Ostgebieten, DN–33–1, nos. 1–195 (June 23, 1941–April 24, 1942)

Report of *Einsatzgruppe* A until October 15, 1941, 1–180

Report by Karl Jäger, commander of *Einsatzkommando 3*, on the extermination of Lithuanian Jewry until December 1, 1941, 0–53–1

Nissan Reznik's account of the activities of the FPO Doc. 649

Avraham Sutzkever's account of the flight to the forests Doc 688

From the Archives of the Jewish Labor Movement, Tel-Aviv

Irgun Brit Zion almanac from the Kovno ghetto III 91 (975) (Hebrew, 1943–1944

From the YIVO Archives, New York

Documents from the German security forces in Lithuania during World War II concerning anti-Nazi activities on the part of the local population, OccE3b 19–63 (1942–1944).

TESTIMONIES AND INTERVIEWS

The following is a list of the people whose testimonies have been included in this research. The method of numbering testimonies or interviews is determined by the archives in which they are kept. Interviews that were done by the author especially for this research on behalf of the Department for Oral History of the Institute of Contemporary Jewry (Hebrew University, Jerusalem), are marked with a "12," and separated from the serial number by a slash (e.g., 12/215). Interviews on the underground in the Kovno ghetto that were arranged by Messrs. Zvi A. Brown and Dov Levin for Yad Vashem are marked E/17a, separated from the serial number by a dash (e.g., E/17a–45). Other testimonies from the Yad Vashem archives are marked 03 and M–IE, separated from the serial number by a slash (e.g., 03/2003). Testimonies from the Moreshet Archives are marked with an A before their serial number (e.g., A43). The number in parentheses after a witness's name indicates that the witness was interviewed or produced written testimony more than once. The names of people interviewed in more than one framework appear more than once in the list. Pseudonyms for witnesses who wished to remain anonymous are marked with an asterisk (*).

ABE*	12/23	Bleiman, Leib	12/49
Adamowicz, Irena	E/17a–37	Bogen, Alexander	A930
	(0-33/415)	Borkan, Chaim	12/34
Akerman, Hinda	12/127	Brand, Shlomo	12/62
Antubil, Sheraga	12/140	Brauner, Sarah	12/158
Auerbach, Aryeh	12/117	Burgin, Yechiel	12/165
Azgad, Baruch	E/17a–52	Burstein, Jacob	E/17a–57
Barak Zvi	12/150	Bushkanitz, Shimon	
Basok, Haim	12/70	and Goldah	12/89
Bat Ami, Masha*	12/31	Chaluzin, Shmuel	12/92
Bat Yisrael, Yaffa*	12/162	Chanes, David	03/1675
Bekin, Shimon	12/35	Charmatz, Joseph	12/124
Belkind, Jacob	03/838	Chazan, Bela	12/100
Ben Eliezer*	12/167	Chefetz, Abraham	12/123
Ben Hillel*	12/170	Chefetz, Jacob	12/193
Ben Menahem, Joseph*		Daitz, Shmuel	E/17a–32
(5)	12/251	Dan, Yehudah	12/139
Ben Moshe*	12,198	Davidovitz, Michael	12/115
Ben Zvi, Yeshabyahu* (3)	12/16	Dayan, Moshe	12/50
Bick, Avraham	12/136	Dekel, Yitzhak	12/156
Bin, Zalman	12/21	Dersa*	12/63

Litvin, Shimon	12/102	Rolnik, Zvi	12/128
Ma'apil, Menashe*	12/122	Rosenberg, Zesia	A55
Magid, Elhanan	12/64	Rosenfeld, Jonah	12/17
Magid, Elhanan and		Rozhanski, Chaim	12/75
Niselevitz, Sonia	A43	Rozovski, Yeshayaku	12/145
Marshak (Papier-		Rubinstein, Reuven	12/146
macher), Nina	12/43	Rudnicki, (Arad) Yit-	
Mazorevitz (Mazor)	12/110	zhak	03/3243
Melamed, Abraham	E/17a–51	Rudnicki, Shemariah	12/119
Meltzman, Joseph	12/139	Schwarz, Yehiel (2)	12/24
Molk, Joshua	12/51	Segal, Eliyahu	E/17a–33
Mor, Lipman	12/76	Segalson, Moshe	E/17a–29
Mozes, Eliezer	E/17–14	Senderovicz, Yitzhak	12/72
Mushkat, Marian	12/148	Shafriri, Joseph	12/160
N-r, Zvi*	12/150	Shapiro, Yitzhak	12/109
Nadel, Chaim	E/17a–47	Shapiro, Luba	12/159
Neshamit, Sarah	12/18	Shapiro, Shalom	12/73
Niv, Ze'ev (6)	12/22	Sheftel, Aryeh	12/106
Nurock, Mordechai	12/4	Shilansky, Dov	121
Olshan, Yitzhak	12/98	Shimoni*, Eliyahu	12/53
Oranski, Ze'ev	12/27	Shimoni (Rabinowitz)	
Oreg*	12/134	Leib	12/137
Orlovitz, Nessia	12/45	Shimonov, Shimon	12/93
Peretzman, Ber	03/1032	Shin, Baruch*	12/66
Pergament, Lusia	12/93	Shiniuk, Yerachmiel	E/17–1.2
Pick, Teddy	12/96	Shumovitz, Mersik	A51
Pildus, Rivkah	12/157	Shutan, Moshe	12/81
Pogir, Gita	E/17a–19	Skurkovitz, Nachum	03/2587
Pugatzki, Malkah	E/17a–8	Skurkovitz, Nachum (2)	12/32
Pumpianski, Yehudah	12/149	Slova, Leib	12/81
Pupko, Moshe	12/38	Smoli, Joseph (2)	12/12
Pur, David	12/82	Solel, Shimon*	12/41
Rabinovitz, Hannah	12/188	Solz, Moshe	12/185
Rabinovitz, Moshe	12/187	Shpiz, Yitzhak	E/17a–69
Rabs*	12/152	Stein, Rivkah	E/17a–41
Rapaport, Elimelech	12/20	Steinman, Jacob	03/1898
Rest, David	03/1560	Stift, Yeshayahu	12/196
Reuveni, Jacob and		Sutzkever, Abraham	12/67
Luba	12/111	Svirski, Bluma and	
Reznik, Nissan	12/59	David	12/61
Reznik, Nissan	E/17a–55	Svirski, Luba	12/61
Rindzunski, Alexander	12/108	Svirski, Noah	03/3134
Rindzunski, Alexander	A.381	Tarshish, Yehudah	12/65
Rochman, Jonah	E/17a–55	Telerant, Elhanan	12/180
Rogalin, Yitzhak	12/47	Tori, Abraham	E/17a–27
Rogovski, Benjamin	12/78	Trigor, Yehoshua	12/126

NEWSPAPERS AND PERIODICALS

He-Avar, Tel Aviv
Izvestiya*, Moscow
Kamah, Jerusalem
Kol Nakhei ha-Milhamah, Tel Aviv
Komunistas, Vilna
La-Merhav*, Tel Aviv
Likutim me-Itonut ha-Olam, Tel Aviv
Lituanus, New York
Ma'arakhot, Tel Aviv
Ma'ariv*, Tel Aviv
Mahanayim, Tel Aviv
Massuah, Tel Yitzhak-Tel Aviv
Nayleben, New York
Nayvelt, Tel Aviv
Nitzotz, Munich
Pergale, Vilna
Pirsumei Muzeyon ha-Lohamim ve-ha-
 Partizanim, Tel Aviv

Pravda*, Moscow
Soviet Life, Washington D.C.
Soviet Russia, Today, New York
Sovietskaya Litva, Vilna
Tarybu Lietuva*, Vilna
Talpiyot, New York
Tiesa*, Vilna
Times*, London
Unzer Velt, Munich
Yad Vashem News, Jerusalem
Yad Vashem Studies, Jerusalem
Yalkut Moreshet, Tel Aviv
Yediot Aharonot*, Tel Aviv
Yediot Beyt Lohamei ha-Gettaot al shem
 Yitzhak Katzenelson, le-Moreshet
 ha-Shoah ve-ha-Mered, Kibbbutz
 Lohamei ha-Gettaot
Zeror Mikhtavim, Ein Harod

INDEX